CARVED IN STONE

To Grange

"If the world had more
people like you, this may
have never happened."

Rosina and Phil Kirk

3/20/10

The survivors are divided into two well-defined groups: those who repress their past *en bloc*, and those whose memory of the offence persists, as though carved in stone.

Primo Levi

MANNY DRUKIER

Carved in Stone: Holocaust Years – A Boy's Tale

UNIVERSITY OF TORONTO PRESS
Toronto Buffalo London

© University of Toronto Press Incorporated 1996
Toronto Buffalo London

Printed in Canada

ISBN 0-8020-0832-1

Printed on acid-free paper

Canadian Cataloguing in Publication Data

Drukier, Manny, 1928–
  Carved in stone : Holocaust years – a boy's tale

  ISBN 0-8020-0832-1

  1. Drukier, Manny, 1928– .   2. Holocaust, Jewish
  (1939–1945) – Poland – Lodź – Personal narratives.
  3. Jews – Poland – Lodź – Biography.   4. Holocaust
  survivors – Ontario – Toronto – Biography.   5. Jews –
  Ontario – Toronto – Biography.   I. Title.

  DS135.P63D78 1996   940.53'18'092   C96-930642-3

University of Toronto Press acknowledges the financial assistance to
its publishing program of the Canada Council and the Ontario Arts
Council.

For Freda
and our children,
Gordon, Laurie, Wendy, and Cindy

Contents

Foreword

The title Manny Drukier chose for his memoirs, *Carved in Stone*, is taken from Primo Levi's words: 'The survivors are divided into two well-defined groups: those who repress their past *en bloc*, and those whose memory of the offence persists, as though carved in stone.' Thus he announces what the reader can expect: personal memories, indelibly inscribed in his mind, going back to the years of the German terror regime.

Drukier, who was born in 1928, has lived in Toronto since shortly after the war, and although he does not say so, one gets the impression that he made an effort, whether consciously motivated or not, to adjust and to forget. Yet he obviously belongs to Primo Levi's second group, as he realized himself when, in the early nineties, he wanted to return to the places where he had lived as a boy.

The organization of Drukier's book reflects the process of rediscovering and coming to grips with his past. What in the early chapters is a tentative and almost reluctant gauging of the attitudes of the people he encounters becomes in the later parts of the book a clear judgment and often a condemnation. The same itinerary from the periphery to the core can be observed in Drukier's focus of attention. Whereas the reader is first acquainted with an almost confusing multitude of relatives, slowly the very personal experiences of the author himself take centre stage. The growing isolation, the uncertainty, the ever-increasing danger of being sent to one of the camps – shrouded in mystery because nobody knows exactly what is going on there, and nobody returns from there – the disappearance of close family members, and the mounting desperation are described in a detached, matter-of-fact tone, probably the only manner of description that holds the author's deeply felt emotions in check.

In the unpredictable game of cat and mouse that the Germans played, their victims were often faced with choices the implications of which they did not know, and were forced to make split-second decisions. Survivors often think that they owe their lives to having been able to make an instantaneous decision. But the voices of those who were equally quick in making the wrong choice cannot be heard to correct that impression.

Drukier makes the surprising remark that he belonged to 'the lucky ones.' Relatively speaking he is right, in that he stayed out of extermination camps such as Majdanek, Treblinka, and Sobibor. Nevertheless, his losses and his suffering were immense: the sixteen-year-old boy was left alone to fend for himself in an extremely dangerous and incomprehensible world.

There is a very extensive literature of personal memories about the Holocaust. Among the best-known writers of such memories, Primo Levi and Elie Wiesel immediately come to mind. Yet Drukier's experiences are quite different from those described by Wiesel and Levi, and bring into focus elements of gratuitous cruelty that are much more dependent on individual whim than is the cruelty one encounters when the functioning of the extermination machine, in its almost impersonal force, is the main subject.

The end of the war does not bring immediate relief for the boy. Gone 'wild,' hungry and unkempt, he continues to fend for himself, never trusting the people with whom he comes into contact enough to reveal his identity.

Ending his story where his new life truly begins, in America, Drukier conveys how difficult it was to adjust to a milieu that was full of good intentions but lacked any understanding of what he had been through.

Drukier's account of his experiences gives the reader a glimpse of aspects of humankind that are far from uplifting. Yet it is of the utmost importance for those who have never witnessed racial hatred in its crudest form to realize to what nadir of inhumanity racial prejudices can lead. Drukier came out of the ordeal with his sensitivity and his humanity intact. By sharing his memories with his readers, he is doing a great service to the cause of tolerance and mutual understanding.

Henry Schogt
May 1996

Acknowledgments

I wish to acknowledge a debt of gratitude to several individuals whose input was invaluable in shaping this book: my editors, Darlene Zeleney and Kate Baltais, Fraser Sutherland, Dr Gordon Drukier, Robert A. Ferguson, Gerald Hallowell, Dr Linda Hershkovitz, Henry G. Schogt, Phil Surguy, K. Zarzecki, and the late John M. Robson.

I dedicate this book to four unsung stalwarts, our children, Gordon, Laurie, Wendy, and Cindy, and to my wife, Freda, whose contribution to the book was equal to mine and without whose love and faith it would not have been written.

Manny Drukier

My grandparents with their ten children. Mother is fourth from the left in the top row. 1928

My maternal grandparents with their daughter Andzia, taking the cure at Szczawnica. 1930

Aunt Hela. 1939

On summer holidays in Wiśniowa Góra, 1936. Seated, from left: Uncle Fishl and Aunt Bluma; my father, Gavril, and my mother, Eadis; Uncle Meyer and Aunt Baila; Aunt Rózia and Uncle Nusyn; mother's youngest brother, Meyer; and Aunt Mania and Uncle Nathan, with their son and daughter (in front). Top row, from left: cousins Moniek, Geniek, and Natek, and I and my sister, Anna.

With Izidor in Hitlerjugend uniforms. Chmelna, Czechoslovakia, 8 May 1945

Milton Zeldis, just prior to departure for the United States. France, September 1945

With Private O'Krepke from Pittsburgh. Marienbad, November 1945

Indersdorf, July 1946

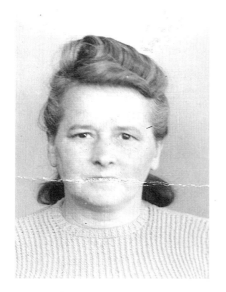
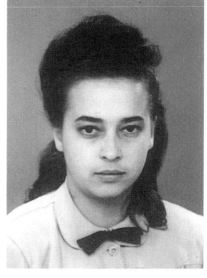

My mother in Borås, Sweden. 1946   My sister, Anna, in Borås. 1946

Children of many nationalities at the children's home in Indersdorf, with an UNRRA official. I am second from the right, in front. Summer 1946

With Izidor (on the left) in Times Square. New York City, January 1947

CARVED IN STONE

Prologue:
The Second Coming of the Jews

After looking around the crowded revolving restaurant at the top of the Metropol Hotel in Warsaw, the chicken rancher from Biała Podlaska, on the Belarus border, leaned forward in his chair and addressed us earnestly: 'I've got a plan for the resurrection of Poland's economy.' Our conversation to that point had centred around chickens, so this showed a side of Stan that we had not anticipated. Handsome and lean, in his mid-thirties, Stan is a self-admitted tax evader in the six-figure range. Nevertheless, he considers himself a true patriot. Tall, fair, broad-shouldered, he walks with a slight stoop brought on by the need, in his line of work, to be bending over constantly, gathering the eggs that his flock lays around the clock every day, including Sundays. My wife, Freda, and I glanced at each other and gave Stan the go-ahead to tell us his plan.

'Our situation now, in 1991, is no different than the predicament King Kazimierz the Great found himself in in the 1400s. And the solution is just as straightforward.' I was thinking fast. Kazimierz's claim to fame was twofold: he had succeeded in consolidating his rule over feudal Poland and he had invited the Jews to settle there. This was getting interesting. Stan, seeing that he had our attention, enthusiastically dove into his explanation.

'Look,' he said, lowering his voice by an octave. 'Our economy is collapsing around our ears. The factories are closing down even if they have orders, because they have no funds to purchase the raw materials they need. Furthermore, the orders are usually from state-run stores that have no money to pay for goods. Our banks cannot grant any more credit to these jokers. Besides, the banks are broke, too. And then,' he sat up in his chair and continued, 'you have the coal mines: too old, too deep, and too dangerous. The steel mills are antiquated and use much too much coke and pollute the air.' Now he was really warming up to his topic. 'The administration in this land is feudal in its actions and outlook. Each department chief acts as though he were the head of a fiefdom. Usually he becomes a partner in a business that his department has a regulatory power over. Then he diverts funds to his deal, and won't let the competition breathe.'

'But that will all be illegal from now on,' I interjected.

'Bah.' Stan dismissed the observation with a wave of the hand. 'They will find a way to get around it. Our education system is a mess. We can't afford new textbooks, so students are still being taught Russian as a second language – and Marxist economics. Smuggled-in vodka is cheap, so the unemployed men drink themselves into a rage, beat their wives, and abuse their children. Everything operates on the łapówka pay-off system. You have to bribe the higher-up in order to be allowed to steal.'

'Surely,' I suggested, 'it can't be as bad as you make it out to be.'

'Little do you know! The only organization that functions is the Russian Mafia.'

'So what's your point?' I pressed.

'Poland,' – and here he paused for effect – 'will invite the Jews to come home!' I beckoned the waitress and ordered another round of beer.

'We are back to a primitive agricultural economy, except that the peasants are no longer indentured to the lord. Neither will they work seven days a week, stand for poor TV reception, and not earn good money. On the other hand, if the government gives in to the farmers' demands and fixes the price of food higher, there will be riots in the towns. This talk of potential foreign investments is a lot of foolishness. The Americans don't know which end is up. The French and Italians just want to sell us condoms, perfume, and soft leather. The Greeks, Bulgars, and Turks have nothing to invest and stuff us with halvah and cheap wine. As for the English, they want to dump their surplus phys-ed instructors here to teach us English grammar. The Germans and Austrians pick off our best firms, keep pushing their old cars and trucks, and brainwash us to think that anything German is the best in the world. If this goes on they will accomplish by stealth what Hitler couldn't do by force. To accommodate and ingratiate ourselves with these new overlords we'll learn to speak and think in German.'

'What about the Japanese and Koreans?' I asked, trying for a global sweep.

'Fuckers. All they come here for is to screw our women,' Stan fairly exploded. 'And the Thais, just about wiped out our poor textile industry. So,' he summed it up, 'our only hope is the Jews.'

'Where? How? *What* Jews?'

'See, the Spanish have passed a law that any Sephardic Jew who can trace his ancestry back to the Inquisition can claim Spanish citizenship.' Stan paused and awaited my response.

'Are you suggesting that any Jew, anywhere in the world, could demand Polish citizenship based on his ancestors' origins?'

'Precisely,' he shot back. 'Think what a grand and noble gesture that would be. It will fly in the face of all the bad press Poland has been getting. The Kielce pogrom of 1946 will be forgiven, anti-Semitism will be a thing of the past. What I'm proposing is a law of return even more generous than the Israeli. It will change the course of history.'

I couldn't believe my ears. But Stan wasn't finished.

'A gesture of this sort will, in one fell swoop, transform the image of Poles from one of drunken Jew-baiters to one of a tolerant and generous people. We would become like the Swiss or the Bahai, only more so.'

'Okay, okay. But what makes you think that Jews in North America, for example, could be persuaded to settle in Poland?,' I asked.

'It won't be easy,' Stan admitted, 'but it can be done. As a sort of a signing bonus we'll offer each returnee an attractive escort for four to eight weeks, depending on the size of the investment.'

'Isn't this a kind of pandering?'

'I call it good business,' replied Stan. 'The religious can obtain, on request, the use of ancient Jewish cemeteries and synagogue sites free of charge. We will even welcome their dead brought to our country for burial.'

'Can you imagine what The Limited, or The Gap, could do with the Polska Moda stores?' Stan was well informed. 'And Walesa could get President Bush to let Michael Milken out of the stockade to take over our banks. After all, Polish junk bonds pay 40 to 50 per cent, so they should be an easy sell.'

'Agriculture will still be a problem,' I countered.

'Right,' he said, 'but a million or so Jews buying chickens, carp, white flour for noodles and kugel – even just for the Sabbath – will sop up a good deal of excess. And sales of corned beef, pastrami, and baby beef will take care of the meat surplus. We won't have to beg the EEC to let our meat in. Mushrooms, we'll sell to your people, also pumpkin seeds.' He was getting bogged down in details.

'What about the Catholic Church? The army? The bureaucracy? Are they going to take this lying down?' The plan had to have a downside.

'One thing at a time. The church will be a problem. But we can talk to our pope. I'm confident that he can be persuaded to issue a papal edict endorsing the proposal. The man is no fool. If he pulls it off he'll have a special place in history. The army, we can slowly disband; we need it like the Russians need more rubles. The military may get us into trouble yet if we don't watch out. Also, if instead of doing service, these young men went to Germany or Switzerland and found jobs, think of all the money they would send home to mamma. The bureaucracy will do just fine. The Jews can be investigated and prosecuted for tax avoidance. They will pay off not to be hassled.'

Stan had thought of everything. One item was bothering me, though. 'What if there is resentment, violence, a pogrom?'

Stan scratched his head. 'Maybe to start with, the Jews should stay put in their neighbourhoods. Keep a low profile, you know – for their own safety. The police can put up watch-towers with search lights, trained dogs can sniff out intruders. Not to worry.'

1
Rehabilitation

Saturday, 4 May 1991. Jerzy Kosinski is dead. Killed himself in his Manhattan apartment, police say. He was fifty-seven. Kosinski was a figure of glamour. I would often come across gossip pieces about him in magazines. A horseman, a mysterious East European, irresistible to society women. Kosinski had had it made. Jewish, for a time he had denied his origins. I should read his first novel, *The Painted Bird*, but because it is painful for me to read about Holocaust experiences, I don't. Like me, Kosinski was born in Łódź, although five years later. His body was discovered at 9:30 A.M. by his wife, Katherine von Fraunhofer-Kosinski. She found him in the bathtub, with a plastic bag pulled over his head. He left a note, but its contents have not been disclosed.

Dr Marek Edelman is another of my contemporaries born in Łódź. A survivor of the Warsaw Ghetto Uprising and hero of Hanna Krall's book, *Shielding the Flame*, Edelman has remained in Łódź and practises medicine there. In 1989 I heard him speak at a public gathering in Toronto. To the question, 'How is the Jewish problem dealt with in Poland?' he replied, 'There is no Jewish problem, because there are no Jews.' This response was not received kindly by the mainly Jewish audience. Unanswered remained the query regarding what motivated Edelman to carry on in Poland. His pleas in Toronto to help Solidarity at a time when the Communist regime was breaking up had fallen on deaf ears.

Another native of Łódź, someone closer to home, is Dr Henry

Morgentaler, the man who pioneered abortion on demand, first in Montreal and now throughout Canada. Morgentaler has suffered enormous punishment and indignity, but he has stuck by his convictions.

Am I reading something into the origins of these three individuals that is merely coincidence? Jewish survivors from Łódź, about 5 per cent of the city's pre-war population of more than three hundred thousand, are probably no different than others. Some of them have made a good deal of money in the countries where they settled after the war. In Canada I built and owned the largest furniture manufacturing and importing firm in the country, only to lose it in the recession of 1991.

Perhaps I am both envious and proud of the accomplishments of my three dissimilar compatriots. Since my arrival in December 1946 I have immersed myself in North American culture. Three-quarters of my life has been spent here, at first in the United States and, from 1948, in Canada. I consider myself an entirely North American product. Why, then, the nagging feeling that something is amiss? Why keep putting ever-more-onerous demands on myself? Why go on pushing ahead to prove that I am up to the test of time? I don't know Morgentaler or Edelman, and I never met Kosinski, but something binds us.

In 1939 Łódź was Poland's second-largest city, with 650,000 residents, almost exclusively provincials. Since the early 1900s it had been a major textile centre, second only to Manchester in output. Fifty per cent Jewish, Łódź was a bustling, brash, unsophisticated place. These Jews, whose command of Polish was at best basic, were in the main nationalistic and ready to make the best of their second-class status. Łódź – or Poland itself, for that matter – without Jews was unimaginable. The bureaucracy, army, navy, farming, and mining were Polish, but industry and commerce were 90 per cent Jewish. It seemed a natural arrangement. Most of the populace was poor, and there was a worldwide recession, but conditions were getting better and there was work in Łódź.

I left Łódź when I was eleven years old. It was December 1939, four months into the Second World War. I remember Łódź as a sunny, crowded city. What is it like now, fifty-two years later? I have avoided visiting the place of my birth. I have not returned to Poland since the war, although in 1985 Freda and I spent three days in Prague. A side trip to the Theresienstadt concentration camp was included in the itinerary, and everyone on our tour went. Everyone but us.

Kosinski, Edelman, Morgentaler, and I are products of a lost milieu. Those of us brought up on the heroes of the historical novels of Nobel prize winner Henryk Sienkiewicz are probably incapable of passivity. Our Polish schooling put the emphasis on courage bordering on recklessness, on a romantic, chivalrous past fraught with danger – for the history of Poland over the last two centuries is strewn with many corpses and few victories. Certainly, a life of comfort and idleness was not the ticket there.

Nothing much is keeping me in Canada this fall except for some complicated, unfinished legal business that I would just as soon leave behind for a couple of months. The people to whom I have mentioned our plans to visit Poland seem doubtful. I'd never spoken about such an idea to my sister or other friends, survivors whose reactions I expect to be unfavourable. When I do speak of it, nearly all our acquaintances and relatives say that the idea has some merit, perhaps, but only if the visit is short. A two-month stay would be madness. Some question whether the shock to my system would not be more than I could handle. Others fear for our safety and decry the lack of decent food.

For decades I have spoken English. My Polish is fragmentary. It is impossible for me to formulate a coherent sentence. I am sure that the language will come back to me; still, looking over Polish newspapers, I realize that I have a lot to relearn. Though Poland is the country of her father's birth, Freda thinks it may seem like any other foreign country to her. Then there is the question of anti-Semitism. Jews and Christians were distinct communities in Poland; this was a fact of life. I am steeling myself for possible unpleasantness.

In North America, it is different. Communities are mixed, and my own family has never been Orthodox. Freda and I do not attend synagogue regularly, nor do our daughters, Laurie, Wendy, and Cindy. The exception is our son, Gordon, who, searching for answers he could not find while doing his doctorate in astrophysics, began to observe the traditional rituals faithfully. He now knows more about Judaism than I ever have.

The happy and productive lives of our children are in contrast to events in their ancestral home. All of my father's and most of my mother's family perished in Poland during the Second World War. My mother, my sister, Anna, and I survived. By the end of this century a majority of concentration camp survivors will have died. We survivors have not been readily forthcoming with accounts of our experience. Rightly or wrongly, we have judged the world to be apathetic about the Hitler years. The reluctance to speak out is also based on the belief that even sympathetic outsiders cannot be trusted to understand the extent and the depth of the tragedy. Often the painful retracing is denied to one's children and grandchildren, partly because one feels ashamed of having given in to the oppressor without a fight, of having valued life above dignity. Uppermost, though, has been a desire not to appear 'different' in the new community. Certainly in my case this has been true. This chronicle is, I suppose, the result of a wish to rehabilitate myself.

2
Warsaw

Warsaw, September 1991. The Lufthansa flight to Warsaw via Frankfurt was uneventful. The immigration officer at the Warsaw airport asked me which hotel we would be staying at. Even though we had leased an apartment, East European officialdom is best told nothing, so I unhesitatingly replied, '*Nie wiemy jeszcze*' ('Don't know yet'). That gave me the confidence to ask a skycap, in Polish, to carry our heavy suitcases and further enquire as to the cost of a taxi into town. The skycap led us to the taxi. The driver consulted with me about the location of the apartment. It was difficult for him to read the map, and I accurately translated to Freda when he said that he had to get his glasses from the trunk of the car. In the end, my newly recovered vocabulary wasn't much help, as the driver took advantage of us anyway.

Pani Halina,* our landlord's emissary, heard the hall door opening and met us outside the apartment door. Thin, grey-haired, and excited, she gave every impression of being very busy. She quickly showed us through the three rooms. Extremely cluttered and containing an immense number of books, they were the kind of safe haven I used to dream of in my tense teens. I went to the window and parted the curtains. To the right was an arch in the red brick walls of the old city. People had their dogs down in what used to be the moat, now grassed over; others milled about laden market stands. It was warm outside and cool inside.

* 'Pani' is the Polish equivalent of 'Mrs.' The standard polite form of address places the social title before the person's given name (in this case, 'Halina').

In the afternoon we walked to the Menorah kosher restaurant at Plac Grzybowski number 2, which happened to be just after number 8, which followed number 6. Not easy to find, and I was too stubborn to ask directions. We were served good chicken soup with kreplach, chicken with rice and vegetables, and a salad. The only visible Jew was the *meshgiach*, the supervisor of *kashrut* (dietary laws), a man with a yarmulke and a healthy black beard. All the others were obviously Poles – both the help and the guests. After lunch we wanted to go to the synagogue and the Jewish theatre. This time I asked directions, and off we went across the boulevard.

The large synagogue, the only one in Warsaw, has a cathedral ceiling and a gallery around three sides. Brightly lit, it has narrow, dark wooden benches and a supply of prayer-books of all shapes and sizes. A few elderly men were gathered on benches in front of an old man with a white beard who sat on a chair, a book open in front of him on a small desk. Continuously rocking, the rabbi was interpreting a section of the Talmud. The others listened avidly. From where we sat it was possible to hear only the odd word distinctly. The recitation had to do with *parnosseh*, the idea that every family man has an obligation to earn a living. A noble thought.

One of the men came over and asked us where we were from. On learning that it was Canada, he whispered to another, who then walked over and told us that he was an *inkashier*, a collector for the shul, which, as usual, needed money. I tried to engage him in conversation, in Yiddish. He said that evening prayers would start shortly. My question as to whether he had lived all his life in Warsaw brought the reply that he wished to collect money. When I asked how many people came to the shul regularly, he impatiently replied, 'Very few.' More came during the High Holidays. I mentioned that we intended to return, and this again elicited the comment that his function was to collect money. He turned on his heel when I gave him a banknote. No one else paid the slightest attention to us. The entire episode was eerie. Obviously, they took us for an American couple slumming. Feeling somewhat hurt and rejected, we put down our prayer-books and left.

Back at the apartment, we decided to call it a day. The pull-out bed was uncomfortable, but we slept for fifteen hours, waking up at half past eleven the next morning. I had hooked up the fax/telephone-answering machine that we had brought with us, and there was a message on it, perhaps from Pani Halina: the female voice exclaimed something that sounded like 'What is this?' before being disconnected. Again, the day was warm and bright. Our first stop was a television and video store. When we asked if it would be possible to rent a TV, we were met with a look of bewilderment: the answer, evidently, was no. After lunch we walked west and north, and bought a cake at the Mirowski Market. Although the label on the cake said 'Baked in Austria,' the outdoor market did have a lot of local produce, priced at half (or less) of what produce of similar quality cost in Toronto. We learned that local wages were about 10 per cent of the North American scale.

After walking through the Saxony Gardens, we watched the changing of the guard at the Monument to the Unknown Soldier. Among the many battles listed on the monument we found 'Ghetto IV 1943.' A group of veterans marched up to the site and laid a wreath. The eternal flame rose and fell in the brisk wind. It was now overcast and much cooler.

We bought half a loaf of bread, half a package of butter, jam, orange juice, and a can of sardines. The salespeople were helpful. Apparently, it is customary here to buy food in small quantities, possibly because people lack refrigeration or have little money. At the market carrots, root celery, parsnips, and green onions were cleverly bundled in small bunches for soup. All of the colourfully packaged goods were imported. On our way home we passed through the narrow streets of the old city and looked into the many small restaurants that emitted wonderful smells. Back at the apartment, we dined on black bread, butter, coffee, cake, and red wine.

Conversation in Polish was still difficult for me, though my reading and comprehension were gradually improving. Freda, hearing me utter strange sounds, was impressed. I tried to sort out my feelings after this second day of our visit, and I did not seem to bear any grudges, nor did I see an anti-Semite lurking in every corner. Of course, our contact with locals had been only minimal.

That evening, I spent some time exploring the library in the apartment. I found a Polish dictionary, *Słownik Języka Polskiego*, originally published in Wilno (Vilnius) in 1861, a time when the Polish language was being suppressed by the tsar. Its publication had been made possible by a grant from a Maurycy Orgelbrand, a Jew. I looked up the word 'Jew' (*Żyd*); translated literally, the definition read as follows: 'A person of Moses-led persuasion; Orthodox; resembling a bent-over tavern [?], like a Jew rocking back and forth in prayer; a sneered-at member of the populace; a wasteland such as that in which the Jews wandered; a dealer or merchant; a usurer; greedy; a thrifty, grasping miser; in handwriting, a sudden ink blot; also, to love in a brotherly way, as Jews do.' Spooky! A current Polish dictionary defined *Żyd* as 'a member of an ethnic-cultural group, historically joined by religion, tradition, and customs; a person whose roots are in ancient Judea, a member of the diaspora.' It seemed that, having virtually disappeared from the Polish scene, the Jews had now received a clean bill of health.

Most of the books in the library were in Polish and of postwar vintage, but there were also some in English and Romanian. The library was varied and had obviously been assembled with care, its owner being a publisher and translator. Half a century of Polish literature had passed me by.

A two-volume account of the Warsaw conspiracy of 1939–43 caught my eye. Among the hundreds of heroes listed was Klepfisz Michal (1913–1943), a member of the left-leaning Jewish Bund and a ghetto fighter who served as a go-between with the Poles. A teacher by profession, Michal was skilled in metallurgy and had learned to make explosives. He left the ghetto in 1942, but returned in 1943 to help in the Warsaw Ghetto Uprising. He was killed on 20 April 1943, about two blocks from where we were staying. His mother was gassed in Treblinka. In February 1944 Michal received a posthumous decoration from the commander-in-chief of the Polish army based in London. His name also appears in Hanna Krall's *Shielding the Flame*. His picture in the Warsaw account shows a young man with distinctly Semitic features, his white shirt-collar out over a dark jacket. All the other names and pictures are of Gentiles.

The library also contained a collection of essays, dating from 1986, from the underground press, typewritten and presumably mimeographed by the *Niezależna Oficyna Wydawnicza* (Independent Publishing House). The masthead states boldly that the publishing house desires to break the Communist government's monopoly on publishing and information, and does not express any particular view. Its continued success and fulfilment of duty depend on a steady supply of manuscripts, help in distribution, and aid in the form of printing materials and money. In conclusion, the masthead reads, 'It is up to us to protect freedom of expression in Poland.' I also found, in a desk drawer, *Malowany Ptak* – Kosinski's *The Painted Bird*.

Our plan was to stay in Warsaw for seven weeks. During this period we would also visit Staszów, Kielce, and Łódź. Warsaw touched me only superficially, as I had never been there before. Łódź perhaps would be more of a shock. I wouldn't know until I got there.

The capital of Poland, and the focus of culture for Jewish and Polish society, Warsaw held a historical fascination for me. In 1941, a year before the 'final solution' was implemented and two years before the Warsaw Ghetto Uprising, its Jewish population numbered half a million.

It was raining the morning we set out for the site of the former ghetto, a drizzle that soon gave way to a brisk, chilling wind and dark clouds overhead. A thirty-minute walk along cobblestone streets with narrow sidewalks led us through rebuilt parts of a city that had seen hand-to-hand combat in 1943 and 1944. Using drawings and photographs, architects were hoping to re-create the town as it had been before the war.

At the perimeter of the former ghetto, we encountered a solid phalanx of tall, drab apartment buildings. Past them, rising from an elevated base in the centre of a large open area, was the Ghetto Memorial, a rectangular, grey monument covered with inscriptions in Polish and English. The wind had extinguished the flames of the memorial candles. Wilted flowers were stuck in crevices everywhere. A dead rat lay on one of the steps leading up to the monument. Parked to the side, a vendor was selling memorabilia, and two uniformed guards passed by, seemingly oblivious to their surroundings. No one else was around. Freda and I took photographs of the large stone plaques that mark the four corners of the cobblestone quadrangle. Their sandblasted inscriptions list the names of some of the ghetto fighters, along with the dates on which they perished.

In spite of the weather, my throat was parched. The vendor had no drinks for sale, but he offered us a xeroxed map of the area. His wares consisted mostly of gritty black and white photographs reproduced from German archives. They showed smiling troopers and dejected-looking Jews.

We walked to Umschlagplatz (Place of Transshipment), the special railway siding from which nearly the entire population of the ghetto had been deported to Treblinka, where they were gassed and cremated. I found I had little to say: I knew what it was like in the summer of 1942. Some had come here resigned to their fate. Others, escorted in by the Jewish police, had tried to get away. All were emaciated. Starvation was the norm for some 300,000 who were still alive. The siding at Umschlagplatz was enclosed by a barbed-wire fence. The gate would swing open only to allow out those who were soon to be put to death.

The white marble Umschlagplatz Memorial forms an inverted U-shaped wall at the back, with a shorter, free-standing wall in front. I assumed there was a plaque inside, but I didn't venture in. Guides and taxi-drivers stood nearby, and three uniformed guards strolled along the siding, smoking cigarettes. A white Mercedes limousine arrived, and a well-dressed man got out. He looked around for about thirty seconds, then got back into the car. I, too, had seen enough.

We moved on to the bunker where the commander and staff of the ghetto fighters had made their last stand, and then we walked past the Pawiak Street Gestapo building that had been used for interrogation and torture. We reached the Jewish cemetery too late: on Fridays the gates closed at noon. Exhausted, both physically and emotionally, I hailed a taxi, and we returned to the apartment. I poured myself a double scotch and dozed off, telling myself it was probably still jet lag.

That evening we went to a movie, *Dances with Wolves* (a bargain at two dollars), but we left three-quarters of the way through, perturbed and restless after the ghetto experience.

Many buildings in Warsaw bear plaques commemorating the fallen in the 1944 Polish uprising. The suffering of the Poles is well documented throughout the city. Of the Jews who worked, lived, prayed, married, bore children, and participated in the life of the city since its founding, however, there is little evidence. Jews are now a minor curiosity in Poland – souvenir stands sell figurines of Hasidim.

3
Grandparents

My maternal great-grandfather, Meyer Frajman, grew up in the shtetl of Połaniec where he learned the trade of shoemaking. In the early 1860s he was presented as a potential husband to the parents of my great-grandmother, Sura, in the village of Osiek, some twenty-four kilometres away. A dowry was negotiated, and the marriage took place.

As was the custom, the groom and his bride were supported by the groom's in-laws for the first year. That is to say, the newly-weds moved in with the bride's parents. This custom (*kest*) was part and parcel of the marriage contract, and it was intended to give the groom free time to continue his religious studies and also to give the couple a chance to get to know each other without the pressures of trying to make a living at the same time. Whether or not Meyer Frajman and his wife enjoyed their first year there, they must have found Osiek to their liking because that's where they stayed.

Great-grandfather Meyer set up a shoemaker's shop and for the next fifty years divided his time between studying in the synagogue, raising a family, and minding his shop. He lived to the age of ninety-five, at a time when a man's life expectancy was around fifty-five. Even in his nineties, he would walk twenty-four kilometres to Połaniec every spring to visit relatives during the mid-Passover break. While being dined by them, he would amuse the children by breaking walnuts with his teeth. Sura, my great-grandmother, gave birth to twelve children in the course of about thirteen years. Two of them died very young.

Poland was a poor country, whose territory had been appropriated and occupied over the years by Prussia, Austria, and Russia. The partitioning of the kingdom took place in three stages, beginning in 1772 and culminating in 1795, when Poland was obliterated from the maps of Europe. Historians have told us that in the hundred years preceding the Second World War, the poverty of the Poles and the population explosion of the Jews combined to produce deep tensions between the two communities. Yet the parts of the country that had become prosperous shortly after the Second World War, such as the northwest – anti-Catholic and formerly occupied by the Prussians – also became virulently anti-Semitic earlier than the poverty-stricken eastern sections.

My great-grandparents' first-born was a son, whom they named Israel. Next came my grandfather, Yankel, then Nusyn, then Moishe, then five daughters, Baila, Tobe, Marmaeita, Esther, and Blema-Rizel. The last-born was also a son, Haim. Two children also died somewhere in between. At an early age, Israel became apprenticed to a ritual slaughterer (*shochet*). Sometime before the First World War he emigrated to Hungary and settled in Budapest. There he became a full-fledged shochet, got married, and raised a large family. The growing Frajman clan in Budapest prospered in the wine-making business.

Grandfather Yankel was born around 1870. By the age of twelve he had acquired a reputation as something of a prodigy. He studied the Talmud and the writings of the sages. At sixteen, he felt confident enough to strike out on his own. A neighbour had a brother who had moved to Łódź, and there Yankel went to seek his fortune. The shtetls where these events were taking place were about 120 miles southeast of Łódź, in Kielce province, a considerable distance to travel at that time. Because of overpopulation, the area was described as 'The Lord of the Poor's Kingdom.' Grandfather found work in Łódź, giving religious instruction to students in their homes. In those days, the affluent engaged a teacher to teach two, three, or more of their children privately. As childbearing was ongoing, at least for the first ten to fifteen years of marriage, siblings close in age would take instruction together.

Yankel went to Łódź in 1890, and by the time he was twenty-one had married my grandmother, Hudys. Grandmother was born in Staszów, the largest shtetl in the same penurious area. This was a marriage of some significance. Hudys was the daughter of my great-grandmother Faigele (Wasercyer), who had made a reputation for herself as a confidante of learned rabbis. Even though she bore at least ten children, Faigele was rumoured to have frequently neglected her husband, my great-grandfather Moishe, and spent a major portion of her time waiting on numerous renowned rabbis. Undeniably well versed in the Torah in her own right, Faigele had selected Yankel for her daughter even though the prospective bridegroom was not likely to provide for a family on his earnings as a teacher. Faigele had previously turned down a young man brought to the family table on a Saturday evening by the marriage broker (*shadchan*) as unsuitable: the wastrel had used a brand new match to light his cigarette instead of using the flame of the multibraided *Melave Malke* candle, lit at the end of the Sabbath.

Within about two years of the nuptials, Hudys had given birth to the first two of her eventual ten children in quick succession; the second child, born in 1899, was my mother, Eadis. Grandfather reluctantly gave up teaching and turned to handling dairy products. Early every morning he would take the horse-drawn streetcar to the village of Kala, at the end of the line. There he would pick up two or more cans of milk, each standing about three feet tall, from the dairy farmer who was his supplier. He would return to Łódź early enough to distribute the milk to his regular customers in time for the children to have a hot drink before going to religious school (*Cheder*). All milk had to be boiled. Grandfather's customers lived in the four-storey apartment complexes of the neighbourhood. The heavy cans had to be carried up the stairs, the milk ladled out in the customer's kitchen, and payment collected. Because there was no refrigeration, distribution had to be even speedier in the summer. As Grandfather Yankel's children got older, they all gave a hand in the milk distribution. By that time, grandfather had bought his own cows, thereby eliminating the need to travel. The cows were kept in a shed at the back of the apartment complex. The shed was behind three courtyards, near the stables where wagon drivers kept their horses. Peasant women were hired to milk the cows. My partiality for farmyard smells dates back to the times when, at my grandfather's, I would watch the docile animals chew their cud while being milked. The apartment complex was one of the largest in the city. Four hundred families made their home there, plus an unknown number of roomers and out-of-town guests.

Like his father, Yankel was a Kohen, a direct descendant of Aaron, first high priest of the first tabernacle in the desert and brother of Moses, who led the Hebrews into the Promised Land. Hence, Yankel had the honour of reading certain passages of the Torah. By middle age, he was renowned for his sound judgment and was much sought after for advice. As he was learned and a son-in-law of Faigele to boot, Yankel the Dairy Man was someone people looked up to.

Grandfather had a large dog, black with white spots, who stood guard over the cows and made sure that the rats didn't annoy the animals and, heaven forbid, make them reduce their milk yield. The dog became quite adroit at killing rats. Not being as fast as the rodents, he tried to corner them, then went for the jugular. He was effective, and the rats kept their distance, except for this once. A rat, cornered by the dog, scampered into an eavestrough and hid for a time. Grandfather's dog waited patiently for the rat to emerge and when it did, snapped at its head. The rat dove into the dog's mouth and down its throat. Unable to dislodge the rat, the dog choked to death. A sad end to a valiant animal.

This incident happened in 1928, the year I was born, and four years prior to my grandfather's death. Not long after my birth, Grandfather Yankel brought a piece of fresh-baked bread with him on one of his visits, and proceeded to rub it over my forehead. This, he said, would make me wise (or at least appear so), for it would ensure that I developed a high forehead. When I was three or four, he let me play with his watch-chain. My memory of him is of a man with a white beard who liked to pat me on the head.

My grandfather was very much in demand for Din Torahs, impromptu tribunals made up of three learned men who would listen to both sides of a dispute, then render a verdict. Both parties to the argument were obliged to sign an agreement that, whatever the outcome of the trial, the party found in the wrong would abide by the verdict. Most of the disputes brought before such courts concerned business or family matters. A common problem was a dowry not being paid in full. Usually the bride's parents asked for more time to make good on the promise, while the bridegroom's parents preferred to have the cash in their son's hands on the grounds that, once the wedding took place, there was little they could do if the in-laws proved unwilling or unable to pay up. Promissory notes were not accepted. To avoid the disgrace of the bride's being deserted at the wedding canopy (*chupa*), the families sometimes negotiated on their own to the last possible moment, at which time a member of one of the families would summon a Din Torah. The judges were unpaid, but as it was considered a great honour to serve on a Din Torah, they performed their duties gladly.

Grandfather Yankel's younger brother Nusyn was called up to serve in the Russian army. Posted to the Siberian city of Irkutsk, he spent the first two years in basic training and the next three repairing other soldiers' boots. Released from the service at the end of five years, Nusyn was given back the clothes in which he had arrived and told to turn in his army uniform. Having received his discharge papers, he was free to go. But the price of a railway ticket, even third class, was beyond his means. Trained to march great distances, he proceeded west on foot. Nusyn got home in 1903, almost two years to the day after his release from service to the tsar. On his long trek he had endured hunger, cold, and heat. He had also learned to economize. He found some of his new habits hard to break, even in the near comfort of the shtetl. One was the knack of using only one cube of sugar to sweeten up to fifteen glasses of hot tea at a sitting. He somehow managed this by holding the sugar cube between his teeth and letting the tea filter through it.

At twenty-seven Nusyn married a sixteen-year-old girl. He

soon moved to Łódź with his wife and his younger brother Moishe – as did a great majority of their generation over the next two decades.

In the city Moishe became wealthy in the sweater trade. Unhappily, he had married a woman who was a hypochondriac. This was no excuse, however, for his getting their woman servant pregnant. The maid had red hair, a colouring not much in demand and extremely difficult to give away in marriage, unless a big dowry was promised. The servant was from another poverty-stricken shtetl and was now, of course, ruined for life. Moishe had been obliged by social pressure to pay the unfortunate girl compensation and return her to her parents.

The youngest brother, Haim, had become something of a free thinker, and the family had almost given up on him. However, he fell in love and married the daughter of a calligrapher of holy scrolls. He then turned religious to the point of fanaticism. Haim's father-in-law's profession – the careful hand-lettering of goatskin scrolls – was highly respected, but paid little. Haim, with an unsteady writing hand, was unable to help in this work. He was devout and prayed three times a day, rocking with the rhythm of the prayers. Eventually, he became a pedlar, often travelling by train to sell his wares throughout the region. On his trips, he would repeatedly recite the morning prayer 'L'man Yerbi,' 'Let our days be multiplied.' Spoken rapidly, the phrase sounded like *tanie ryby*, which in Polish means 'cheap fish.' 'Cheap fish' thus became his nickname – used only behind his back, of course.

Haim's wife, Shprintza, a spirited woman who had hoped to break out of her cloistered home life by marrying Haim, was dejected when he turned ultra-Orthodox. The marriage deteriorated, and Shprintza deserted her husband and turned to prostitution. What made the situation singularly distasteful was the fact that Shprintza's regular beat (where she was much in demand) was on a street corner not far from her former home. Remarkably, she and Haim eventually reconciled.

Of my five great-aunts, Marmaeita stands out because of her dominating personality. She prodded her husband to become a pedlar in the far-away province of Poznań. Unheard of in those times, they travelled as a team, she in the wig that all married Jewish women wore in those days. It was through her machinations that two of my mother's sisters married first cousins. Marmaeita was convinced that the Frajman blood line was second to none and that it was best to keep it in the family. The exception was my adventurous Aunt Frieda, who had emigrated to Canada, sponsored by my great-aunt Brancia (Faigele's youngest sister), who had married a local man who'd returned to Poland from Toronto to find a bride. In Toronto, Frieda married a man from Lithuania, a rather drastic step, since *Litvak*s were thought to be rather peculiar people. But Frieda was then in her twenties and had no time to lose. Altogether, there were three sets of marriages between cousins. The first was Aunt Bluma's marriage to Uncle Fishl, whose mother was Bluma's Aunt Baila.

Fishl became a wealthy textile wholesaler who supplied goods to many of the pedlars, including Marmaeita. Marmaeita and Fishl, aunt and nephew, had a falling out a few years later. It had something to do with her son Garshon, who had gone out peddling yard goods on his own and had gotten a certain farmer's daughter pregnant. There was no thought of the couple's marrying, as their religious beliefs were incompatible. The farmer, not surprisingly, was pretty sore about the whole thing and was heard threatening to do harm to all pedlars. Fishl and his aunt had words about the matter. Garshon, the errant son, got a job in town, where he had a chance to practise the tango, at which he had become something of a maven. Unable to find a match with a girl of good lineage, Garshon married an older girl who had no dowry, and remained in Łódź until the family was deported to Auschwitz in 1944. His wife died, but he somehow survived, and in 1946, after Liberation, married his cousin Rózia, my mother's younger sister. (Rózia's first husband was Nusyn, also a first cousin.) The net result was that Marmaeita stopped buying from Fishl and refused to speak to him for the rest of her life.

Pedlars sold yardage to customers in the Poznań area for a down payment, and what remained owing was paid in the form of promissory notes called *weksel*s. The weksel was an early forerunner of the credit card. Cash was scarce, and the Polish national bank was keeping the money supply tight. Bank loans were unheard of, so the business community created their own currency. The weksel circulated like cash. Each time it passed from hand to hand, the person had to endorse it, thereby becoming a co-guarantor of payment on the due date. Some long-term notes had 'tails,' or strips of paper glued onto them, bearing the signatures of endorsees. A good endorsement made the weksel more valuable, even if the original debtor was not considered good for the money. Failure to redeem a weksel on the due date was commonly called a 'protest,' a term that came up often in adult conversation.

Pedlars often presented weksels to Fishl as payment for goods bought wholesale. By keeping track of the addresses of the original issuers, Fishl could extrapolate information as to which specific village or town would be easy pickings. These data he supplied to customers' relatives – but not to Marmaeita.

Fishl had a form of security in his apartment, which doubled as a warehouse and store: he had trained a large dog to let people and goods in but to bark and bare his teeth at anyone trying to pass him on the way out carrying parcels. He obeyed only Fishl's command to let them pass.

The war brought changes: In late 1939 the Germans had ordered all Jewish businesses to shut down. The air was rife with talk of deportation. Mother's cousin Leon (the middle son of grandfather's brother Nusyn, of the two-year-march fame) had, early in the war, crossed the Bug River into the Russian-occupied half of Poland. In December he had returned to Łódź bringing important news: an underground railway had sprung up in Wilno smuggling Jews out of German-occupied Poland. For a fixed price, to be paid in gold coin, valid passports from an obscure Central American country were provided. Entraining on the Trans-Siberian, the lucky ones would be taken overland to the railway's terminus on the Pacific, the port of Vladivostok. From there they could obtain ocean passage to America via Japan or the Philippines.

A meeting was called in Uncle Fishl's flat to discuss the proposition. Father and all the uncles on Mother's side were present when Cousin Leon gave details as to the costs and the time frame. He spoke of the tensions between the Germans on the west bank of the river and the Soviet army on the east bank. Each side was wary of the other's intentions. Refugees on either side of the partition line were suspected of spying. To cross in either direction was possible only at night, with guides. It was dangerous and likely soon to become impossible. A decision had to be made immediately.

Only Uncle Fishl and Aunt Bluma were in a position to take advantage of the offer. They had a hoard of gold pieces that had been minted by the Imperial Russian Court and were referred to as 'little piggies.' Such coins were in clandestine circulation throughout Central Europe. But Uncle Fishl was reluctant to walk away from his possessions, and Leon returned to Białystok empty-handed.

About two years later, after conquering all of Western Russia, the Germans first herded the Jews into ghettos and then proceeded to murder them en masse. Leon made his escape into the near-impenetrable forests of the region, where he joined a partisan group. Polish maps identify the forests as *puszcza* (wilderness). The area was home to bison, wolf, and wild boar and became a base for the many guerilla bands sniping and disrupting the German supply lines to the eastern front.

There are times when you wish people would not forget to remember. Leon, the only man in the family who waged war and killed Germans, could recall in minute detail his experiences in the forests. He couldn't remember, however, who it was that inquired about my father in the summer of 1945, after Leon had returned to Łódź and again taken up the manufacture of underwear. Leon emigrated to Canada in 1950, and, almost until his death in mid-1995, I kept after him to try to remember who it was. My prodding was futile. Leon merely shrugged his shoulders. After fifty years the strange man was just a blur. Leon insisted, though, that the man was a relative of Father's.

On the Frajman side, I have had help in reconstructing the family tree. I know little of the family on Father's side. The Germans succeeded in killing them all. The name Drukier is the phonetic spelling of the Dutch/Flemish word for printer, *Drukker*. In German the word for printer is *Drucker*. I believe that my Drukier ancestors settled in Ozorków, in the Łódź province, many years ago. My paternal grandmother's family name was Domankiewicz. Beyond that, all is darkness.

History tells us that Jews settled in the Kielce area in the late sixteenth century. Despite a lot of inbreeding, the original genetic stock must have been solid, good enough to produce so many forceful personalities. The Kohen line passes by oral tradition through the male family members, and it is now finished in our Frajman family branch. The fate of the Budapest branch remains unknown.

4
New Year 5752

On the first day of Rosh Hashana 5752, Freda and I walked for about twenty minutes from our apartment to the Warsaw synagogue. Freda sat in the gallery with the other women and I with the men in the main sanctuary downstairs. There were about forty men, some with prayer shawls (*tallitim*) wrapped around their shoulders, several – mostly younger men – in suits and ties, and a few, of various ages, in everyday clothes.

I was supposed to meet Konstanty Gerbert, a political commentator who wrote under the pseudonym Dawid Warszawski, and, as arranged, I kept visible a copy of *The Idler*, a magazine I publish, as I.D. But Gerbert didn't seek me out. As the service proceeded, I kept looking about trying to determine which of the young men milling around might be Gerbert. No luck.

In front of me sat Aaron, a young man in his mid-twenties, with brushed-back, light-brown hair, glasses, a dark suit, and polished shoes – Ivy League all the way. During the break in the service he and several other young men in North American attire met to chat near the entrance. When the service was about to resume I learned that Aaron was from Alabama via Maryland and was helping *Gazeta Wyborcza*, the Solidarity newspaper, install state-of-the-art computers. Aaron knew Gerbert and pointed him out to me. I moved over to the backless bench where he was sitting beside Stasiek Krajewski.

I had heard about Krajewski in Toronto. He had become extremely Orthodox, unusual in a young man born of a Jewish

mother and a Gentile father, and there was talk that he would
study to become a rabbi. His devotion was unmistakable. This
section of the shul was composed of local people who seemed to
know each other well. Some were absorbed in their prayer-books;
others looked out of place. I had difficulty following the service
but Gerbert assured me that others, even Warsawians, did no better. Krajewski, however, was doing very well. A man just in front
of me, a retired colonel who was introduced as the vice-chairman
of the Jewish community association, kept pointing out to Gerbert inconsistencies in the way the *Baal-tefilah*, the prayer-leader,
was conducting the prayer. I suspected that Gerbert was being
charitable with me. I plodded on. There were perhaps sixty men
in the sanctuary now: about twenty-five older men, ten younger
natives, fifteen or so foreigners, and a few Russian-speakers. That,
according to Gerbert, was the most expected at High Holiday services. At Yom Kippur a few more 'once-a-year Jews' turned up.
After services Gerbert had to rush home to meet a deadline. The
services had begun at ten and ended about eleven-thirty, being
much shorter than the services at home in Canada.

An older man told me that during the war he had hidden out
in Warsaw on Aryan papers. He was pale, had blue eyes, and
stood six feet tall, with erect posture. He was, he declared, still in
mourning for his wife, who had been trapped in the Nazi net in
1943, even though she had dyed her hair blonde and could easily
have passed for a Pole.

At the Menorah Restaurant a group of us from the synagogue
sat down together. Andy, from Denver, was just passing through.
Max and Emil, brothers in their early thirties, were in the elec-
tronics business in Warsaw. They had emigrated from Poland to
New York in 1981 with their parents, who had spent the war
years in Russia, and the brothers had returned to Warsaw in 1989,
but did not intend to stay. Jeffrey, a twenty-six-year-old Toronto-
nian, slightly built and with a full head of dark, wavy hair, had
come to Poland to seek his fortune. Aaron, as well as Abram, an
Israeli businessman operating a halvah-manufacturing plant outside Warsaw, and his wife, Ruth, completed the group.

The wine was deplorable, but the food and company good. We

were a group who shared a common heritage, but whose backgrounds were very different. Andy and Aaron were undoubtedly third- or fourth-generation American. My mention of the fact that I had spent time in Buchenwald brought a moment of respectful silence.

On the second day of Rosh Hashana we were late for services. I was befriended by Dr Simcha Wajs, a slim, grey-haired man in his seventies with a neatly trimmed beard and moustache. His twinkling blue eyes had drawn me to him the first day, when we shook hands and wished each other 'Shana Tova' (Good Year). Hoping to see the many new friends I had made the day before, I was disappointed. Attendance was down by half.

Dr Wajs had taught medicine at Warsaw University and been the editor of a quarterly medical journal. The Polish/Yiddish newspaper, Folk Sztyme, had published an article by him that identified the Polish officers of Jewish faith who were among those killed by the Russians in 1940 and buried in a mass grave near Kharkov, in Ukraine. According to the doctor, there were 200 Jewish dead. His biography of the 250 Jewish doctors buried in the Warsaw cemetery was nearly completed. He gratefully accepted the High Holiday prayer-book I had brought with me, as he had been trying, with difficulty, to follow the complicated Holy Day service with the aid of a daily prayer-book. Our whispered colloquy was interrupted when a short old man who had his tallit pulled over his bald head remarked that the Baal-tefilah had poor lungs. The blowing of the ram's horn – the Shofar – was indeed uneven. The old man, a former butcher, pointed out that he himself had been the Baal-tefilah when the shul was first reopened after the war and that he had, by all accounts, done a creditable job. But this Baal-tefilah, sent from New York for the holidays, a tall, skinny youthful individual with a flowing beard, was unable to sing the prayers with an Ashkenazi melody and, consequently, lost a few marks. Our butcher friend, speaking loudly and telling stale jokes, was shushed by the rabbi. When I asked where he had spent the war years he said that, because he had always been honest in his dealings with the farmers, he had managed to roam the countryside for more than two years without being caught. He did not stay very long with any one family, in order not to endanger his hosts, and no one ever reported him to the authorities. That, I agreed, was remarkable, and possibly unique for that era. He now wished he could repay his friends in some way, and wondered whether I could help any of the farmers' sons to emigrate to Canada.

When I first entered the sanctuary I was asked by the attendant if I were, perchance, a Levite. Like Kohanim, Levite men are descended from the tribe of Levi and, by tradition, perform certain functions during prayers in conjunction with the Kohanim. The rituals, clearly spelled out in the Torah, date back to the time of the first Temple in Jerusalem. A male child is told of his lineage at an early age by his father. (About 98 per cent of the Jews in the world are descended from the tribes of Judah and Benjamin, and the balance from the tribe of Levi. The Assyrians exiled, sold as slaves, or killed off the other ten tribes of Israel.) A special New Year's blessing on the congregation can be given by a minimum of two Kohanim, I was told, but Rabbi Joskowicz used his prerogative and allowed the only Kohen in Warsaw, a man named Wasserman, to bless us on his own. Wasserman, an older, bald man wearing glasses with thick lenses, repeated the prayer in a voice that sounded as though it were coming from Mount Sinai.

After the service Dr Wajs urged us to make haste in getting over to the nearby community centre. A hot lunch of chicken soup with rice, a dish of noodles topped with a slice of salami, and tea with lemon, preceded by gefilte fish and matza, awaited us, but not before we were pushed and shoved at the kitchen serving window.

Crowding around us were what I assumed to be most of the poorer, older Jews left in Warsaw. Several had come directly from home, only for the meal. I learned that seventy to eighty meals were served daily, paid for by the American Joint Distribution Committee. Heavy-hearted, I contemplated the group gulping down what was conceivably their main daily meal. One man and a woman were obviously not Jewish. At first, Dr Wajs told me that he could vouch for their authenticity, but as an afterthought, he remarked that some Christians who had hidden Jews during the 1940s had been given permission to share in the bounty.

At this point, a tall man entered the small dining room. Except for his grey beard, he was a casting director's ideal Rasputin. He was wearing a long coat and a fur hat despite the warm weather, and he was carrying a Bible. He went to each seated male in turn and, shouting to make himself heard over the din, recited a sort of blessing that started with 'Shalom,' and the man's name and concluded with a series of words that sounded like gibberish. In the harried, melancholy setting, no one seemed to mind the man's intrusion. Within twenty minutes the crowd dispersed. Freda pointed out that some of the group were squirrelling away leftovers in purses or bags.

A slight, wizened old man named Kagan approached Freda and began speaking to her in Yiddish. His companion, a man in his late thirties, was decidedly not Jewish. Kagan lived in the town of Międzyrzec Podlaski, near the Belarus border. The only Jew in the area, he tended the old Jewish cemetery. He was married to a peasant woman and had a young son. The nearest other Jew lived some sixteen miles away but was unfriendly and did not practise his religion. Kagan and his companion, a farmer named Zanycki, were neighbours and had come to Warsaw by train for the services. They were now returning home. The words *Babcia Israelita*, spoken in passing by the farmer, caught my attention: it seemed odd that a Gentile would have a Jewish grandmother.

This is the story Kagan and Zanycki told: In the 1980s, an old Jew in the area, who had been ill for years, died, leaving his third wife, a Russian Jewish woman of advanced age, destitute. The farmer, Zanycki, who sold his produce in the market, routinely undercharged the widow; eventually, he was giving her vegetables for free. The relationship evolved to the point where he was calling her 'grandmother' (*Babcia*). Kagan noted that Zanycki had embraced some aspects of his 'grandmother's' faith and described as 'one in a million,' this mitzvah that he had performed. Zanycki depended on the woman for advice, and, on the grounds that she had 'suffered a lot,' had bought her a new black-and-white television set. He had also given her a new washing machine, and other things. Just before her death, Zanycki delivered a colour television, but she rejected it, saying it was extravagant and frivolous. After she died, her body was brought to the Warsaw Jewish cemetery for burial. Zanycki's mourning period of one year was almost up. It was a remarkable story, from a remote and forgotten part of the old Pale.

5
An Apartment in Łódź

In Polish, the word *'miasto'* (city) always precedes Łódź for the following reason: The word 'from' is 'z,' so the statement 'I am from Łódź' translates 'Ja jestem z Łodźi.' However, the word for 'thief' is *'złodźiej'* – pronounced almost identically to *'z Łodźi'* – so one could easily be taken to be declaring oneself a thief. To avoid the trap, one says, *'z miasta Łodźi.'*

We arrived in the city of Łódź late in the afternoon. After foolishly missing the nine-twenty from Warsaw, we had had to connect in Koluszek, about halfway to Łódź, with a rattling old local train. A hard rain was falling when we arrived, and the taxi-driver was not very pleased with the short run taking us to the Grand Hotel on Ulica Piotrkowska.

We had intended to rest for a while but I was too excited, and so out we went. Though the rain had abated, the air was chilly. We pushed off to Plac Wolności (Liberty Square), a formerly elegant circle in midtown where, in pre-war days, sections of the wide sidewalks were lined with the chairs, tables, and umbrellas of luxury cafés. The massive baroque buildings are still there, but nothing remains of the cafés. At the intersection of Piotrkowska a large sign pointed to a sale of second-hand clothing (*Ciuchy*). Piotrkowska is no longer elegant; the buildings, with carved cornices and sculptures, are mostly in a state of sorry decay. The few that have a fresh coat of paint make the others appear even more drab. The streets are full of people shopping, but there is none of the leisurely strolling that was notable in Warsaw. There are no tourists. The people here are simply going about their daily business.

We sought number 11 on November Eleventh Street. (November 11 is the anniversary of Polish Independence, gained in 1918, as well as of the First World War armistice.) The street had been renamed Defenders of Stalingrad. We found numbers 9 and 13, but 11 was no more. Number 11 was the building in which my family had lived until 1935. The intersection of Ulica Zachodnia (West Street) had been widened to allow for streetcar lines, and my old building had apparently been demolished. It took me a while to become certain of this. The rain started up again. My doubts were dispelled when I correctly directed us to the next intersection, Gdańska. There, the building on the corner that had housed a liquor store in my youth was gone. The empty space was now occupied by a couple of street vendors, one selling bananas and the other lottery tickets. I led the way to number 6, where my family had lived for the next four years. Entering the courtyard through the arch, I noticed that the double gate, though very old and dirty, was not the one that I remembered. The original gate had been of heavy wood, rich brown and highly polished. It was locked every night, and thereby became a source of income for the janitor, whom latecomers would tip about twenty or thirty groszy to let them in. I would often find empty vodka bottles behind the open double doors, where drunks had stopped to quickly down the contents. I would turn the bottles in at the corner liquor store for a caramel candy worth a grosz – the smallest unit of Polish currency – per bottle.

We lived at number 6 at the time that I started school. The four-storey wing on the left hadn't changed much. I could see the small windows in the attic over the fourth-floor apartments. This was where Mother and the washerwoman hung the laundry to dry after a major wash. Such a wash took place about once every three months, certainly before Passover and Rosh Hashana. The hired washerwoman came early in the morning and set enormous pots of water to boil on the kitchen stove. All the bedlinens, cotton garments, and underwear were first boiled, then dropped into a large tub constructed along the lines of a barrel, with staves and metal rims. Each piece was carefully lathered with a large chunk of yellow laundry soap, then scrubbed on a washboard. A rinse in cold water and a run through a wringer completed the process. The wet laundry was then put into large baskets and carried up to the attic, where ropes strung under rafters provided a permanent, airy drying space. The important white bed sheets were hung in the centre, and the smaller items along the walls. To create a cross-breeze and thereby speed up the drying process the washer-woman would open the small windows.

Mother seldom got a night's sleep when our entire lot of bedding, shirts, and underwear was up in the attic. In Łódź, gangs of second-storey men specialized in stealing laundry. Fortunately, it hadn't happened to us, but my mother's older sister, Baila, had had all her laundry stolen.

The next day we would take the bedlinen, dry and folded, to the mangle. That was the best part of the whole affair. The mangle was operated by a family consisting of a father, mother, and several daughters. They took our linen and passed it through a large machine that had a series of heavy wooden rollers. The father did the cranking, and the girls handled the linen. The mother took the money. The shirts and underwear were ironed by hand by the washerwoman, who stayed behind in our kitchen.

As Freda and I stood before number 6, my gaze travelled to the lower part of the building, where changes were evident. The frames of the two windows of our main-floor apartment had been painted a bright yellow. The door to the hallway was locked, and there was an intercom board listing the dozen or so apartments in the wing. The tall poplars in back, by the church that faces another street, were as I remembered them. They must have been replanted once or twice over the years, as this type of tree has a relatively short life span.

To the right, there was the same row of two or three low-rise apartments, but they seemed closer together now. The courtyard seemed narrower as well. Cobblestones were missing; in their place were bare patches of wet sand. Unlike in the past, the court-yard was eerily still and deserted. Children once played there, their mothers shouting to them from the windows above. Itiner-

ant entertainers would saunter into the yard – magicians, acro-
bats, jugglers, musicians, singers, and even dancing bears with
muzzles. Men with monkeys on their shoulders played accordi-
ons or cranked music boxes. Gypsies came, the men offering to
mend pots and the women to tell fortunes. The neighbours tossed
coins from the windows, and the performers acknowledged them
with courtly bows. Often a pushcart appeared, pulled or pushed
by a bearded man who shouted 'Szmaty!' ('Rags!') and paid cash
for worn-out clothes and used glass bottles.

Our presence alerted a woman who was looking out a window
two floors up. My inquiry as to the name of the person or persons
occupying the main floor brought the reply 'Kowalczuk.' I hesitated, just for a second, then buzzed. We were let in. A tall, blonde
woman in her mid-sixties came out to see who the visitors were.
Behind her was a man of perhaps forty. The hallway was dark. The
doors had closed behind us, and the only light came from the open
door of the apartment. Taking off my cap, I announced that I had
lived on the premises before the war, that we had come from Canada, and that I only wished to see what the place looked like now.

Poles get nervous when people return from foreign parts and
seek out their former homes. They assume that they have come to
reclaim property and that the present occupants could be forced
to leave. In fact, the pogroms after the Second World War had
their origin in the Poles' fears that the Jewish homes and shops
they had taken over would one day be returned to the former
owners or their descendants.

The Kowalczuks, mother and son, graciously invited us into
their living room/bedroom and offered us tea. In passing the
small kitchen, I noticed that we had interrupted their dinner and,
apologizing, declined the offer. The floor of the apartment, once
painted red, had been covered with beige linoleum. I would have
loved to lift a corner of it to verify my memory. Instead, I just sat
on the couch searching for words. How long had they been in the
place? 'Since 1949.' Mrs Kowalczuk, now quite at ease and curious, had at first attempted to deny the possibility that it was I
who had lived here. Likely, it had been only my parents. I
repeated that I had lived here too, up to the age of eleven.

The kitchen was microscopic, mostly because of the addition of an undersized bathtub behind a curtained partition, as well as of an enclosure containing a toilet. The stove was now on the opposite side of the kitchen, and the sink was where the stove had originally been. There was room for only a small table and two chairs. Proudly, Mrs Kowalczuk showed off these improvements. Certainly, the gas stove was an improvement over the wood-and-coal-burning stove we had had, as was the toilet over our common outhouse in the back of the courtyard. Otherwise everything was about the same. A large wardrobe stood against the back wall. Our wardrobe (*szafa*) had been taller and had mirrored doors – that I was sure of. Often I would turn a chair towards it and play-act cowboys and Indians. Putting my arms over the back of the chair, I would pretend that I was on a horse, rocking back and forth, to my mother's displeasure, while making threatening faces in the mirror.

We chatted, Mrs Kowalczuk and I, my Polish still halting. Was she born in Łódź? Mrs Kowalczuk changed the subject. The reluctance of provincials to admit to having been born elsewhere than in Łódź persists to this day. (Snobbish native Łodźians proclaim their birthplace proudly.) The Kowalczuks had moved in when the place was in disrepair. She said there had been an arch in the back wall that led into the pastry shop facing the street, and I told her that, before the war, it had been a pharmacy and had had the only working telephone in the building. Mrs Kowalczuk suggested that a bomb must have fallen on the spot, because, when her family moved into the apartment just above, the windows of the shop were smashed and there was debris all around. I observed that since there had been no damage during the September 1939 campaign, the likelihood of damage later was remote. She reluctantly agreed. They had closed off the wall to the pastry shop, fixed up the kitchen, and replaced the window frames. She had been there forty-two years. Her son had heart trouble. So far, holding a lit cigarette, he had said little.

The place was smaller than I remembered it. On one of the walls hung a tapestry depicting Pope John Paul II, and there were two couches that I supposed were turned into beds at night.

I rubbed my eyes and turned to the wall. Of course! Where I was now sitting there had been a fireplace, a closed fireplace about four feet wide, with a filigree metal door and shiny white tile that extended up about as high as I could reach. It was gone.

On Saturday afternoons in cold weather, mother would gingerly remove from the fireplace a pot of *cholent* that had been simmering since Friday. It contained lima beans, barley, whole or grated potatoes, and kishke (a steer's intestine stuffed with flour, fat, and seasonings). The cholent was good and brown, ready to be served when father returned home from synagogue. When father later leaned against the warm tiles and dozed off, we children would tiptoe out.

Mrs Kowalczuk still wasn't entirely satisfied with my credentials, but I dispelled her doubts when I identified the landlord as being a lady of White Russian origin. I correctly pointed out her second-floor apartment above the main gate. The old lady had died, and her three daughters had inherited the building. Yes, the building was still privately owned. The rent was being paid to a remaining daughter who now lived upstairs. Neither the Germans nor the Communists had dispossessed the owners.

In the one-storey building across the yard, where the janitor now lived, there had dwelled an old German with his grandson, with whom I often traded books. Early in the war, we could hear the faraway sounds of artillery salvos, and would look up to spy for enemy planes. The neighbours noticed that the old German had climbed up onto the low roof, perhaps to better observe the night sky. The tenants, alarmed, clutching folded pieces of gauze over their mouths in case of a gas attack, shouted at him to come down immediately. They thought he wanted to send smoke signals to the Luftwaffe to drop a bomb on our place. The struggling man was dragged off the roof, and no bombs fell.

Łódź had escaped damage in 1939. The Polish armies, outnumbered, outgunned, and outmanoeuvred, had made a stand in Kutno, near Łódź, and again in Warsaw, which was heavily bombed from the air and by artillery. In January 1945 the Germans abandoned Łódź to the Russians without a fight.

In September 1939 my father and uncles had walked off

towards Warsaw at the first sign that the Germans were approaching Łódź and that the Polish armies were pulling back. My Uncle Nathan, a junior cavalry officer, was present at the siege of Warsaw with his army unit. When the Poles capitulated, he exchanged his uniform for civilian clothes in order not to be taken to a prisoner-of-war camp. Nathan was big, so it wasn't easy, but Cousin Leon had managed to find him a three-piece suit.

Again, the Kowalczuks asked us to take tea. The son, still not very talkative, continued to chain smoke. When I said that I was born in 1928, our hostess admitted to having been born in 1922. We complimented each other on how well we looked. Freda and I made our excuses and apologized once again for having interrupted their meal. Mrs Kowalczuk asked us to come again, and hoped that, if I started a business in Łódź, I would consider employing her son.

I left number 6 Gdańska holding on to Freda's arm.

6
Yom Kippur in Łódź

On the way back from our visit to my old home we stopped at the address which, according to Cousin Leon in Toronto, was the Jewish community centre. No luck; no one there knew the place. We returned to our hotel, The Grand (which it had certainly been when I was a little boy), changed clothes, and went down to dinner. After the meal we asked the desk clerk for the location of the synagogue or Jewish community centre. He seemed puzzled, looked something up, and referred us to number 6A Południowa (South Street). We found the street, but there was no such number, so we continued walking to the spot the clerk had marked on the map. The number there was 62–64, and the numbers were still rising. It was now after 7 P.M. We walked briskly back to the lower numbers. There were few pedestrians, and those we did pass rushed by. It started to rain again, having drizzled or rained on and off all day. Freda watched for potholes in the sidewalk – there were plenty. Dogs came out of doorways and sniffed us. Twice I asked for directions to either 6A or the synagogue. No one could help. I kept my eyes peeled for any sign of a gathering. It was Yom Kippur Eve.

The buildings facing the street were all three or four storeys high. Some had two or three stores at street level, and a central archway that led into a courtyard surrounded by more buildings, of various heights. Some of those buildings also had passageways, into other courtyards flanked by wings of other apartments, stores, warehouses, and repair shops. Above, invariably, were living quarters. In many cases, the numbers on the buildings had been obliterated. The street name had been changed in the 1950s to 'Revolution of 1905,' then changed back to the original 'Południowa,' but only some of the signs on the buildings reflected the more recent change. We were getting anxious: the numbers were now in the teens.

Unofficial information gives the number of Jews now in Łódź at no more than three hundred. Most are not practising; we were told that even the few who do not deny their Jewishness prefer to keep a low profile. The telephone book lists no Jewish organizations.

The street lights overhead threw off only a dim light that was further diffused by the steady rain. Into this scene strode a tall man with a long grey beard. He was wearing the traditional dress of the Hasid – a long, black, shiny coat, tied by a sash around his waist, and a round fur hat (*shtramel*), flat on top and about two feet across. Accompanying him was a woman wearing a traditional wig. I stopped, stunned. Motioning Freda over, I approached the Hasid and requested, in Yiddish, his assistance in finding the synagogue. My approach startled him a bit, but he recovered and suggested that we follow him. At number 28 we entered through the gate into a courtyard, then proceeded through an archway into a second yard, and then a third. To the right stood the synagogue. It was locked up and dark. Rabbi Moreino, our guide, muttered that he could not depend on his flock to hold services. I expressed surprise that there were no services for prayers on Yom Kippur Eve (*Kol Nidre*). We walked back out onto the street, Freda with the *rebbitzen* (the wife of the rabbi). We were making our way to Zachodnia (West Street) where, the rabbi said, a service might be in progress. It was now half past seven, and it was raining hard. The rabbi told us that he was Chief Rabbi of Łódź and Poland. I was mystified.

The story that unfolded was so engrossing that I tripped a couple of times. I stole a look at the rebbitzen, who was pretty and quite young. Rabbi Moreino, I guessed, was seventy or so. We stopped in a doorway so that he could cover his fur hat with a sheet of plastic. He showed me a bottle of what he said was nitroglycerine, for his angina. It is contrary to Jewish religious law to carry anything but a handkerchief on the Sabbath or Holy Days. Medicine is specifically exempted, but, just to be safe, the rabbi placed the vial in his hat. This is not considered carrying.

The rabbi resumed his story, moving easily between past events and present circumstances. He had spent the war years in concentration camps. Afterwards, he had lived in Łódź until the early 1980s, when he moved to New York. During the postwar period, the Communists had jailed him for two months for refusing to toe the line. Two months ago, he had returned from New York to look after the Jews of Łódź. When I asked him how often he made this trip, I was ignored. His dealings with the government used to be acrimonious but were getting better. Their apartment in Łódź had been let to someone, and they had had to move to Widzew, a suburb. According to the rabbi, the local Jews were an ungrateful bunch. He blamed their absence for Kol Nidre on their old age and their tendency not to go out in the evening. At number 78 Zachodnia we stopped at a nondescript door. This, the rabbi pointed out, was a prayer room (*Bet Midrash*), not a proper synagogue. The place was padlocked and dark. The rabbi shrugged his shoulders and announced that a private service would take place in his apartment.

I scratched my head, as we certainly were not going to Widzew at this hour. On Sabbath or Holy Days, Jews are forbidden to use any type of transport, including elevators. But the rabbi was already moving away. Curious, we followed him to a doorway about seventy-five feet to the right, passed through a broken door, and climbed three flights of stairs in complete darkness. The rabbi dropped a key that he'd retrieved from under the mat. 'The rebbitzen will pick it up,' he said. We entered a sparsely furnished apartment lit by only two Sabbath candles and a small night light. When he removed his coat, we saw that the rabbi was wearing a prayer shawl. We washed our hands, and the rabbi motioned to the east wall. He started chanting the Kol Nidre passages, and the strangest service we have ever attended began.

The prayers went on for an hour and a half, without pause. The rabbi and I were on our feet the entire time – I felt that if *he* could hold out and not sit down, so could I. Certain passages of the prayers may be sung to different tunes or melodies, which vary in origin, Sephardic or Ashkenazi. But it was impossible to pick out a melody in Rabbi Moreino's chanting: it was flat, monotonous, fast, and slightly halting in spots. My own prayer-book was nearly useless, and I couldn't follow or even pick out the familiar passages. The rebbitzen sat for the most part, and kept her eyes on the prayer-book.

As soon as he ended the prayers the rabbi apologized for not being able to offer refreshments, as it was the start of the twenty-four-hour fast. However, if we wished, we could join him and the rebbitzen in breaking the fast after sundown the next day. But it was not too late, he said, for me to examine the numerous letters he had written to the authorities regarding the desecration of Jewish cemeteries.

Evidence showed that schools and other public buildings had been erected on the site of several old Jewish cemeteries. According to religious law this is illegal, even if the graves are exhumed and the remains moved to other sites. The graves of our ancestors, some dating back to the sixteenth century, are inviolable, the rabbi said. His letters promised investment in Poland by Jewish entrepreneurs in the West on condition that the Polish government show good faith in protecting the cemeteries. The government's replies, addressed not to Moreino but to Fundacja Nissenbaum (the Nissenbaum Foundation) of West Germany, pertained to the cemetery in Kalish, the oldest in Poland. The government conceded that it was possible to move the school that had been built on the cemetery elsewhere, but only if funds to cover the cost were found abroad.

Rabbi Moreino had written to Polish authorities with respect to other matters as well. He wrote to the governor (wojewoda) of Łódź about the possibility of producing kosher chocolates and candy for export. He also suggested moving thirty Yeshiva students from New York to Łódź on a rotating basis, in order to form a nucleus of Torah study in Poland. The tradition of study must go on, declared the rabbi. His meeting that same morning with the wojewoda had been fruitful. The man was sympathetic to the idea of reviving Jewish life in Łódź.

Fascinated as I was, I couldn't help overhearing the rebbitzen telling the rabbi that Freda appeared to be very tired. Undaunted, Moreino proceeded to tell me about the many shortcomings of his flock. Without exception, they were members of the underworld dating back to the ghetto and before. They cooperated with the Nazis and Communists and continued to thwart and frustrate his efforts to restore them to the path of righteousness. The rabbi's descriptions of the doings in the Warsaw synagogue were hair-raising. Rabbi Joskowicz, he claimed, who lived in Israel but was officiating in the Polish capital, was a fraud. Not a rabbi at all. He had done time in Israel for dealing in suspicious meats, and was a charlatan who had cooperated with the Polish authorities and given permission to remove graves. The entire Warsaw Jewish executive committee, according to the rabbi, was a group of col-laborators. Moreover, since they cohabited with Gentile women, they could not be regarded as true Jews.

Our conversation was conducted in Polish, Yiddish, and English, with quotations in Hebrew. Quoting from the Talmud, Maimonides, and other sources, the rabbi explained, at some length, that even though a congregation of ten adult male Jews is thought to constitute a quorum (*minyan*), those men are qualified to join in prayer only if they are observant Jews, guardians of the Sabbath (*Shomer Shabbat*). The inclusion of even one man who is remiss in his observance of the Sabbath and the rituals makes the prayers invalid in the eyes of the Lord. The rabbi said that, with respect to his own congregants, he overcame the obstacle by intoning, at the end of the prayer, 'We are here to learn.' Although the phrase negates the official nature of the prayer, it makes the attempt credible in the eyes of the Almighty by defining the pro-cess as a learning session that will prepare the way for proper prayers in the future – presumably once all the men have become devout. The rabbi confessed that he had misgivings about the solution he'd devised. He held us in his spell.

It was now half past eleven. Outside was total darkness, relieved only by a flickering light across the street. Where we sat, the fifteen-watt bulb in the night-light dimly illuminated a large, low bed on one side of the room, a buffet, a table, and two chairs. On the wall between the windows hung an enormous set of antlers, either moose or reindeer. The rabbi's tall figure became invisible when he moved into the dark side of the room. He would occasionally bob into the light, bringing me more and more letters that he kept in a thick file. Trying to concentrate on the material and make sense of the colloquy consumed all my attention.

Quoting the scriptures, Moreino explained that a rabbi's acceptance of payment for the services he performed, such as a marriage ceremony or a divorce, or delivering judgment on a question of *kashrut*, invalidated those services. He also explained that, in civil or criminal cases involving Jews, only a properly constituted rabbinical court could render judgment. No Jewish person was ever to take his complaints to a civil court within a rabbi's jurisdiction. Should a verdict handed down by a rabbi be ignored by either of the parties, however, the rabbi could (and should) ask the civil authorities to enforce the verdict. This was not a denunciation of the delinquent party, but a request of the authorities to carry out the judgment. The rabbi further insisted that an infraction of rituals made a person non–Shomer Shabbat. 'But,' I protested, 'surely one cannot be expected, in today's world, to follow each and every one of the hundreds of precepts.' Cunningly, the Rabbi asked, 'If you were a soldier, would you carry out only the orders that you liked and ignore the ones you didn't?' Fumbling, I replied that being forbidden to carry the prayer shawl to services was a bit much and that I didn't think it could be much of a sin if I did. He pleaded that I wear the shawl under my coat to avoid breaking the commandment that prohibits carrying anything in one's hands or pockets. Then he asked, triumphantly, 'After all, aren't we soldiers in the service of the Lord?'

Out of the corner of my eye, I saw Freda conversing with the rebbitzen in hushed tones. Just then the rebbitzen declared again that '*Ona jest zmęczona.*' And Freda *was* tired. As we were leaving, the rabbi again invited us to return to the apartment the next evening so that we could break the fast together and discuss his projects further. It was, he declared, improper to discuss business

on a Holy Day. We left, neglecting to ask where and when the services would take place the next day. We would have to trust in
our luck.

Next morning we found the main shul still locked. We proceeded to the synagogue on Zachodnia. There were two guards in
front, which led us to believe that something was indeed happening. Inside, we found about twenty-five men, and a few women
sitting behind a makeshift curtain. Services were in progress. Our
rabbi was on the *bema* (podium), leading the prayers. This was, as
he had said, a Bet Midrash – larger than a *shtibel* but smaller than
a synagogue. The ramshackle room had benches, two rusted
chandeliers with half the bulbs burned out, and a cupboard for
storing the Torahs. The *bema* faced east, towards Jerusalem. The
walls needed a coat of paint badly, the wooden floorboards
creaked and hadn't been waxed in years. The faces around us
looked familiar, such as are seen in certain older parts of Miami
Beach – the faces of Jewish men and women who have been
through a lot. Some wore suits, others mismatched jackets and
pants. About a third wore work clothes, some of which were quite
soiled. Few had prayer shawls.

Heedless of some indignant looks, I engaged a few of the men
who seemed not to be paying attention to the proceedings. One
told me he had settled in Łódź after returning from Russia at
war's end. Too weary to move on, he had stayed behind when
others emigrated. Now he was retired, and regretted not having
left. But it was too late – his wife was ill. I had correctly guessed
that he survived the war years because he had been deported,
first to Archangel'sk and later to Tashkent. In 1940, living in eastern Poland under the Soviets, he had registered to return to
German-occupied Poland. To the Russians, refugees who wished
to return to the Nazis were obviously Nazi sympathizers. Consequently, they were rounded up and sent to the far north and to
the east, where most survived the war. My four unmarried uncles
had crossed over to the Soviet side before it was closed off in late
1939 and had no intention of returning, even though their living
conditions were deplorable.

Another man had worked as a shoemaker and now subsisted

on a pension. He wore torn shoes, soiled jeans, and a zippered-up windbreaker. On his head rested a blue peaked cap that he wore at a rakish angle. He regretted not having had the ambition to move on in his youth. He repeated the proverb 'The worm that bores its way into horseradish thinks it has entered paradise, not having tried other vegetables.'

Taking advantage of a break in the service, I shook hands with others. My claim that I had been born not far from this spot brought no response.

Leib, a functionary of the Jewish executive committee (*kehilla*), told a sad story. About two months before, the Bet Midrash had been broken into and three *Safer Torahs* had been stolen. The police were informed, and a drag-net was set up at western border points, but Leib was certain that the Torahs had been spirited out to Belgium that very night. When I expressed surprise that there would be a market for stolen religious objects, Leib's melancholy reply was that some Belgians had been seen about the previous day asking questions about the habits of the community. 'It was,' he declared, 'a pre-sold project.' Someone had pre-ordered the scrolls, which had a retail value of nearly twenty thousand dollars.

Leib, I recalled, was the man Rabbi Moreino had singled out as the most corrupt of the Łódź Jews. About seventy, tall and slim, with a gentle, sad face, and wearing a shabby, grey-brown suit, Leib, according to Moreino, was the relative of a man who had collaborated with the Nazis.

Just then, a dispute was taking place on the bema. The rabbi had decided to delay the memorial service for the dead (*Yiskor*), in favour of continuing, and expanding on, the Torah reading. The men seemed to be incensed by this, and insisted that Yiskor be said immediately, according to the traditional sequence and schedule. The shouting, in Yiddish and Hebrew, escalated to a feverish pitch. Among the most vocal of the dissenters was a short, slight, grey-haired man with heavy eyeglasses who had come from Israel to visit the graves of his dear ones in the Łódź cemetery. He was shouting in Hebrew and making threatening gestures. The rebbitzen hid her face in her hands. Suddenly, the rabbi gave in. Immediately after the memorial prayer, attendance dropped by two-thirds. Freda and I left as well, promising to return for the afternoon services. It was about one o'clock.

At 3:15 P.M. there were three police guards outside, but only five men inside. Among them were David, twenty-three years old, tall, dark-haired, a Parisian of Moroccan ancestry; a short, corpulent man of about seventy-five who identified himself as the chairman (*Prezes*), and who was blind; Skowroński, a handsome, blond, bearded man of twenty-six wearing gold-framed glasses, an open-necked white shirt, and a double-breasted black worsted suit from which protruded the religious fringes (*tzitzes*); and an older man with a dark moustache who was wearing soiled clothes, pants with the cuffs rolled up over his ankles, and a floppy cap with the peak pulled to the side. Leib darted in and out to make telephone calls. His efforts to raise the group to the minimum of ten for a minyan seemed fruitless. The rabbi was nowhere in sight.

I pieced together the events of the past two hours: The men had ganged up on Rabbi Moreino, demanding that he let someone else lead the prayers. Their main complaint was that his chanting brought them no pleasure. It wasn't melodious, it followed no known sequence, it was a one-man soliloquy. It was dull, and his droning was driving everyone crazy. The rabbi put up a brave fight but finally departed in disgust.

As we waited for the services to continue, I learned that the Polish government, while acknowledging Rabbi Joskowicz's appointment to the highest office by agreement between the Ministries of Religious Affairs of Israel and Poland, also dealt with and respected Rabbi Moreino. However, Leib cautioned me not to take the rabbi at face value. Where had he been during the war? It was unclear. Wasn't it unfair of him, at his age, to marry a girl of sixteen and to make her a rebbitzen, a position that carried great responsibility? Although he was undoubtedly an extremely learned man, his attempts to mould everyone in his image were doomed. Skowroński added that he had tried hard to respect the rabbi, but found his methods of dealing with opposition to be in poor taste. For instance, Skowroński had been in the Warsaw synagogue when a dispute arose between Moreino and Joskowicz. At some point Moreino pushed Joskowicz off the bema. Wherever Moreino went there were fights, disagreements, and verbal abuse: people now viewed him as a fanatic who brooked no opposition. What was more, Moreino, according to Leib, coveted Chief Rabbi Joskowicz's six-thousand-dollar monthly salary.

I found out that Rabbi Moreino had been a chaplain in the Polish army. At a point when he began to object to certain actions by the Communist government he was sent to a lunatic asylum – and not to jail as he had told me. As for Rabbi Joskowicz, people said that, in spite of the generous salary paid by the Estée Lauder Foundation, he was unhappy in Warsaw. During the Passover Holidays, they alleged, he was with his family in Israel instead of tending to his flock in Poland.

David was shocked that Jews would argue on Yom Kippur, the holiest day of the year, and said that the experience left him numb. It was some time before I stopped thinking about the fierce rabbi. With his pale face, bulging dark eyes, high forehead, and prominent nose, he reminded me of Fagin.

Skowroński had recently landed a job as coordinator for the American Joint Distribution Committee. He would be going to Warsaw to oversee a group of young men and women who had formed a social and religious organization. His life story – not unique in Poland, he assured me – was of a man's quest for an identity. His grandfather, with hair as 'black as tar,' was an assimilated Galician Jew who served as an officer in the Polish army. Within a few days of the 1939 blitzkrieg he was taken prisoner by the Germans. For almost six years he was kept with other junior officers in a camp supervised by the *Wehrmacht*. Try as they might, the SS and the Gestapo couldn't persuade the German army high command to treat commissioned Polish POWs, and Jews in particular, differently from Allied POWs. The potential for reprisals on German officers taken prisoner by the Allies was clearly on their mind. Some Jewish officers were turned over to the SS, but the decision to halt the violations of the Geneva Convention was made final with the enormous disaster that befell the Germans when two hundred thousand under Field Marshal von Paulus surrendered at

Stalingrad. However, under the pretext of needing non-commissioned Jewish POWs for work gangs, the SS demanded they be handed over to them – and they were never seen again.

At war's end Skowroński's grandfather returned to Poland to find his wife, who had been hidden by Poles, ill. His teenage daughter, blonde and blue-eyed, had been working under forged Aryan papers in a German-run factory. After his wife died, the grandfather remarried; his new wife was Polish. The all-Jewish daughter, Skowroński's mother, married a young Christian. At the age of five, Skowroński began to wonder who he was. Stories his grandfather told him spurred him on. As soon as he learned to read he explored the libraries in search of anything about Jews and their religion. At all times he felt he was a Jew. As soon as it was possible he went to Israel to pursue his studies. He now spoke Hebrew with a Polish accent. Having been born of a Jewish mother, Skowroński was accepted at face value in the many subsects in Jerusalem. He favoured the Lubovitchers, but was interested in other groups as well. On his return to Poland he married a girl whose father was Jewish but whose mother was not. His wife, he remarked, would have to undergo a formal conversion to Judaism, as having only a Jewish father didn't count. (At some point during the Crusades many Jewish maidens had been raped by the knights. Abortion being frowned on, the rabbis declared that any child born of a Jewish mother was Jewish. The edict had stuck.) The Skowrońskis kept kosher and observed the rituals. The young man's declarations were so fervent and genuine that I felt uncomfortable about my lack of dedication.

According to Skowroński, many young people of mixed parentage were also returning to the Jewish faith. In Warsaw and Kraków there was some sort of support system for these people, but elsewhere they had nowhere to turn – there were few Jews around. The study of Hebrew and religious texts was conducted in private. Their lot was sad, Skowroński said, but not hopeless. Former communists in Warsaw had returned to the faith. This 180-degree turn could be explained only by historians. Some detractors said that the returnees hogged all the donations, squeezing out the rest of the country.

Just before five o'clock, a tenth man wandered in, and the prayers resumed. Visiting from Israel, the man had served in the Russian and then the Polish Red Army that had fought its way to Berlin. Originally from the Łódź area, the man had spent the past forty years in Israel. A teacher by profession, he was now retired. Unfortunately, since he had fought against the Germans, it was impossible for him to claim a German reparation pension. Those who had survived the concentration camps could apply for a pension; those who fought, couldn't.

During the afternoon break in services, I went to find my old school. Fifty years had left their mark – the paint was peeling, the walls were cracked. It was now a trade school, but I had spent grades 1 to 4 there. Across the street the Jewish private school had been converted to an apartment building. The schoolyard where we used to play was smaller than I remembered it, and was now paved. There were sheds in the back for cars.

I clearly remembered that during recess the girls skipped rope, and we boys played tag. In teams of six or more, we chased each other – if you were as much as grazed it was an automatic 'out.' Teams took turns being pursued. A chap by the name of Flamenbaum was by far the fastest runner. Whenever it was his turn to pursue my team, he invariably caught us. At one point, fed up, I split up my team, and we played our own game of catch-me-if-you-can. Flamenbaum could go to blazes.

At the drop of a pencil, boys challenged each other to fight. Bullies picked fights with me, perhaps because teachers sometimes left me in charge while they went out to do whatever teachers do when they leave the classroom. I would then read the day's lesson while condescendingly eyeing my classmates, possibly playing to the girl with long braids who sat at the desk next to mine. I don't think I was all that pompous. Anyway, I didn't back down and fought when attacked. My tactic was to delay the start of the boxing or wrestling to just moments before the bell sounded for class to start. It worked – sometimes.

Comic books used to take up a fair amount of my time. *Terry and the Pirates, Prince Valiant*, and *Tarzan* were my favourites. One boy, hoarding them, had assembled a huge collection, which I thought was unfair. Saturday noon was movie (*kino*) time. I could get in for twenty-five groszy. The Kasino movie-house was the best, concentrating on action pictures, westerns with Tom Mix and Ken Maynard, pirate films with Douglas Fairbanks and Tyrone Power, and, of course, Tarzan with Johnny Weissmuller.

I prided myself on being able to draw and my art was prominently displayed on the classroom wall. But I had trouble with three dimensions: given the assignment to draw the teacher at her desk, I failed miserably. I managed to convey the impression that the teacher's chest rested on a floating square. I made up for the deficiency by colouring the wall a bright yellow and the floor red. The teacher accepted my spectacular art without comment.

The public school system was segregated into Jewish and Roman Catholic, and we went to school six days a week, Sunday through Friday for the Jewish kids and Monday through Saturday for the Gentiles. There was a shortage of school buildings to accommodate the rapidly expanding student body, so we had morning and afternoon shifts. The private Jewish school across the street was named Kacenelson, after a Zionist educator. My three cousins, sons of my Aunt Bluma, attended this school, where the curriculum included Hebrew. The idea was to prepare youngsters for emigration and life in Palestine. The public school curriculum was taught in Polish only. Some of our kids must have been undernourished, because the Kacenelson would send over daily baskets of sandwiches. The discreet, regular drop-off of food suggested charity (*tzedaka*) of the better type, where the donor and the recipient remain unknown to each other. I remember peeking at the sandwiches: very interesing stuff. If there had been some way of swapping my own lunch for one of them I would have liked to do so. But there was no mechanism for this sort of deal.

Possibly I *was* becoming pompous. Just about then I had my first documented personal trauma. It happened in grade 4, and concerned a cat. The homeroom teacher, a pleasant lady whose fair-haired boy I was, taught an afternoon class to a younger group than mine. She was tall, dark-haired, blue-eyed, and had dimples. She had a husband who was also a teacher.

My trauma began one sunny spring day, when this, my favourite teacher, asked me to run an errand for her after class. I was to walk over to her apartment, get the housekeeper to give me her cat, and bring it to school. She explained that a demonstration of feline anatomy was to take place. The students of grade 1 or 2, who knew nothing about cats, were to get a treat. An honour for me, indeed. Imagining that I would nonchalantly drop the cat on the teacher's desk to an accolade of hushed whispering, I departed. I was confident that the mission would be accomplished successfully. Needing a witness to my triumph, I asked Finkelsztajn, one of my 'followers,' to accompany me. I was to carry the cat, and he would open doors.

The teacher's apartment was a few flights up in a nice building several blocks from the school. I leaned on the doorbell and brusquely asked the maid for the cat. Tom Mix probably was my model. The woman wanted to know how I was going to manage. I replied that the class was waiting and to please give me the animal. Presumably my teacher had told her about the pick-up, because without a word she handed me a rather large cat. Down the stairs I went, cradling the squirming creature in both arms. Finkelsztajn plodded behind me.

I had forgotten to ask the cat's name, which might have helped. The cat was definitely uncomfortable. No amount of moo-mooing on my part would stop it from squirming. I'd had little experience with animals. The previous summer, I had helped to stone a large mother cat who had recently given birth to a litter and had made her home in a corner of the vacant basement of the building next door. She had a flat head and a bunch of us thought that by getting rid of her we would be doing the community a service: we knocked her off because she was ugly.

But now, my teacher's cat had been in my possession for no more than five minutes before, practically without effort, it leaped out of my arms and vanished down an alley. Finkelsztajn and I looked for it for a while, but the cat was gone. I took off for home.

I spent the night in bed tossing and turning, wondering how to face my teacher the next day. My humiliation was total. I thought I might try feigning sickness. Toothache, headache, stomach cramps – anything. In the morning I decided to face up to it. What rankled me most was the fact that I had run home immediately after the cat bolted and had not reported the loss to school that same afternoon.

The teacher and I exchanged good mornings the next day as if nothing had happened. I wondered if the cat had made its way home right away. Was it possible that my teacher had guessed what had happened? The most likely explanation was that the cat had arrived home before the teacher and that the teacher assumed I had simply forgotten the assignment. I made a mental note that it was best not to trust preconceived ideas about how any particular crisis might turn out.

7

The Last Hours of Childhood

The Łódź civil registry office was not hard to find. I was asked to fill out a slip giving details, and after fifteen minutes and payment of six thousand złoty – about sixty cents – I received a typewritten, stamped, and sealed version of my birth certificate. I was Mojżesz, my father was listed as Gabrych, and my mother as Idessa. I was shown the original entries in my father's handwriting. For good measure I also got and paid for a copy of my sister, Anna's, birth certificate. In a few minutes Freda and I were back in the sunlight. My hands trembled a little.

A short taxi ride brought us to the Jewish cemetery, reputed to be the largest in Poland. Surrounded by a crumbling, eight-foot-high, red brick wall, the cemetery is huge. We entered through a small gate. The monuments, engraved in Yiddish, Hebrew, and Polish, are in decay. Many have been vandalized. There are mausoleums of families long gone. Inscriptions on monuments from the late nineteenth century are barely decipherable. The mausoleum of the rich Poznański family, resembling a Greek temple, was boarded up when we were there. Enclosing it was a fence with barbed wire strung along the top: a sign that was obviously old proclaimed that the municipality of Łódź was in the process of putting the structure in order. I wondered whether it could have been pangs of conscience for all the properties of the Posnańskis that had been confiscated that made the authorities put up the sign. The stone edifice was in terrible shape. The cast-bronze Hebrew lettering was missing, but one could make out the impressions it had left, which were several shades darker than the stone.

More recent graves make the others seem all the more ancient. A woman in her sixties approached us and asked if we spoke Polish. Until then, we had been the only ones there. She burst out that she had been looking for someone to whom she could tell the good news: She had found the burial place of her father, who had starved to death in the Łódź ghetto. The family had been present at the funeral, and she remembered the location of the grave. She and her sister were the only family members to survive Auschwitz after the remaining Łódź ghetto population was sent there. They had gone on to live in Israel. This was her first chance to visit Poland; her husband was waiting at the exit gate. I offered to take a photograph of the site or slab, but she said she had already taken a video of it and intended to make a copy for her sister. We embraced briefly.

I had been told that there was a record book identifying all the graves, with a plot map that pinpointed their exact locations. Perhaps only my mother's parents could be found here. They had died of natural causes in their sixties, the normal life span in the 1930s.

On one of the brick walls near the entrance are plaques, in Polish and English, mourning relatives who perished in the Holocaust. Whether by accident or by design, each has a different way of saying 'criminal.'

Back in town, we came upon a shop with a sign in the window that read 'MIĘSO I WĘDLINY.' Inside the white-tiled store, behind the counter, hung wreaths of salamis in an assortment of thicknesses. Strings of cocktail wieners lay sprawling on top of a crate. Displayed under glass were chunks of fat kielbasa; a pale pink liquid seeped onto waxed paper from the cut end of a blood sausage. At the far left, a plump woman in a kerchief and white coat tended the counter.

When I was a child the Łódź shops sold kosher salamis (*ofshnit*) – turkey salami, red with white ovals of good fat, beef salami showing eyes of white, goose salami, white veal, knackers, dry salami, garlic salami. Bought Saturday night when the shops reopened after the Sabbath, the double wrapping of waxed paper removed, the salami sat in the middle of the kitchen table beside a jar of congealed goose fat. In the fat were *gribben*, pieces of crisp skin. The feast lacked only fresh bread; Jewish bakers did not work on the Sabbath. Friday's bread, salt, and sour pickles completed the treat. We spread the goose fat evenly on the bread, sprinkled it with salt, and overlaid it with slices of turkey, beef, and goose salami. We ate silently, savouring every bite. This ritual usually followed a week of good business in Father's shop.

Father's wholesale textile store specialized in gentlemen's fabrics. It was a two- or three-way partnership with an uncle and a cousin. Passing it this day in 1991 I saw how small it had been. It was now a shoe repair shop.

Mother and Father sometimes reminisced about the good old days just after they were married, when *tatuś* (daddy) would arrive home on a Friday afternoon from peddling in the Poznań area and give mother the week's receipts to count while he went off to the barber's for a shave and a trim. Tatuś had a heavy beard and delicate skin. Occasionally I would accompany him to the barber-shop, eagerly awaiting the stropping of the razor. The barber had a long leather strop, greasy and glistening from strokes of the steel. To me, the rapid stroking of the razor, followed by two or three loud, flat smacks, was tinged with drama and danger. Father had a pronounced Adam's apple, and sometimes the barber, attempting an extra-smooth shave, nicked Father, and tiny droplets of blood would appear. The barber applied cotton, and Father, not paying attention, leaned back in the chair and kept his eyes closed.

In those honeymoon years Father was a travelling salesman (*foorer*). On his rented cart he carried a range of gentlemen's suiting. Checks, pinstripes, and flannels in grey, black, blue, or brown were cut into three-metre pieces, sufficient for a man's suit. Getting off the train at one or another of the rural stations near Poznań, Father would go from village to village peddling his wares. There were no hotels in the villages, and he usually slept in someone's hayloft. He told us how he once frightened a farmer when he emerged from the barn for morning prayers with his phylacteries and a large prayer shawl. The man, startled, spilled his pail of milk.

The Poznań province had a large proportion of Germans who had money to spend. Father did good business there, probably because he spoke the language, having attended a German school during the German occupation of western Poland during the First World War.

It must have been a lonely and hard way to earn a living. Distrusted by his often anti-Semitic customers, he had had to tread carefully. Poland in the 1930s was a semi-fascist state. Everyone had to register with the constabulary. Staying over a weekend in Poznań, or moving there, would have made my father's life easier, but that was impossible: there were restrictions on Jews settling in the area. Still, my father went about his work cheerfully. Mother said repeatedly that the first few years of their married life, the years of Father's travelling, were their best. It ended when I was five, and he needed to stay closer to the family.

Some Saturdays, in good weather, we all walked the twenty-odd blocks to visit Father's parents, Grandparents Hunnoh-Leib and Channah-Leaha. They lived on the main floor of a building similar to ours. Previously, they had owned the grocery store that adjoined their apartment and faced the street, where sacks of flour, sugar, barley, salt, and kasha sat on shelves and the floor.

Before my grandparents moved to Łódź they lived in the small town of Ozorków, just outside our sprawling city. I believe my father's family had lived there for many generations. Before I started school Mother would take me to Ozorków in the summer and leave me with my grandparents for a few days. As I was the first grandson – and, as it turned out, the last – they made a fuss over me.

An electrified tram ran from Łódź to Ozorków. There, one very hot day, I laid myself down on the tracks, spread-eagled, preventing the streetcar from moving. It took some persuading by my grandmother and the streetcar conductor to get me off the line. I'll never know what possessed me to do it.

Once, when I was about three months old, my father, who was in the habit of taking off his wedding band when washing his hands, put the ring down on a table. My sister, Anna, two at the time, started to play with it. I was in the cradle nearby when she dropped the ring into my open mouth. Mother heard me choking, saw that I was turning purple, and demanded that Father do something. At this point Father noticed that his ring was missing and figured out what had happened. Father called on the neighbours for advice. All this time I lay choking.

The consensus was that holding me by the feet and shaking me vigorously would release the ring. And so it did.

There were two other mishaps during my childhood. When I was about three and a half, Mother had put a bowl of hot chocolate pudding on the table to cool off. Ever inquisitive, I came over and pulled the bowl towards me. The spilled, near-boiling liquid left a permanent mark on my chest where the skin had come off in strips.

The other episode involved our landlady's retarded brother, who, in my preschool days, sometimes took me to the cinema. One Saturday afternoon we had returned early from seeing a black and white film that had sequences in which people leapt out of windows, followed by objects such as boxes and then more people. In imitation of the scenes, the brother put me out a window, head down facing the street, and held me by one foot. The simulation was fairly accurate as we were about twenty feet up. Mother became alarmed and scolded the poor fellow. After that incident she refused to entrust me to him, and I saw few movies.

In Łódź my grandparents on my father's side had two sons and two daughters living at home. All of them worked. My aunts Esterka and Andzia, in their twenties, were seamstresses. Uncle Meyer, a carpenter, and Uncle Abram, a barber, were in their late twenties or early thirties. My father, the oldest, was the only one married, and at the outbreak of the war he was thirty-eight years old.

When I stayed overnight at my grandparents', I slept with grandfather in a narrow bed with a cold metal headboard that was brown and had leaves and flowers painted on it in yellows, reds, and greens. Staying over had something to do with going to shul with grandfather on High Holy Days and getting back late.

Grandfather was a thin man with a short, greying beard; he usually wore a round, small-brimmed black cap and a black satin coat. Grandfather and I never talked much. Grandmother was the outgoing one in the family. A short, plump woman with dark hair, she was always busy cooking or baking. I looked forward to the taste of her pickled squash.

The aunts fussed over me. Once, while I waited, one of them cut and sewed a short-sleeved sailor-type shirt in blue and white stripes for me. It was a hot day, and I wore it when we went to the park and sat on a bench under a tree. I was about seven at the time. A woman walking by greeted my aunt and recommended that I wash my eyes when I got back home, since they were much too dark. There was a chance, she observed, that I would break women's hearts.

With Father, I once visited Uncle Meyer in his workplace, in the basement of a building not far from Father's store. The floor was covered, ankle deep, in shavings and sawdust. Uncle Abram was spoken of as a bit of a black sheep – something about forged banknotes. He was tall, with a head of blond curls. No pictures of the family exist. My grandparents and aunts perished in the Łódź ghetto, my uncles probably in Majdanek.

During one of my visits in preschool days, a man walked by the window, yelling something in German. My aunt told me that the man had been born deaf. His family, comparatively well off and determined to give him an education, had sent him to a special speech therapy school in Germany. After finishing his course he returned to Łódź. He had learned German, and it was the only language he could speak. His family was not entirely pleased with the progress he had made. My aunt explained that whereas previously he had been a quiet, pleasant young man, he was now often agitated. The story fascinated me. I sat, cross-legged, on the window sill, waiting for him to pass by again. He emerged wearing a brown jacket and pants, and he had a hat on, even though it was a hot day. Clean-shaven, he had a large head on a medium-sized body, and his head shook up and down. His hands were bent out at the wrists, with fingers moving and twisting. His voice was loud, and this time I could hear him distinctly: he yelled 'Wir sind verloren, alle Juden verloren!' (We are lost, all the Jews are lost). He moved on, still shaking his big head up and down, his hat slipping to the back. At home I mimicked his outcries for my parents' benefit.

Łódź had its share of Jewish thieves, extortionists, and beggars. The regular beggars had routes. Mother could expect a visit from the same man or woman once a month, almost to the day. Clever beggars scheduled most of their calls for Fridays, when the Jewish homemakers baked challahs and boiled fish and chicken soup: feeling guilty because of their own good fortune, they would be apt to give a little more. Mamusia never turned anyone away. A grosz or two had to be found. If not, special little challahs were included in the baking, to be given away.

Our family did not show affection in public. As a matter of fact, we didn't much in private either. These were not Hasidic Jews but middle-class business people living in a big city. Not much overt affection was shown the children, either. We knew that our parents and our aunts, uncles, and grandparents cared; they just didn't go in for hugging and kissing. Perhaps it was a carry-over from the shtetl and the religious upbringing that prevented them from being demonstrative.

We were brought up to kiss our aunts on the hand or cheek, to say please and thank you, and to be careful to observe a certain ritual when visiting, not taking the fruit or cookies until they were offered and refusing second helpings, even if we were dying for them. Mother and my aunts expected to be asked at least three times before they would partake.

Talk about anything relating to sex was rare, certainly when children were about. Expressions of endearment in various shades and degrees are not common in the Polish vernacular, and are even less prevalent in Yiddish. Had they been required, they would have been invented. The difficulty I have with expressing fondness may have its roots in the culture I knew as a child.

It makes sense that Jews and Poles, two peoples living side by side for more than five hundred years, would develop similar habits. One is a certain disrespect for authority. As the saying goes, 'Where there are four Poles you find three political parties' –

a mirror image of the scene in Israel. There is one major difference though: with exceptions, Poles drink a lot and Jews don't.

When I was eight years old my father's wholesale fabric shop was a few blocks from where we lived, in a place called Halle. In long, low rows of cheaply built structures that faced each other across a wide walkway were shops displaying every conceivable type of textile product. The open shops were about six to eight feet deep and had folding doors. The Halle was a wholly Jewish enterprise. Ostensibly wholesale, it also sold retail. Haggling was a part of any purchase. On one occasion, I probably ruined a potential sale for my father. I was sitting on the counter when, in the midst of a transaction, I ventured the opinion that the price quoted was a lot of money. That, I believe, was the last time I interfered in my father's business.

Hundreds, even thousands, of business people passed through daily. Strong men called *tragers* (porters) went about with coils of rope over their shoulders. For a fee these men would carry off one's purchases to the railway station or one's place of business. They would also deliver, on their backs, merchandise from the factories to the Halle shops. The tragers, organized and having set their fees, didn't allow others to undercut them. As well, goods stolen in transit could be ransomed by getting in touch with certain tragers. The parade of hawkers selling delicacies was of most interest to me. My favourite pastry was the napoleon, a custard square. The shops were open to the elements, summer and winter, the only protection being the roof. To measure out yardage in the winter, for a better grip, my father used gloves with the fingers cut off at the tips.

Some merchants had grown moderately wealthy as the economy expanded. One of the richest Jews in Łódź was Poznański, whose family owned a very large textile factory that covered several city blocks and was surrounded by a red brick wall. At one corner of this complex was the Poznańskis' baroque palace. The factory had a tall chimney (*komin*) that spewed smoke day and night. We could see the chimney from our home. In fact, in Łódź anything big or important was always jokingly compared to the *Poznański komin*.

When I would visit my father's latest upgraded street-front shop, I had to pass an exclusively Polish housing development. The trip was always undertaken with trepidation. Polish boys would accost me and challenge me to a fight. At an early age I must have considered it cowardly to cross the street to avoid danger. From overheard conversations I learned that one dealt with anti-Semitism in the only way possible: negotiate around it, never confront it head on. One learned early in life that the rights of second-class citizens are often trampled. The adults found that the least troublesome manner to deal with anti-Semitism was to bribe or navigate around the difficulty. The bottom line, even in pre-war times, was survival.

The housing complex where I had the problems with the Polish boys had been erected by Poznański to house his employees.

The middle-class Jews of Łódź, newcomers from the shtetls, tried to blend into the big city. Their children spoke Polish at school and often at home. Family ties were strong and marriages were frequently arranged. But, unmistakably, rapid changes were under way. My mother and father had an arranged marriage. My mother was two years older than my father, which was not unusual. My grandfather had paid a dowry of perhaps five hundred dollars, a good deal of money in the mid-1920s.

At the age of twenty-four, my father, just released from the army, was introduced to the textile business by my Uncle Fishl. My mother's sister Bluma was married to Fishl, her first cousin, who by that time was established in the business. My mother's sister Rozia married Fishl's brother Nusyn, and her younger sister Andzia married their second cousin Moniek. In fact, my parents' marriage was the only one in the immediate family that bound two individuals who were unrelated or who did not share a common small-town family history.

In our apartment complex there were families who produced articles of wear in their living quarters. The people directly above us had knitting machines and employed young men and women in manufacturing sweaters. (Some of them marched in the big May Day parades in our city. They would return the next day sporting black eyes and bruises inflicted by policemen's batons.)

The two daughters in the family across the courtyard gave piano lessons. We all did our grocery shopping just outside the gate of the complex. Facing the street were shops selling dairy products, fruits and vegetables, meat, and baked goods. Directly opposite our complex, in front of three buildings that had no commercial outlets, was a *droshky* stand. There, waiting for fares, drivers dozed on their high seats while their horses ate from sacks filled with oats that were strung around their necks. At the corner was a confectionery and liquor store. Adjoining it was a candy store that sold wonderful ice cream in the summer.

When it came to buying fall and winter clothes Mother would take us to a street where many shops specialized in children's and teens' clothing. The stores facing the street were considered a bit expensive. Through the gates in the courtyards were shops that gave a better deal, and still further into the complex, or even up a flight of stairs, prices were even lower. A tout (*reefer*) would transmit this message to Mother as she walked along the street holding my sister and me by the hand. The reefers' livelihood depended on enticing people from the street into shops located deep inside a complex. Working on commission only, they persistently sang the praises of their particular shop. I often wondered what made Mother decide to follow one tout over another. To me, they all seemed equally menacing. Once inside, unless the shop did not have the right size, it was difficult to leave without buying. The salespeople were persuasive and always complimented Mother on her children's appearance. A certain amount of haggling was expected. Invariably, the owner insisted that he was losing money on the transaction.

Stray dogs and cats wandered about in our neighbourhood. Dogcatchers tried to keep the streets safe, but they were not always successful. One beautiful Saturday afternoon, in about 1938, a stray dog wandered into our complex from the street. Some of us were sitting on chairs in the courtyard when the peculiar-looking dog began to circle us. It had a leonine mane and a long tail with a clump of fur on it, and it was foaming at the mouth. As Father tried to shoo it away, the dog leapt and bit him in the chest. The police were called. They came and shot the dog dead. I recall two policemen, one with a rifle, cornering the hapless animal and shooting it. Stretched out dead it was every bit as lionlike as it had been when it was alive. The carcass was taken away, analysed, and declared rabid. Father had to undergo a number of painful anti-rabies injections.

I don't think I took any interest in books until I started school, at which time my sister, Anna, had entered grade 2. She could read, after a fashion. I demanded that she read to me her school lessons and homework. Her grade 2 stories I considered much superior to my own first grade fables. Impatient to get to the source, I learned to read for myself. From that point on I was invariably one year ahead in my school material, as I would go through Anna's school books as soon as she got them.

Books were scarce and expensive. I never bought one or got one as a gift. The school lending library had few books, and those were graded and lent out according to the age of the student. I could get an advanced book through my sister, who had been assigned to a different school, or I could swap with someone in our building. It was tricky, and I had to be nimble. When visiting relatives I would sometimes come across books. This helped. I was considered a bit unsociable as I would often devote the entire visit to catching up on my reading. By the time I completed grade 3 my need to read had become all-consuming.

I found a better way to satisfy that need in the summer of 1939. Our family didn't rent a summer cottage that year. I suspected that we couldn't afford the expense. Nevertheless, I insisted on compensation for my lost vacation, and a deal was struck. Father and I went to the local private library and signed up for two months, at a cost of three złoty per month – a large sum for a ten-year-old, about sixty-five cents in pre-war dollars. The catch was that subscribers could take out only one book per day, which translated into six per week, hardly a bargain and far short of my requirements. I resolved the problem by exchanging books with a boy who lived across the courtyard and who found himself in the same predicament.

The summer of 1939 was hot and dry. Early each morning I would set out for the library about nine blocks away. The book I'd picked out the day before would be very much on my mind, but should it be out, I already had my alternative selections planned. My favourites were adventures, especially of the American Wild West, such as those by Karl May. May had written marvellous stories from a jail cell somewhere in Germany, and he had never set foot outside his own country. With his and other books in hand, I had a glorious time that summer.

From the beginning we knew that there would be war.

Prime Minister Chamberlain's peace efforts notwithstanding, my aunts and uncles repeatedly said that we were in for it. At first Hitler said he only wanted Austria and the Sudetenland, then he demanded a corridor through Polish territory to the Free City of Gdańsk (or Danzig). The sabre-rattling went on all summer, but it was common knowledge that wars don't start before the harvest is in.

I sometimes listened to my mother's unmarried youngest sister, Hela, say that the situation might get worse and that the Poles were foolish to grab from the beleaguered Czechs the Zaolzie region, a strip of southern territory that had a mixed Polish and Czech population. The younger generation of Frajmans, my mother's family, occasionally met on Saturday afternoons at Aunt Rózia's. She lived directly across the street from us in a fourth-floor walk-up, but hers was a three-room apartment. Since she had only one little boy there was ample space to sit and talk.

One reason I liked to go there was that Aunt Rózia had all sorts of cookies, chocolates, and fruit. That is, I knew she had them but it was a fifty-fifty proposition whether she would offer them to me. Rózia was known as a skinflint. There was apparently a defective gene on my mother's side of the family that surfaced every other generation: it magnified normal thriftiness to miserliness of a malignant kind. Mother said that her sister couldn't help it. I was sure, though, to be offered oranges that had begun to go soft or chocolates that were old.

In my Aunt Rózia and Uncle Nusyn's bedroom hung a picture that took up most of the wall. It portrayed King Solomon in his court issuing the famous 'cut the baby in half' judgment. The blood-chilling choices proposed to the true mother were similar to those facing Poland. By then Stalin and von Ribbentrop, the German foreign minister, had signed a non-aggression pact. They had also secretly agreed on the partitioning of Poland. The signing was received as bad news by our side. It left only France and Great Britain as guarantors of Poland's sovereignty. Whether they were ready to fight Hitler was debatable, and the grown-ups debated it frequently.

I liked Aunt Hela, who was usually the most outspoken but who had become morose and silent lately. Having overheard my parents talking about it, I knew that she was in love with a certain Srulek, employed as a salesman by Uncle Fishl. (Hela was in Fishl's employ as well.) They had been going out for some time, but when they began to talk of marriage, Uncle Fishl put his foot down. Fishl was against the match because he suspected Srulek of concealing the fact that he had tuberculosis, which is, of course, contagious. As Fishl put it, referring to Hela, 'A healthy person does not lay down willingly in a sick bed.'

Among the Frajmans, there was apparently also a gene that produced domineering personalities. Fishl was a good example. Short and pudgy, with light hair cut short, he had a round, boyish face that could lull you into believing he was an unassuming person, until you looked into his unblinking blue eyes. His wealth made him even more formidable. Hela, he declared, was an educated, intelligent, good-looking girl who could do better than Srulek. Fishl broke up the affair. Srulek was a rabid communist – another reason for Fishl to dislike him – and he soon departed to the Soviet Union, never to be heard from again. Hela never forgave Fishl and Aunt Bluma for forcing her to break up with Srulek. At the start of the war she was unmarried and still angry; in January 1940, when most of the family left for Staszów, she insisted on remaining in Łódź and was eventually deported from the ghetto to Auschwitz, and to her death.

On 1 September 1939 German army divisions crossed into Poland at a dozen points. The fully mobilized Polish army was no match for the German panzers and Luftwaffe. Blitzkrieg, being perfected, called for pushing hard with everything and not giving the opposition a chance to regroup. The Poles kept falling back, often leaving behind their horse-drawn supply wagons. The enemy forces pushed ahead so rapidly that soon they were near Łódź. We heard but didn't see the artillery fire. The Luftwaffe was dropping bombs and machine-gunning the retreating Polish troops, who were going to make a stand at Warsaw. The reserve brigades were moving as fast as they were able in an easterly direction to a defence line on the Wisła or the River Bug. Abiding by the secret pact, the Russians moved into the eastern half of Poland on 17 September. There the Polish armies were disarmed and interned. Eventually the enlisted men were let go, sent to the far north, or east; most of the officers' corps were shot.

During the first days of the war, a radio was placed in the courtyard of our complex, and neighbours gathered to hear the news. It was all bad. At one point the Germans were within a day's march of Łódź. That evening a rumour made rounds that the Germans had executed all the Jewish men in every city they had taken. Panic set in. Father and all my uncles packed knapsacks and, on foot or hitchhiking, made for Warsaw. Only Uncle Fishl stayed behind. A few days later my father was back, unable to get through because of the heavy bombardment of the roads. Others made it to Warsaw, only to return after it had surrendered. Still others continued east, and they did not return. All my unmarried uncles, from both sides of the family, stayed on in Białystok, where the Germans found them in 1941.

With the men away, and the artillery salvos sounding close by, the old men and the women and children from our wing assembled in one apartment. We children would stick our fingers in our ears and cower with each thud. Expecting a gas attack, we each had folded pieces of gauze and bottles of powdered soda to use as makeshift gas masks. I refused to be intimidated by the noise and slept through the shelling. This was a great irritation to Mother, who wanted my attention.

No sooner had the German troops entered the city than they posted a number of troublesome regulations. A dawn-to-dusk curfew was imposed. When we were out on the street, all of us, men, women, and children, were required to wear yellow Stars of David on our clothing – one on our chests and another on the back of our coats. Fabric stores soon ran out of yellow cloth. Mother cut up our curtains to make the six-pointed stars. I was upset that my school was closed, only three days into the school year. Not having much to do, I read whatever I could lay my hands on.

Within two short months of occupying the city on 8 September, the Germans had made life unbearable for the Jewish population. For one thing, Łódź and other areas of western Poland had become part of the Third Reich. Łódź was renamed Litzmanstadt, and neither the Jews nor the Poles were wanted there anymore. Altogether, up to ten million people were affected. Some Poles with German ancestry or non-Slavic-sounding names declared themselves German nationals, *Volksdeutsche*, and put on swastika armbands.

Several members of our extended family decided to stay put, but most chose to abandon everything and leave. Through Cousin Meyer of Osiek we arranged for a couple of his Volksdeutsch neighbours to escort us out of town. On an evening in December the two men arrived in a horse-drawn wagon. Into it we piled up our clothing and bedding. There was no room for anything else. Father slipped all the money we had behind the back of a framed family photograph. The bills were in large denominations, soon to be declared worthless by the authorities.

In the morning of the day of departure Father suggested that either I or my sister go with Mother and the bedding. Nusyn, Rózia's husband, was to go as well and, together with Mother, try to find a place for us to stay in the city of Kielce. Father, Rózia, and her three-year-old son Mietek, and either my sister or I were to follow later. At the time Mother opposed moving to her birth town of Staszów because she still had nightmares from her experiences there in the last war. We discussed who would accompany Mother. I wanted to go right away.

During the upheaval of getting ready to leave town, I read books. My friend across the courtyard, whose grandfather was German, attended school and borrowed books regularly from the library. These he graciously lent me, but only for overnight. Interfering with my reading was my little cousin, Mietek, who was staying with us for the duration. As I was hurrying to finish read-ing a book which I had promised to return pronto, Mietek leaned over his bowl of cereal and tugged at the pages: he ripped out at least three. Now I had a serious situation on my hands. The book, a fable called *The Secret of Blue Almonds*, had been below my expectations, but it had to be returned in good shape. I realized that honour and reputation were on the line. I casually dropped off the tightly closed book at my friend's and, not mentioning the incident, left town for good. Fifty-two years later I still have not forgotten this act of cowardice.

The wagon, loaded high with bedding, moved out. In the dead of night we came to the newly erected border post. Here, the Third Reich joined the Generalna Gubernia, as the balance of our truncated country was now called. On being challenged by the guards our Volksdeutsche flashed their swastika armbands and hollered, '*Heil Hitler!*' The barrier went up, and the horses trudged on to Kielce. Our escort had gotten us safely across, with-out a search of the wagon.

8
Kielce

Freda and I drove to Kielce in a rented car in the fall of 1991. Our first sign of the town was a series of four- and five-storey apartment buildings erected after the Second World War. After we passed a street flea market specializing in automobile parts, the streets began to look vaguely familiar. We followed the signs for *centrum*, hoping to find there the place I'd called home for about six months in 1940. But the road led to a dead-end street and then to a pedestrian mall. On foot, we located the old town square, renamed Plac Partyzanów (Square of the Partisans).

There have been changes. There is a small park in the centre of the square. Across from what had been my former home is a fairly large, pillared building. The buildings around the square have been painted pastel shades of blue, green, and pink. Ours was an undistinguished two-storey edifice with a small metal plaque affixed to the wall declaring the structure a historical site. The wrought-iron front gate and the former grey stucco are now painted a pale blue. Inside the courtyard the three surrounding buildings are the same grey as I remembered. The window of my former room over the archway was partially open, and white curtains billowed in the light breeze. It was a beautiful, sunny fall day. Beyond the courtyard arch I saw the traffic passing by on the street. In 1940 a series of low sheds closed off the rear courtyard from the street, and to the right there was a gate that opened into a side street. In its place there is now a low structure over which hangs a sign advertising video rentals. It was through this side doorway that, at age eleven, I led my troop of five boys to do battle with a group of Polish kids from across the square.

In early 1940 Mother and Uncle Nusyn had rented a room in an apartment overlooking the square from a bachelor who retained for his own use one large room and the kitchen. This bachelor was a tall, balding Jew of about forty who said little and didn't seem to do much either. There might have been some hanky-panky going on between him and a Polish girl who used to come to visit, ostensibly to clean his place, but that was strictly gossip. I had no idea what people were talking about, and frankly, I didn't care. More to the point was the fact that I had little to do and, at least initially, no one to play with. Mother insisted that I stay close to home, and she didn't dare venture anywhere either. The shopping could be done just outside our door. Twice a week the square filled up with horse-drawn farmers' wagons from which all manner of stuff was sold – chickens, geese and ducks (which had to be taken to a *shochet* for ritual slaughtering), and unkosher kielbasa, as well as eggs, butter, cheese, sour cream, potatoes, parsley, onions, garlands of garlic, fresh and dried mushrooms, apples, pears, carrots, and green vegetables in season.

The war seemed to have come to a halt. France and England were not fighting the Germans. The weather improved, and I ventured out and made friends with other boys in the courtyard. To impress them, or out of boredom, I fashioned a shield and sword out of bits of wood I'd found in the yard. Carrying the arms, painted and marked with heraldic symbols, I paraded to the envious stares of many. The idea of forming an army naturally followed. It was wartime, and armies were marching everywhere. Often I watched German squads in formation, singing lustily as they marched through the square. They had rucksacks covered in brown and white horsehide, shining rifles, and dark helmets. Sometimes they escorted a group of Polish men, some in priest's cassocks. The rumour was that these were important people whom the Nazis didn't like and were taking to jail.

We were now an army of five. To produce a likeness of firearms was beyond my ability or resources. Swords, lances, and shields were to be our weapons. Slowly, over weeks, I picked up odd pieces of wood, board, and wire and fashioned the equipment for my army. Embellishing the weapons took some doing, since everyone wanted his own particular emblem. Lolek, one of the recruits, turned out to be talented in painting and decorating the shields.

Unlike my other friends, Lolek was a new arrival. His family had come to Kielce from Łódź a little later than we did, but they must have been well-to-do. Their apartment, above ours, had at least two rooms. They had also brought along their live-in maid. Lolek was my age but taller. I admired his grey eyes, blond curly hair, and rosy complexion. He dressed well, and he was apparently more sexually advanced than I was as well. His stories of climbing into bed with their maid I found interesting, but irrelevant. He reported that she asked him to hold her, and that these carryings-on were to be kept secret from his parents. The maid was a tall, heavy-breasted redhead who kept her mouth partially open at all times, wore short skirts, and had bare legs, even in the winter. Although it was nice to be with her, Lolek claimed he could take it or leave it. He said her freckles were all over her body.

My army trained and ready, I went in search of the enemy. I didn't have to look far. Across the square, in one of the buildings no different from ours, but occupied mainly by Gentiles, there was a group of ten- or eleven-year-olds who gathered occasionally on the square and taunted us. They were our foe. Negotiations took place, and time, composition, and choice of weapons were agreed on.

Appointing Lolek my second in command, I advised my troops of the task at hand. We were to meet at two in the afternoon on the coming Sunday, in the very centre of the square (which was usually deserted at that time), to do battle. Five to each side, sticks only, shields permitted, and the first to give ground was to be declared the loser.

At the appointed time, to avoid the possibility of encountering a parent, we sneaked out the side gate and marched smartly over the cobblestones. My squad was in formation and ready for my orders to go on the offensive, but we were swarmed by a group of about seven or eight boys, yelling and brandishing black sticks. As my men put up their shields, I gave orders to join battle. A stick had touched my shirt and left a black mark. I grabbed it, hoping to wrest it away, but my hand became covered with sticky, black tar. It was an uneven fight. Our clothes, faces, and hair were tarred. We were no match for the larger, better-equipped enemy. I shouted an order to retreat, which really wasn't necessary, since my group had started to flee towards home and security. For my sceptical mother I concocted a story of having fallen down and gotten soiled in tar.

Having done with fighting, I explored the town. One of my former troopers, Isak, had an aunt living several blocks away. I tagged along on one of his visits to her. The complex the aunt lived in was similar to ours, an edifice facing the street, with an archway leading into a cobblestone courtyard partially enclosed by three wings of apartments. The only difference was that all the kids playing in the courtyard were girls. The games played were hopscotch or other girls' games. Calling out to each other to skip ever faster, they seemed to pay little attention to Isak and me.

On one such occasion Helka looked up, and our eyes met. Helka had very white skin, the bluest of eyes, and long, straight, shiny black hair. Our eyes met again as I waited for Isak to come out from his aunt's. In those days, girls – even eleven-year-old girls – did not speak to boys first. Isak assured me that Helka liked me. What I was to do with that kernel of information was unclear to me. I wanted desperately to speak to her, and for us to become friends, but I couldn't get up my nerve to say a word. I was certain that her response would be favourable, but I didn't utter a sound. The last time I passed Helka, just before we packed up and left town, she and I stood for a while looking at each other. She definitely had the bluest eyes and the shiniest hair I'd ever seen. I never learned her full name. Exploring the town now, I couldn't even recollect which building it was where I was first smitten with the feeling called love.

In February 1940 my father, my sister, Anna, and Aunt Rozia and her son Mietek joined us in Kielce. The seven of us packed into one room. Father had got out shortly before the walls of the

Łódź ghetto went up and the gates were shut. We learned later that my grandfather and grandmother and Father's two unmarried sisters had walked, carrying their belongings, into the ghetto. So did my mother's sisters and their families, including Hela, my unmarried aunt. We heard that they were living eight or ten to a room. The boys in the families had crossed over to the Russian side.

Hardly a day went by that we didn't learn about a misfortune that had befallen someone we knew. One day that winter three members of a family related to the husband of my mother's younger sister Andzia showed up on our doorstep. How they had found us was unclear. The story they told confirmed our fears for the inhabitants of Łódź. As elsewhere, the Germans had cordoned off their street and, after curfew, ordered all the people out onto the street, giving them fifteen minutes to gather their belongings. They were allowed only one small suitcase per person. Amounts of money exceeding twenty-five złotys were confiscated. The Germans then herded them to the railway station and packed them into cattle cars.

Travelling southeast, the train stopped hours later in the middle of a ploughed field. The people were ordered to get out. Our unexpected guests had walked ever since, staying off the main roads, until at last they reached Kielce. They sought comfort and advice. We had nothing to give them except a hot meal and space on the floor to bed down. Unable to help and not wanting to be burdened with additional bodies, my father and uncle urged them to return to Łódź by whatever means possible. They had friends and relatives there who could help them with clothes and money. Reluctantly, they agreed and left for Łódź the same day. At the time, I felt that Father's and Uncle's advice was simply a way of getting rid of them. Ultimately, I suppose, it didn't matter.

After Mother and I had left, Father had stayed on in Łódź for a time to try to salvage something of his inventory and the moneys owing him. Nothing materialized. Debts were secured by promissory notes issued by small-town shopkeepers. No one was willing to pay off debts, even if they had money. The Germans had ordered the Jewish shops to be closed. Soon after, they ordered all owners to produce accurate inventory sheets, under threat of death. Following that, a demand went out that the goods be delivered, at a specific time, to the railway yards, for shipment to Germany. Father had to arrange for transport to take his entire stock to the station. The items checked off against the inventory list, he unloaded and was given a receipt. He said goodbye to his parents and sisters and left with Anna for Kielce. A lifetime of hard work and self-denial had come to nothing.

9
Majdanek

Back in Warsaw, Freda and I met Beata for lunch. Beata is a busy woman, the publisher of *Ex libris* (a book review insert to *Życie Warszawy*) and two other papers. She had been a delegate to the round-table discussions with the Communist martial law government in 1989, representing journalists on the Solidarity team. She knew Walesa, Michnik, Kuroń, and Mazowiecki personally. A lively, slim woman of perhaps thirty-five, with short, ash-blonde hair and expressive blue eyes, she was well dressed, smoked a lot, and used her hands to make a point.

After rejecting a foul French, then an equally bad Bulgarian, red wine, we settled down to a satisfactory Bulgarian. A delightful person, Beata speaks English a lot better than I do Polish. Her family originally came from the eastern part of Poland, now the Republic of Ukraine, and settled in Warsaw after the war. She told me about an octogenarian whom she had recently interviewed. He had been a courier sent by the Polish underground to London in 1942. He was to inform Churchill about what the Germans were doing to the Jews. Fifty years ago he couldn't convince London and, as Beata talked to him, he wept. He blamed himself for not having found the right words to describe the horror. He had failed because words had failed him.

Beata believes that the Jews went to their death largely without opposition because of a kind of fatalism consistent, in her opinion, with Jewish religious philosophy. I countered that in 1942, in the ghettos of Poland, we would not accept as fact that the Germans meant to put to death every man, woman, and child. It was incomprehensible. We blindly believed that the war would end before any harm would come to us. The Białystok and Warsaw ghetto uprisings took place only when it was abundantly clear to those left behind that their fate was sealed. The Jews of Hungary, more than four hundred thousand of them, were sent to Auschwitz in mid-1944 having no idea what awaited them.

I related how, towards late summer in 1942, our family and neighbours would gather and discuss the inevitable *wysiedlenie* (expulsion). We children sensed the danger but, being young, did not give in to despair. Our parents wrung their hands, tried to make plans, and thought and rethought ways to make it through to the war's end – which was believed to be near.

One warm evening in Staszów, in July or August of that year, we children were listening to the adults in the yard speaking in hushed tones about the towns and cities that were being cleared of Jews. To where, no one knew. I spoke up, saying that the transports must be taking the people east to work, or to new ghettos. I wanted to believe it, as well as to reassure my troubled parents. The statement was met with silence. Our turn would come. The Jews' hope was in hiding out for the duration or, if possible, finding what we thought would be secure work indispensable to the Nazi war effort.

The incentive for a Pole to turn in a Jew trying to flee the ghetto was a posted reward of twenty-two pounds of sugar, worth a small fortune at the time. Consequently, the chances of survival on the outside were virtually nil. As for rising against the Germans, in the smaller towns it was inconceivable. There were no weapons to be had. There was no organization. Malnutrition undermined efforts at clear thinking, let alone resistance. Moreover, common sense told us that fighting the combined Germans and unfriendly Poles would be futile. Finally, the Germans diabolically kept us divided among ourselves, making us believe that those who worked for them and the Jewish administration (the Judenrat), who in turn recruited the Jewish police, would not be harmed. As a matter of record, the Jewish police assisted the

Germans in rounding up the people. The Poles were, for the most part, indifferent or hostile. 'Enough was done only by those who died while giving aid,' I quoted to Beata.

Beata brought up the ever-present question of anti-Semitism or philo-Semitism in Polish society. Neither, in her opinion, is, or was, a factor in intellectual circles. Below this level, however, anti-Semitism has always been endemic, but so has a curiosity about the vanished Jews. In the next few days Freda and I confirmed this, noticing in numerous shops an array of books on Jewish topics and by Jewish writers. In Beata's view, the place of Jews in Polish culture, history, and civilization is secure. It seemed grotesque that the near-total annihilation of the Jews during the German occupation and the forty-five years of Poland's Communist experience were lumped together by the Poles as one dismal half-century that was best put behind them.

The topic shifted to the economy and the lack of business and managerial expertise in the country. Beata said there was now a greater selection of merchandise in the stores than there had been two or three years before. Russian tourists, she maintained, considered the consumer goods available in Poland to be the very best the West could offer. Commerce was taking root.

Returning to our apartment, I thought about Beata's comment that she didn't perceive me as a typical war victim. Such victims felt that they had been wronged, that life hadn't been fair, and that others had had all the luck. Soon after liberation I had made up my mind to look to the future rather than to dwell on the past. It seemed a sensible alternative to feeling sorry for myself. Some people have found my matter-of-fact façade somewhat baffling. They could not know the depth of the pain that it hid.

Freda and I lunched with Hanna Krall, a celebrated author, and Jurek, her husband, a writer on economic matters. Hanna, with a full face and her very dark hair loosely pulled back, looked younger than her years. I was curious to learn about Dr Marek Edelman, the subject of Hanna's book *Shielding the Flame*. Hanna found Edelman to be a cantankerous man. She confirmed that he waged a perpetual war with his God, a God who had let his people down. Edelman had been witness to unspeakable crimes and consequently had become an atheist. His quarrel, then, was with a God that did not exist.

In mid-summer of 1991, Dr Edelman had announced his candidacy for a senate seat on the Union Demokrat list. (In the October voting the doctor came in seventh in a field of twenty-six, polling 159,000.) Interviewed by the newspaper *Politika* before the election, Edelman expressed a number of interesting views. We discussed the interview, in which, among other things, Edelman contended that the Polish nation was running the risk of falling under the rule of a new dictator, and that the Jews' mission was to protect the weak, particularly from the excesses of their rulers. Edelman believed strongly that one should never compromise one's principles, and that, next to life itself, freedom was our most important commodity. Having seen as much death as he had, he realized that life amounted to 'nothing.' He believed that anyone who comprehended the meaning of 'nothing' understood death. He went on to say that only those Jews who had kept busy in the ghetto did not go mad. They had fought hunger; they had battled for their lives. It was one's duty to oppose oppression, he insisted, to never give in. In passing, Edelman mentioned that the West German government had offered him a pension, but that he had refused to accept it. He had fought Germans, he said, and therefore was not entitled to one. Sons and daughters of wartime SS officers had come to Łódź to beg his forgiveness. He had dismissed them with a curt, 'I have nothing against you, children.' Edelman declared that he remained in Poland to 'mind the shop,' to stand guard over the ashes of those he had watched embark from Umschlagplatz. To the last question in the inverview – 'What do you like best?' – he replied, 'Caviar and pretty girls.'

Hanna was leaving shortly for Rio de Janeiro, on a trip sponsored by a friend, the former secretary to Bolesław Bierut, first president of postwar Poland. Hanna's friend, a biologist with a U.S. oil company in Brazil, had hid out in Warsaw proper during the occupation. Hanna told of how his and another Jewish family had crowded into a small apartment belonging to their building's janitor and spent the entire period of 1942–4 there, never venturing outside the four walls. The janitor was a drunk whose behaviour could be erratic at times. At some point during the 1943 ghetto uprising, two young Jewish men, having made it out through the sewers, had come into the building seeking refuge. A certain Gentile woman, unhappy with the visitors, perhaps anti-Semitic or vindictive, declared that she intended to report the two to the Gestapo. Taking her threat seriously and not willing to endanger the lives of his protégés, the janitor rushed out and reported the fugitives to the SS. This action effectively put his own apartment above suspicion. The two men were executed, and the janitor got a reward. The Polish underground learned about the episode and, after a trial in absentia, handed down a verdict of death on the janitor. The first attempt to have him executed failed. Though he'd only been wounded, his life was now in great danger. The two Jewish families nursed him back to health. Together, they survived until liberated in January 1945. Hanna had learned that the janitor died of old age a short time ago, and the others had long since dispersed. The question of who brought food to the expanded family from 1943 to January 1945 remained unanswered. Jurek suggested that the nasty woman, at some point contrite, may have done the shopping.

Hanna is proud of her ability to make a special type of gefilte fish. Her recipe calls for cutting up a carp into slices about an inch thick, and removing the flesh while leaving the skin and backbone intact; grinding the meat, mixed with onion, salt, pepper, sugar, egg, and bread crumbs, to the texture and consistency of molasses; and filling the cavity with the mixture. To complete the ritual, Hanna slides the portions into boiling water, along with carrots and onions. The aroma of such fish simmering on the stove evokes memories of Friday afternoons, of a world in ashes. Hanna prepares the fish only twice a year, once for the High Holy Days and again at Christmas, when her and Jurek's guest for dinner has been the Warsaw Vatican apostolic delegate. Her one regret was that she had, at a time when she did not think she had any more use for it, given away her cleaver, the *hack-messer*, necessary for putting the finishing touches to the blend. She likened it to a jeweller's tool, with which she had, in her words, 'created art.'

At one point during our lunch, Hanna described her trip to the Majdanek camp, a few days before, to observe the anniversary of the deportation of hundreds of thousands of Jews – including her father – from the Warsaw ghetto to Treblinka and Majdanek. Treblinka was levelled by the Germans in 1944, just ahead of the advancing Red Army. Hanna feels certain of the date her father met his death. As she put it, 'In my heart I knew when he gave up his soul.'

'Majdanek' was a name familiar to me since 1943. Whispered, it spoke of massacres, brutality, gas chambers, and flaming ovens. It had been only partially destroyed by the Germans and was a reasonable distance from Warsaw. Next morning Freda and I boarded a train east to Majdanek-Lubelski.

We arrived about one o'clock. When we stepped off the train, it seemed to me as though the Lublin station and the streets leading from it had been frozen in time. Around us were low structures in disrepair. In front of crumbling buildings, on crowded sidewalks, were pedlars selling produce and toilet articles displayed on plastic garbage bags. I become tongue-tied and disoriented. I asked a young man and woman where the centre of town was, but they looked startled and recoiled from us. From twenty feet away the man turned and gave us a baleful look while at the same time shoving the woman hard to keep moving. I bought stale buns at a bake shop that could have been out of Dickens and hailed a wobbly taxi. I had no idea of the distance to Majdanek but bravely asked the driver to take us to the Jewish museum.

This might seem a routine method of getting from point A to point B, unless you are a Jew, a stranger, in provincial Poland. The driver didn't acknowledge my request, nor did he turn his head. Within ten minutes, however, the taxi came to a hard stop in front of a single-storey structure on which a sign read, 'Majdanek.' To the right, about two hundred yards away, set back on a rise of land, loomed a monument, as if suspended in space. My heart skipped a beat. We were shown the way to the barracks. The place was huge, isolated, windswept, and deserted. I felt threatened and more than just a bit anxious.

The apartment buildings of Lublin's suburbs are within sight of Majdanek. The monument erected by the postwar Polish government stands at the front of the former camp. Rectangular, about fifty feet across and thirty feet high, an enormous, rugged, grey-black rock, it towers over a long narrow pit with walls of jagged rock. A ramp leads down the length of it. The barracks are in the distance. The effect is unnerving. A plaque lists crimes committed by the Nazis. Not unexpectedly, it states that the criminals were '*Hitlerowcy*' (Hitlerites), rather than, simply, Germans. Perhaps the Poles, having to live next to the German state, were opting to give the Germans a way out.

Lager means 'camp' in German, but it also means 'warehouse' – in this case, a warehouse for bodies. Here was one of the most notorious *KZ's* – *Konzentrations Lager* – ranking with Auschwitz as an efficient extermination machine. Built by slave labour beginning in 1941, it initially held prisoners of war, Jews from the Polish army, and Russians. Before the spring of 1942, when transports of ghetto Jews began to arrive, tens of thousands of POWs were first starved, then shot and buried in the neighbouring forest. Some of the wretches had come down with typhus, and the Germans, fearing an epidemic, killed them all. As experienced extermination personnel, like Karl Otto Koch from Auschwitz, were transferred to Majdanek, mass brutality became routine. Some 360,000 men, women, and children were beaten, starved to death, or gassed at Majdanek, most of them Jews from Poland, Slovakia, and Hungary. The large crematorium contained a separate enclosure for the officer in charge to freshen up, to have a shower or bath and a quick change of clothes. Outside the gas chamber a strategically placed small window gave the jailers a vantage point to observe the stages of agony that those being gassed went through. The bestiality of the Germans and their Ukrainian helpers, male and female, knew no bounds. Lining the walls of one of the barracks is page after page giving graphic descriptions of their cruelty and greed.

The former wooden barracks are about one hundred feet long. One is full of shoes in wire cages; some cages are filled with only children's shoes. There are areas full of ripped, dirty, striped pants and shirts, some with traces of congealed blood.

The clothes hang neatly in rows, scarecrow-fashion. On one wall are striped caps of a deadly ash-grey hue. On another, hung in neat, even rows, are more caps of every sort. There are store-rooms containing human hair, batches of toothbrushes, and other personal effects. The gold and valuables were periodically shipped to the Reichsbank in Berlin; the last shipment was made just before the arrival of the Red Army. This is verified by care-fully signed shipping receipts, now neatly arranged on desk-tops. Some members of the SS also diverted gold and precious stones to their own personal treasure chests. Among them was the same Karl Otto Koch, who was sentenced to death by an SS court for the transgression.

The silence of our surroundings was broken by the sound of an engine accelerating. A boy was taking his girlfriend for a motor-cycle ride. Up and down the bleak and barren lane they sped, the throttle wide open, the motor responding lustily to the surge of gasoline and air. I lost sight of them when they swerved left at the far end, around the base of the mushroomlike concrete mauso-leum. Our footsteps were once again the only sound. We pressed forward to where we could peer into the huge stone bowl in which several tons of ashes rested.

A certain Kwiatkowski, a Gentile survivor of Majdanek, pro-vided most of the information about the camp for the years 1942–4. At one point, the Lublin Polish underground planned, in con-junction with the inmates, an attack and uprising at the camp. At the last moment, an order to cancel came from higher up. There was a risk that the Germans would retaliate on the Lublin civilian population.

Throughout the war the Polish Home Army units (AK) were operating in areas where the death camps were located. It would have taken only a small effort to blow up the rail lines that linked the ghettos to the gas chambers. This was not done. Throughout the period 1942–4, there were reports of sightings of Polish parti-sans in our region's heavy forests. The Germans were afraid to enter these enclaves of Polish resistance. Nonetheless, had my family managed to escape and make our way to the woods, we feared that we would find no assistance there. Rumours of the partisans turning Jews over to the Germans persisted throughout this time.

On 3 November 1943 reports came in of uprisings in the camps of Treblinka and Sobibor by the crematoria's Jewish *sondercomandos* (crews). The SS in Majdanek, in response, slaughtered forty-two thousand Jews in a single day.

Systematic dismantling of the barracks for shipment west began in the spring of 1944, as the eastern war front drew near. In the camp at that time were held skilled Jewish prisoners, Russian men and women (some with children), Polish peasants who had failed to deliver their compulsory quota of grain or potatoes, and thousands of hostages held as surety against acts of sabotage by partisans. Mass evacuation of Majdanek took place on 2 April 1944: twelve thousand inmates were sent to Auschwitz and other camps. For reasons unknown, the Home Army did not attempt a rescue, although they were aware of the Germans' plans. When the Russians marched into Lublin in July 1944 they found Majdanek deserted.

Freda and I made our way up to the main road, hoping to find a taxi. Silence. Nothing. The Majdanek reception office was closed for the day. My watch showed 3:50 P.M. I would not even consider our spending the night in Lublin; we simply had to make the 4:30 train, the last one. Still no traffic. Miraculously, a taxi finally appeared, and we made it to the terminal by 4:20. The line-up at the single window precluded any chance of purchasing tickets. Breathless – and ticketless – we boarded. Inside, we sat down in a compartment that already had two male occupants. One of the men on my left, about forty, tall, blue-eyed, and handsome, leaned over to his companion and said something. For an instant our eyes met. We knew each other from another time – he, the anti-Semite; I, the Żyd. A raw nerve had been touched. To stay in the compartment for the next three hours, or even three minutes, was inconceivable. I motioned to a mystified Freda that we had to move on immediately.

In our new seats, I tried to wipe from my mind the feeling of shame. Shame was apparently a traumatic response common among former KZ inmates when confronted with the brutal past

– it was the shame that I had known so well after each selection in the lagers, in the ghetto, and again – intensely – immediately after liberation.

The Majdanek memorial states that 5.7 million European Jews were murdered. About half were Polish Jews. Sheltering Jews was a crime punishable by death, and more than nine hundred Christians were executed for it. About a thousand Poles were awarded medals by the Israeli government for aiding and saving Jews. Possibly because of Poland's central location, all the major extermination camps were on Polish soil. Poland had no puppet government as Slovakia did, nor any Vichy-like collaboration. After the Jews and Gypsies, the Polish nation had suffered proportionally the most. The Germans systematically exterminated the intellectual élite, as did the Russians. The loss in lives, including those on the many battlefields, was staggering. Nonetheless, as the lesser of two evils, Poles preferred the Germans to the Soviets. Their loathing of the Russians was older and deeper. A good deal of Poland's postwar political and economic problems stemmed from the painful fact that its brightest Poles and Jews hadn't survived the war.

Many Jews consider the behaviour of the Poles during the occupation reprehensible. Poles were not recruited to guard the camps; the Nazis preferred to accept volunteers from among the Ukrainians and the Balts, who could be relied on to remain loyal. I assume it was their long, shared history with the Poles that caused Polish Jews to believe they had earned the right not to be abandoned by their neighbours. Zofia Kossak-Szczucka, the Polish novelist, put it aptly: 'Whoever remains silent in the face of murder becomes an accomplice to that murder.' Not all Poles remained silent, but many did rejoice that the Germans were getting rid of the Jews for them. There were also Poles who blackmailed or denounced Jews who tried to pass themselves off as Aryans.

On the return trip to Warsaw I looked out the window at the harvested fields, still so green, and could think only of how the doomed thousands taken from the ghettos forty-nine years ago had travelled through this same, unchanged landscape.

One could either live resolutely in the present, or drive oneself mad.

Most survivors of the concentration camps were now in their seventies or eighties. Many had died in the past few years. People in their twenties or early thirties were considered ideal for selection to the labour camps. (For their own amusement, however, the Nazis routinely killed the most handsome men and the prettiest women.) A few exceptionally hardy or lucky ones made it, some older or younger than the norm. Those who made it to 1945 and emigrated to the West or to Israel were, for the most part, ready to start a new life. As a rule we managed well in the new environment. Some of us became wealthy. Many have maintained ties with compatriots with a similar history. Settled comfortably, they have clung to friends and neighbourhoods. After half a century some remain immigrants.

When I came to North America, in 1946, I was eighteen. I had to work to earn a living but I also felt strongly about catching up on my education, which had been so abruptly interrupted. Night school five nights a week was my schedule the first year, down to three the next. In the third year I gave up, because the possibility of ever completing high school and going on to university had come to seem unrealistic. Besides, my reading had given me a handle on, and an opening into, English culture. What I didn't realize at the time was that education is a process that goes far beyond formal learning: it moulds the way one thinks.

My mother, may she rest in peace, was almost illiterate. Years later, she was known to sigh and say that she had made a crucial mistake. 'I should have gone to work and sent you to school.' She never forgave herself for this apparent error in judgment.

So there I was, eighteen, my faculties intact, eager to absorb whatever North America had to offer. On the surface, I was perfectly assimilated into society; I had friends of various ages and mostly of non-immigrant backgrounds. I had made it, or so I thought. My short visit to Poland and to my roots, however, upset my equilibrium, making me aware that there was a critical gap in my make-up which had, somehow, to be bridged. I realized that I had lost my teenage years, that I had never experienced all the games and recreations of youth that had come so easily to my children.

I never encounter old school friends, neighbours, pals from summer camp, or old flames. Nostalgic pictures do not exist. There are no yearbooks with funny inscriptions, no phone calls from someone passing through town saying, 'Hello, remember me? We were in Miss Jones's class together.' No kindnesses or considerations received, to be remembered and cherished, no warm spot in the heart for the memory of a sunset, or of skinny-dipping with friends. No song or tune of that period means a thing to me.

There are no reunions to go to, no old textbooks to unearth; forgotten class photos don't turn up among dusty souvenirs. There are no funny hats on the top shelf, no favourite toys in a bottom drawer. No thrilling memories of a first kiss in adolescence or of a driving lesson before the legal age. There is just a blank where all this was meant to fit.

I and others like me made up for the deficiency with bravado and hard work. But the feeling that it was all a waste of time persisted, that the only thing worth our attention was the memory of the war. So, we plodded on.

One Sunday, Freda and I went to the Warsaw zoo. It was sunny and warm, a perfect day. We watched the throngs of people. There were children of all ages, some feeding the animals, some just having a good time. A mother scolded a little blonde girl who wouldn't sit still for pictures. Another parent spanked a boy of about seven for walking along the parapet. Cameras and video-cams abounded. It was a big day for ice cream (*lody*).

This was a day for family outings. The faces around me were Slavic, some with wide cheekbones, others with sharper features and darker hair. People came in all sizes. The young women were slim, the older ones, a bit overweight. The dress code was neat casual or Sunday best. Little girls wore pretty dresses and had bows in their long, shiny hair.

For some twenty-five generations, Jews had lived in and around Warsaw. Intermarriage was unheard of. But where peoples live side by side for so many years, one assumes that sheer propinquity would have left some trace. I sought Semitic features among the crowds, concentrating mainly on the adults. (The children were invariably blue-eyed and blond, their skin almost translucent.) The adults with darker hair had features that one could not assume to be Semitic. Their mouths were thin, sometimes hard. Straight hair, brushed back, didn't fit either, nor did the thick waists and bulging muscles on the men. The women were harder to define. Eliminating the very fair ones as obvious Slavs, I kept a lookout for dark-haired, sharper-featured ones. Once again, I was in for disappointment. I decided to disregard faces and pigmentation, and sought out people's eyes. I watched for a certain softness combined with chutzpah, for signs of smugness, wisdom, artfulness, cunning, and compassion. A few times, I thought I was on the right track, but then I detected a gaiety that was conclusively un-Jewish. What I sought was a bit of despair in someone's eyes. Then I could have made a positive identification.

10
Staszów Then and Now

In that first summer of the war, and over Mother's misgivings, Father hired a driver with a horse and wagon to move us from Kielce to Staszów. Mother's sister Bluma and her brother Nathan had gone there from Łódź with their families. Kielce, her preference, was a major city, the province's capital, whereas Staszów was a 'shtetl,' a small town located in the midst of reportedly rich farmland. In Kielce food was becoming increasingly expensive and harder to obtain.

Aunt Rózia argued that we needed the family for comfort, and that, in our reduced circumstances, we would be better served in Staszów, where bread and potatoes were less costly. Father agreed that it served no purpose for us to sit out the war in isolation in Kielce.

Staszów became our home in the summer of 1940. Aunt Rózia, Uncle Nusyn, their small son, Mietek, and the four members of my family moved into a one-room 'cottage' on Ulica Rytwiańska.

In September 1991, Freda and I drove north, from Kraków to Staszów. We would be passing through Działoszyce, a town Freda's father, Al, had insisted we visit and photograph. It was his home town.

The fertile countryside north of Kraków is lush and green and shows signs of prosperity: there are plenty of newer homes, with more under construction. We were travelling during the sugar-beet harvest, the last harvest of the year. We passed trucks and horse-drawn wagons taking loads of beets into a large yard that might have been a storage depot for a sugar refinery. We saw cows grazing in pastures, flocks of white geese feeding near the farm buildings, chickens parading out into the road, children walking to school, and people in the fields burning weeds. It seemed a world at peace with itself.

We drove on, through Miechów, which had at one time been almost entirely Jewish, but was now clean of Jews – *Judenrein*. We soon reached the line that had separated Czarist Russia from Austro-Hungary before the First World War. Działoszyce was just half an hour away. The farmhouses along the road were becoming older and poorer.

Działoszyce was the birthplace of Freda's father. He had left in the 1920s, at the age of six. On arriving in the town, we saw that the houses were old and sinking into the ground. There was not much of anything beyond the immediate circle of houses around the square and along a single street to the west. The only kiosk in the square offered no souvenirs identifying the town. However, the plump young man came out from behind the counter to talk to me. 'Have you come from Israel?' he asked. He hoped we had. Some time ago several Jews, natives of Działoszyce currently residing in Israel, had applied to the local authorities for permission to erect a monument. He noted regretfully that, even though all the formalities had been completed, nothing more had been heard from them.

The town's synagogue was in ruins; a sign warned of the danger of falling bricks or timber. In the centre of the town square were trees, bushes, grass, and three or four benches. My father-in-law had been quite specific in his descriptions of the square and its farmers' market. I realized that the Communists had done away with unwanted free enterprise by simply landscaping the square. Similar work had been done in all the towns we visited.

Freda and I drove on, to Staszów. Ulica Rytwiańska, where we had lived, was dug up part way for what looked like a water main. The shed we had lived in for more than two years was gone. In its place was a pile of rusted metal and car parts under a corrugated roof. Our landlords', the Sznifers', house, in front facing the street, seemed smaller and was painted a light green instead of its former white. The structure next door to it was a two-storey affair. It occupied a lot that was once half overgrown with weeds, and that had a shed on the other half. Under that shed had been the basement in which we hid in November 1942. The cottage just to the right of ours was still there. Possibly used for storage, its small windows were nailed over and there was a large padlock on the door. Aunt Rózia and Uncle Nusyn, with their little boy Mietek, had lived there for about a year after they moved from our one-room cottage.

Like my mother, I have a touch of rheumatism. I trace the affliction to the time we occupied the uninsulated cottage in Staszów. We lived in dwellings with thin walls that acted as conductors for whatever the climate happened to be. The inside walls of our one-room house were moist in warm weather, with rivulets of water coming down in the rainy season and with a cover of frost in the winter. Sleeping as I did, with Father, in a bed next to a wall, I woke up mornings feeling damp and cold.

At the far end of Rytwiańska Street, farthest from the square, there was once a big chestnut tree. I would go there in the autumn to gather fallen chestnuts. They were not edible, but they were clean, shiny, brown, and nice to play with. There, I was once attacked by a Polish boy about my size, for no other reason than that I was Jewish. He came at me with both fists, possibly wanting me to grovel. He cut off my only escape route by planting himself across the path that led to my house. Running in the other direction would have been foolish, as it meant going deeper into the boy's territory. We were probably evenly matched, but it wasn't a fair fight: fighting a Pole, I could only lose. The consequences of winning, with his father or brothers coming after me, were even worse than losing. I did the next best thing. When he closed in on me and grabbed me by the waist I put my right arm out, held his head, and bit him on his close-cropped scalp. The boy screamed and let go of me. I pushed him aside and ran past him, towards home. This incident happened when I was twelve.

I went to see if the chestnut tree was still there, but it wasn't. The missing tree was a reminder of that time, and the memory was painful.

I had no trouble locating the house and barn that had belonged to our neighbours the Myśliwieces (that was all that was left of their farm). Right behind the barn, where the stables, sheds for farm implements, and a vegetable garden used to be, there were now new, two-storey houses. The barn, now in poor shape, had been a large, imposing structure in 1942. This was where my family hid from the Germans under a great mound of sawdust that year.

The dwelling that Aunt Bluma and Uncle Fishl had rented was also gone. The lot was empty and overgrown with weeds and there was no indication that there had ever been a house there. The family who once lived above Bluma and Fishl's kept hides for tanning in outside barrels filled with toxic chicken excrement. In the basement lived the shoemaker who had sold shoes to my parents – shoes that I never wore. Later, in the same basement, near the end, a Mr Hauer – who survived and eventually came to live in Toronto, where he became a successful builder – had established a broom factory, making a product in demand by the Germans. In mid-1942 I worked for him for a time, making brooms; I liked the work because the brooms, made out of stiff, green, strawlike material, swept well. We polished the clean and natural broomsticks to a high lustre. Some days we loaded wagons full of fine brooms. I was sure that the Germans were fond of our brooms, too.

Walking back to our former house, I noticed that the well was gone, too. It had been near Aunt Bluma's, downhill from us – easy to carry empty pails to, but not so easy to return with them full. The town now has running water and possibly sewers, not open gutters as before. A man, the occupant of the former Sznifer residence, eyed us suspiciously.

A number of families shared the adjoining house in wartime. Possibly they were all locals. Father and Mother had little to do with them, and there were no children my age. They were even poorer than we were – if that was possible. One of the occupants, a short, fast-moving woman with two little girls, had tried to make ends meet by dealing in live chickens. She would steal out of the ghetto and buy one or two chickens from farmers who were forbidden to sell to Jews. It had to be a fast transaction. She would then resell the chickens at a small profit. A few people were still buying chickens, mostly on Thursdays or Fridays, for the Sabbath. Sometimes the woman bought from farmers coming in just to the ghetto line – her profit margin was then greatly reduced since the farmer expected a premium for his rooster or chicken if *he* took the risk. The woman bought and sold three or four chickens a week. Her husband had been picked up by a German patrol and shipped out somewhere. Towards the end, her situation must have become desperate. Up and down our little street she moved on her sales rounds, sometimes with a chicken under each arm. It could be that people did not want to deal with her because of her irritability. One day I heard her yelling in front of the gate, 'I'm ready, let them come and put us into the sealed wagons.' I was sure she and her children didn't resist, nor lag a bit, when, on 11 November of the same year, the call for everyone to come out was heard.

In the same house lived an older Jewish lady with her son. I am not sure what, if anything special, they did for a living. The woman was often heard quarrelling with her neighbours. Her voice, raspy and loud, came over the fence one hot day in response to someone doing something to what was obviously her property. 'Hah,' she said, 'sure, on someone else's bedsheet it's nice to screw.' I expect she was speaking figuratively.

Our street now has a few newer buildings. The next street over is almost entirely of recent vintage, except for one structure, where the kosher butcher once had his shop in a backyard shed. Until 1941 it was still possible to buy kosher meat, though at a price. Mother would send me sometimes to pick up a piece for soup or stew. The front of the house is the same, but the shed is gone. The butcher was a heavy-set man with a squeaky voice. He was called *Kaczka* (duck). Mrs Kaczka ran the business. One of their sons survived and eventually came to Toronto. Mother, father, brother, and sisters all perished.

With one of the butcher's sons, I and perhaps seventy-five other Jewish men and boys worked together to improve the road that led to town. That was in 1941, when the big battles were east of Kiev. Daily the Judenrat delivered men to improve our local roads. When it was Father's turn to report I sometimes went instead. I felt like a real man getting up early, having Mother pack me a sandwich of bread, margarine, and a hard-boiled egg, then marching off to break stones. It wasn't bad, except for the dust. The other, stronger men brought wheelbarrows full of rocks that had been unloaded from horse-drawn wagons, and I used a sledgehammer to break the rocks into the little pieces needed to fill in the spaces between the cobblestones that made up the surface of the road. The Germans had to have good roads to move their heavy guns to the Russian front.

The road I worked on was not finished until the German construction company Omler formed a proper brigade of older Jewish boys and trained them. When the road was finished, the boys were deported. Prior to that, the Judenrat had received an order to assemble a group of two hundred boys aged eighteen to twenty-five to be sent east to help the armies cut trees, build roads, and the like. The rich paid not to have their sons taken away. The Jewish police rounded up the poor, those without families, and those who were abnormal in some way. As compensation, the boys were each given a brand-new navy blue suit made out of woven paper. One orphan boy, who occasionally came around begging, was mentally handicapped and always had a runny nose that he wiped on his sleeves. Neighbours gave him bread or soup. A day before he was scheduled to be shipped out, he came around to show off his crinkling, spanking-new suit.

There is now a hotel on the town square where there was none before. Freda and I sat in the cool lobby, drinking espresso and orangeade. Comfortable, in a deep leather chair, sipping my coffee, I was aware that some three hundred years of Jewish existence in Staszów had left no trace. Town records showed that in the mid-seventeenth century, shops in the city hall were leased to Jewish merchants. The faces in the street today are all Slavic.

Walking along the two familiar parallel streets, I recalled the times I had followed the German infantry men on their door-to-door combat-training missions. This was in early 1941, before Germany attacked Russia. They usually started out early in the morning from outside of town, where the two streets petered out into fields, and fought their way towards the square. The white-armbanded soldiers, firing, crouching, diving into doorways, pushed back the red armbands, who had men firing from positions on the roofs of houses. The officers alternately yelled for their men to fall back, to resist, to regroup. Hand-to-hand combat took place in the town square, the whites taking the reds prisoner. Showing little imagination, the officers had the training take the identical route every time. I watched the soldiers out of curiosity, and to pick up anything they might leave behind.

One time I found unspent rifle shells strewn over the sidewalk. Gathering them quickly, I sped home, and, fearing that Father and Mother might confiscate them, I removed the wooden caps and emptied the powder into a paper bag. With a few of my friends clustered around me, I lit a match to it and stepped back. Fortunately for us, the small amount of powder went 'poof' and was gone. I was twelve and bored out of my skull.

That spring large numbers of troops passed through town on their way east. I would stand for hours watching caterpillar trucks carrying tanks or soldiers. Regular trucks full of all kinds of gear passed by, along with large wheeled guns and men on motorcycles. The soldiers wore clean uniforms and belts with shiny buckles. The buckles had raised lettering that said *Gott mit uns* ('God is with us'). The men's high boots were of black leather; the officers wore riding boots and trousers to match. When it rained they all wore capes of waterproof material, and they drove by splashing us – especially the motorcycles, which usually had a side-car attached in which another German sat, with only his head and shoulders showing.

I noticed a marked improvement in the Germans' equipment. Back in September 1939 the invading army included many horses, foot soldiers, and sergeants on bicycles. Some of the smaller trucks were marked 'Skoda,' and my school friends said that the Germans had stolen them from the Czechs. Then, the soldiers were laughing and looked joyous; now, they were silent. They paid little attention to the town and even less to the people. Sometimes a column stopped for the men to stretch their legs, but they didn't linger long and were back on their seats in the trucks within minutes.

As soon as the authorities announced that the German armies had carried out a 'preventive strike' against the Russians, things got a lot more exciting. Posters went up all over town proclaiming that it was the 'mission of the German Reich to liberate the east.' In bold type, they spoke of the need for '*Lebensraum*,' living space.

Once we had settled in to our one-room cottage, my father talked about earning money. Jobs were non-existent, and all commercial activity was *verboten*. It became evident that Father, having delivered his entire store's inventory to the Germans, had left us with nothing to sell or barter. Others, perhaps with more foresight, had risked hiding some goods from the Germans for later use. But Father wasn't the type to dwell on the past; he would simply find a way now to solve the problem.

Food, particularly flour and bread, was a necessity. The Germans had shut down most of the flour mills, and those that were open were allowed to grind wheat and rye only on a restricted basis. The flour was either for the Germans or for civilian rations. Our monthly rations for a family of four were about five or six loaves of bread, at controlled prices. At the time the occupiers were still bothering to pretend that we were being fed. One day, Father went on a trip, saying that he would be gone for a few days. Restrictions applied to travel outside one's town or village; Jews found outside their area were shot.

What form of transportation he used or where or how far he went, I will never know. One day he returned, with a hand mill in a sack. The green-painted, cast-iron mill had a large crank and could be fastened to a table. Taken apart, it revealed two metal discs with sharp ridges running sunburstlike from the centre outward. When the crank was turned, the grinding wheels rubbed against each other, one clockwise, the other counterclockwise. The grain was fed from the top through a funnel or hopper. The mill looked like a large meat grinder. Father mentioned that during the First World War his parents had also resorted to grinding grain.

Since the mill was to be our business, Father set it up profes-
sionally. He obtained sieves of graduated density, bags, tubs, and
other containers. The wheat – purchased clandestinely from farmers forbidden to sell grain except to the authorities at a fixed price
– cost a lot.

And that was how, at the age of twelve, I became an expert
miller. Since the grinding was done by turning the crank, all the
family members would do their share. Once ground, however,
the wheat had to be carefully sifted to extract the cream-of-wheat
cereal, the fine white flour, the chaff, and the residue. Just a few
lessons by Father on sifting were enough – I took to it immediately. The knack of sifting was full of tricks of the trade. After the
first rough pass-through on our hand mill, with one parent and
one child turning the crank, the ground-up wheat was put
through a sieve with openings of about one-thirty-second of an
inch. What remained in the sieve was ground up again to produce
flour for baking whole-wheat bread. Of course, it wasn't whole,
as we had removed the best part of it. But, during the war years, it
was considered first-rate. The mostly white flour that had been
removed on the first sift went to me for sorting. Using a much
finer sieve, I separated the heavier kernels from the fine particles.
The very fine flour, still containing an amount of fine chaff, was
placed on a copper sieve with very tiny openings. I had learned
the centrifugal movement of wrist and elbow necessary to bring
the chaff to a place on of the sieve where it could be scooped up.
The sifting had to be kept up until no chaff remained. The heavenly white flour was placed in linen sacks for later sale by Mother.
The process was repeated with the coarser particles so that, by
eliminating the chaff, we had cream of wheat. Eventually we also
found use for the sweepings. We certainly made sure that 100 per
cent of the grain was accounted for. Nothing was wasted.

My vocation as a miller came to clash with my appetite for
books, now restricted to Zionist volumes obtained from one of
Aunt Bluma's neighbours and Polish historical novels, mostly by
Henryk Sienkiewicz, from Polish friends of Aunt Mania named
Myśliwiec, spinster ladies whose brother had a farm nearby. They
had a collection of about thirty books.

At night – the power shut off, and candles and kerosene being expensive – I hit on the idea of using smouldering kindling wood held close to the page as a reading light. Mother was forever nagging that I would ruin my eyes. What actually happened was less serious: I regularly got smoke all over my face, and with soap in short supply and no hot water, my appearance suffered more than my eyesight.

One day I was absorbed in *Zew krwi* (Call of the Wild), by Jack London, when Father demanded that I resume the grinding. I refused flat out. Had he known that I had read this book at least once previously, it would have made him really sore. As it was, I just went outside to read. But it wasn't fun any more.

Our one-room house, about twenty feet by fifteen feet, in which lived, first seven people, then our family of four, was also the site of our grist mill. The attic, accessible by ladder, held our sifting implements and chickens. There was a small cellar under a trapdoor near the stove. A covered lean-to shielded the door from the elements and served as a pen for four or five geese kept for fattening.

The milling of flour begets by-products. There was stuff that did not fall into any category – for example, the sweepings, dirty flour mixed with straw-ends, sand, rodent droppings, and dust. Father, ever resourceful, came up with an idea to turn this mixture into a profit centre. Geese will eat anything. In order to speed up the fattening process to two or three weeks, we intended to force-feed them. We mixed the sweepings with water, rolled the dough into cigar shapes, and boiled them. Twice a day I would grab the geese, one at a time, force their beaks open by firmly pinching them on both sides, and force the dumplings down their gullets. As each goose's gullet expanded, I would let go and move on to the next. I stuffed until all the 'food' was gone. If we ran out of dumplings, I substituted any kind of cheap grain and poured it down the birds' throats using a small vodka bottle. Whether the geese preferred one or the other I could not tell. But very soon they got fat. The fat was sold separately from the meat. The foie gras was another specialty item. Our own feast consisted of the feet, neck, and organs. We also sold the feathers. When we first got the geese we plucked their down, and after they were slaughtered, we plucked the regrown down feathers.

The attic where I did my sifting was shared with a dozen or so chickens and a rooster. Roaming through the attic, the fowl would climb up to a perch and crow whenever an egg was laid, usually when I wasn't there. I would clamber up the ladder and retrieve the egg. The chickens laid their eggs only in daytime. They prospered on a menu of grain and water.

Our enterprise flourished, inasmuch as we ate three meals a day. There was no margin for error, waste, or inefficiency. It was a classic market economy, with a twist.

The Germans made periodic searches and confiscated illegal material, which meant practically anything. There was also a risk that the man of the house would be punished. A curious ploy to find hidden geese was used by the German soldiers then billeted in town. They would enter a courtyard, one of them holding a goose under his arm, and stick a pin into the bird's flesh to make it honk. This would cause any geese in the area – ours included – to reply. Germans would then follow the trail and confiscate all found-ins. During one of these tame-goose chases, our entire family held our geese by their throats.

The risk of having the mill discovered was greater. That was where the cellar, with its trapdoor covered by a bed, came in. But we were lucky in that regard as well.

There were other, similar mills in town, but none could match the variety we offered. The other flour-producing families usually had smaller hand mills and could compete with Father's operation only because they had more family members to lend a hand. Of course, these families also had to be fed, so in a sense they had no real competitive advantage. Furthermore, because the grinding discs in their mills had finer ribs, they could not sift out the grades of product Father did, and consequently they sold their flour as truly whole wheat. Since they did not grade their product, their cost factor on the end-sale didn't make sense. But compete fiercely they did, proving that there is always someone who will sell for less.

Buying and storing the grain presented problems too. Fast

turnover was key. There had to be enough grain for three or four days of production, and it would have been sun-dried whenever possible in order to avoid clogging the grinding discs. If the grain was slightly damp, cranking was difficult. Limited capital also played a role.

The expression 'fled like a rat' does not give rats the credit they deserve for courage and determination. I encountered rats in broad daylight staring me in the face and not giving way. The narrow snout, glistening black eyes, and long, thin tail on an elongated body indicated ferocity and ruthlessness. Ultimately, it was I who gave in.

By choice, rodents feed on garbage and crop gleanings. But in the Hungry Forties, garbage pickings were slim, and the farmers left nothing edible in the fields. The rats, unchecked, invaded the towns. Our home-cum-flour mill was fair game, and was under siege. Night after night ominous sounds of tunnelling could be heard. Father would chase the rats with a whip. In the mornings we would examine the damage and fill the tunnel openings with broken glass. The winter was hard on the rats, and they became bolder: there were now tunnels on all sides. At times several rats attacked at once. The answer to our troubles was a cat, and the task of getting one was left to me. Armed with a flour sack and a piece of blood sausage, I set out to find a large cat. There were many homeless animals around. My prize was a yellow-and-brown tom-cat who fought like the devil trying to get out of the sack. Let loose in our house, he took charge by sniffing around the rat holes and peeing all over the place. Never having had a cat, we did not know about litter boxes – nor, I suppose, did the cat. In a short time the smell of cat urine permeated everything and everybody. This was a big, big cat accustomed to living off the land. We kept the door shut for fear he might bolt.

The first night we were awakened by the noises of a ferocious battle. Then it was silent. In the morning we surveyed the arena – two half-eaten rat carcasses, blood drippings here and there, and the big cat curled up, sound asleep, under a bed. It was Cat 2, Rats 0. The following night, and the next, and the next, identical encounters took place, followed by an uneasy peace. The rats began to venture in only occasionally, and the big cat grew bored and hungry. Unexpectedly, he ran off. Now defenceless, with the rats back in force, we decided we had to have another cat, and I set out to find one. Unbelievably, I found our own tom and brought him back. The same night the awesome creature dealt the rats a decisive blow. Victory was complete: three rats dead. Never again did the rats attempt a frontal attack. The cat soon vanished again, this time for good.

Living with lice was wearisome. From about 1941 to the end of the war I shared my bed, my clothes, and my blood with lice, as well as bedbugs and fleas. But lice were the main enemy. From the ghetto onward, lice began to appear in great numbers. We were crowded into tiny quarters, with no clothing to change into, scarce hot water to bathe in or wash clothes, and almost no soap. In the early days we were embarrassed to be seen delousing.

Lice are small, wingless, almost translucent parasitic, disease-carrying insects, with short legs adapted to clinging to any surface. They feed on blood by means of piercing and sucking mouth parts. A female lays about three hundred eggs in her lifetime, cementing them to body hairs and elsewhere. The louse has a life cycle of about sixteen days, during which it can cause a lot of grief. Infection can result from crushing lice or their faeces into the skin. All in all, the louse is not a good neighbour. The larva looks about the same as the mature insect, except that they vary in size and the adult is often red – red with sucked blood. First you feel the bite and then an itch, something like the itch of a mosquito bite, only louse bites are somehow different and invariably more numerous. After a while you know where the expression 'getting under your skin' comes from.

The lice that were consuming me alive were everywhere, and particularly in the brown wool sweater that I wore day and night. They preferred the snug portion around my belly. Perhaps I was ashamed, in those early days, to admit that the lice were getting the better of me. Maybe if I had reported the problem to Mother she would have tried to do something about it, like boil the sweater. But I didn't.

We kept up the pretence that the problem didn't exist. How

else can I explain my frequent trips to the outhouse to pick off the vermin? The outhouse was no picnic, either. Four families shared it, and in the summer the smell and the varieties of flies it attracted were revolting. Everyone dreaded going in. The winter brought relief from the flies and the odour, all right, but our bottoms froze. Every fall a farmer came and drained the ditch under the outhouse by pulling up pails of excrement and emptying them into a metal holding tank. The stuff was used as fertilizer in the truck garden business. So there I was, in the cold, huddled, with my sweater off, plucking off lice and dropping them into the hole. The lice kept multiplying ever faster. We were, it seemed, in a race. I learned since then that lice can, if they feel like it, produce up to twenty-four generations annually. Finding the sweater, and my blood, to their taste, my lice went the limit. Over the next three years I defended myself as best I could, and always lost.

Desperate for some sort of soap, Father decided we would make our own. Smelly animal fat was boiled down to a liquid and mixed with soda powder. The mud-coloured stuff was poured into a wooden crate lined with paper. Next day we lifted out the strips of wood that criss-crossed the bottom of the mould and removed the cakes of soap, a type of soap that produced no suds. It was better than nothing.

11
Szifra

At one time or another we have all had problems with ill-fitting shoes. Along any shopping street, only food-related outlets outnumber shops selling shoes. Why shoes? Apparently the comfort and pleasure derived from well-fitting, attractive shoes outweigh other considerations. Pinching, blister-producing footwear is nothing short of a calamity. The mood sours, digestion suffers, tempers flare. A perfectly calm, rational person can turn into an ogre when plagued by sore feet. A sizeable proportion of discretionary spending is on shoes – possibly more than on any other item connected with bodily comfort. A good friend once said to me, 'I would pay a thousand dollars for a pair of shoes that fit properly.' In the Far East, especially in Singapore, professional foot reflexologists treat thousands of people. Many there believe that foot massage promotes healing, relieves stress, and increases virility in men. Our contact with terra firma comes via the feet. Evidence is available that sensitive zones of feet and arches are imprinted in our genes. Imelda Marcos collected thousands of pairs of shoes. Our first impression of a person is based as much on the footwear as on the face and eyes. Is there a primordial instinct that directs our attention to our feet?

Isaac Bashevis Singer tells a story in which a married woman takes her case to a rabbinical court. She asks to be granted a divorce from her husband, who she claims is a dimwit. To substantiate her assertion, she offers as evidence the man's absurd, scuffed boots.

When I was almost thirteen, in the third year of the war, I had outgrown my only, worn pair of shoes. I had to go barefoot.

Working and living in cramped quarters, I spent my free time outdoors. Father and Mother were presumably concerned about my shoeless condition, but new shoes would have ruined the household budget for weeks, if not months. Besides, shoes were not readily available. We had been grinding wheat, and I was a productive member whose strong arm was much in demand. I was also the family water-carrier, and certainly I couldn't be expected to lug water barefoot in bad weather. The well was a good distance away, and to pay the professional water-carrier was unthinkable. Obviously, shoes had to be obtained. They had to be good enough to last through the war, with thick soles to forestall repairs. What we were after was an all-season type of footwear, something that might even be resalable once outgrown.

A certain shoemaker was known to have stashed away hides from before the war. He was approached, tentatively at first. A deal was struck. The price was high, but so was the quality of the shoes. Any sort of leather was hard to come by, as the Germans were keen on keeping it all for their own use. Cattle were numbered and registered, and all hides were accounted for. The well-dressed SS officer wore riding boots and a leather coat. Our order was for a pair of smart brown shoes, the only colour offered, not unlike a Brooks Brothers model. My feet were sized, the deposit paid, and delivery arranged for five to six weeks hence. The wait had begun.

My social life at this time involved getting together with boys my own age at a vacant lot after my grinding and sifting shifts were done. The better-off local kids kept pigeons, which they let out to meet other pigeons high above, to no particular purpose that I could discern. Card games were popular, too. Other than that, we just talked. Everyone had a nickname. Mine was 'Whitey,' which, since my hair was dark, didn't make sense.

All the time I spent at home allowed me to get to know our neighbour, Szifra. A girl of about my age, she lived across the yard in a modern, two-storey house, actually a duplex occupied by her own family and an aunt and uncle with their teenage daughter and twenty-year-old son, a Jewish policeman. Szifra's parents were our landlords. They may have lived in our one-room cottage before they built their new house, the result of a prosperous shoe business. With curly dark hair, brown eyes, a small waist, and a warm personality, Szifra liked me and I liked her. She was a neat dresser, and at all costs I was determined not to give in to my miserable state – I wasn't about to look like a loser. While my new shoes were being made, I managed to keep my feet out of sight. Szifra didn't read much, but I did. That gave me an advantage. Talking knowledgeably about a book was a sure way to dazzle someone who didn't read. Small talk could get tedious, invention could only go so far, but discussing books always worked. I kept Szifra interested and managed to keep my feet out of sight using the simple stratagem of staying indoors and talking to her through an open window that was waist high on the outside and just above my knees on the inside. The arrangement worked well in good weather. On rainy or windy days we didn't meet. If Szifra thought my behaviour peculiar, she never let on. It could be that she thought these were the ways of big-city folks.

Szifra also benefited from my up-to-date knowledge of the German war effort. The newspaper provided information about the progress of the war on all fronts. About that same time I decided to save the local paper. That was to be my contribution to the family fortune at war's end – a complete collection of German propaganda.

For the time being, the rout on the eastern front was complete. After France, Norway, and Greece, entire armies were giving up daily. There was no reason to doubt it: the German war machine was insatiable. Periodic searches of homes were taking place. Anything of value was confiscated. Such a search was scheduled for our area shortly, so Szifra's policeman-cousin informed us.

Szifra's father had been fortunate to hide away some of his pre-war shoe inventory, hence the family's relative prosperity. The imminent search could jeopardize the cache, so they asked neighbours to hide boots in their homes. Our allotment was nine pairs of shoes, and we were told to disperse them, stuff socks in them, and put them under beds. Our frantic efforts to hide the shoes met with partial success. No extra socks were available, and we only had two beds in the room, so an extraordinary number of shoes under them would be suspect. Certainly, it would serve no purpose to have the Germans think that our family was wealthy. A more thorough search would follow, and they might decide to take Father in for questioning. What if they found Father's good, pre-war overcoat or the three-metre piece of fine, dark grey men's suiting? Those two items were to be our capital for a start in business in the postwar world, and they were not to be sold to buy food or anything else. We hid the shoes as best we could, and made them less conspicuous by rubbing a bit of mud on them. Mother tried on one pair of ankle-high boots and found that they fit. We agreed that it would be incongruous for the four of us to walk around in tatters, or barefoot, when good shoes were sitting around everywhere. Later, it occurred to me that it would have been easier to buy my shoes from Szifra's parents than to order them custom made. But we hadn't known then about the secret cache.

Shoes those days were hand-sewn, the soles fastened by puncturing the leather with an awl and then hammering in wooden pegs, one at a time, in rows of three across, right around the entire sole. The same procedure was used for fastening the heels. It was time-consuming, but the result was solid. The excess wood on the heels was neatly filed off with a rasp, and the leather edges were finished off with a coloured wax to match. We waited for the Germans, and for my shoes. There I was, barefoot, and our home smelled like a shoe emporium.

This was the inventory of our worldly goods: a table, four chairs, water pails and pots, hooks on the walls, one bare lightbulb (not functioning, because the power had been turned off in the ghetto as a conservation measure), a wood-burning clay stove and oven, two beds, one shovel, one axe, and one hidden, handoperated mill with several sieves.

The search by the police did not take place that week, but much later. By then most of the shoes had been given back to their owner. Apparently the Germans, as a matter of policy, mixed false tips in with the true alarms they passed on to their Jewish contacts. It made for a more exciting game. Mother somehow forgot to take off the shoes she wore, and they remained with us. I suspect the owners didn't keep a strict inventory count, for not a word was heard. We all felt guilty about the matter, but as time went by, it became unthinkable to return worn shoes. By then I was sharing the shoes with Mother.

When the shoemaker handed over my new shoes, I pranced over to show them to Szifra. But all was not well. Either I had outgrown the size taken two months earlier or I wasn't used to wearing shoes or the shoemaker had made a mistake. The shoemaker tried stretching them, but it was no use. Blisters developed; my big toe swelled up. The shoes had to go. Naturally there was no exchange or refund on custom-made articles, nor any question of buying a replacement. We had spent all we had on this pair. My stylish brown shoes were bartered to our baker. They were last seen being worn by his eleven-year-old daughter, a girl with dirty blonde hair and thickish legs.

Mother and I shared her shoes throughout the fall and winter. This was embarrassing. Mother's feet had bunions, and the shoes developed unsightly crease marks on the uppers. None of my friends noticed, but I was aware of it. Of course, I tried to keep the cooperative shoes away from Szifra's sight, even though I realized that she couldn't be conscious of the trauma I was going through. Through the window my torso, and not much else, was in evidence to Szifra, until it got really cold. Then I wore Father's high, black-felt boots with the rubber soles, while he stayed home.

My best friend was my cousin Natek, the youngest son of Aunt Bluma and Uncle Fishl. They had come to Staszów in January 1940, directly from Łódź. Our family had followed from Kielce in June. Natek and I were the same age. We liked the same books and talked about world politics and what husbands and wives do. Natek informed me that in order to bring babies into the world a husband and wife engaged in an awkward act. Somehow I couldn't imagine Tatuś and Mamusia involved in such a freakish exercise, but I couldn't offer an alternative scenario. By mutual agreement we decided to drop the topic. Yet the subject kept coming up in some of the books I wangled. As I indiscriminately read Jack London, Dostoyevsky, Dickens, pulp novels, and historical romances, I tried to skip the suggestive scenes. It just wasn't decent.

The war was in its third year, and the situation looked bad. Not as bad as it would become, but dismal nonetheless. By now two aunts, an uncle, and their families were in Staszów. We were shut up in a ghetto, and made to wear white armbands with a blue six-pointed star. Our meagre savings from Łódź were gone. My clothes had patches over patches. I had no shoes. In October I would be thirteen.

To a Jewish boy, thirteen is pretty significant – it's Bar Mitzvah time. In 1941, a few *shtibels* were in operation. Not an official synagogue, a shtibel (meaning, literally, a small room, which it usually was) is a room in a learned man's home where a *minyan* of ten Jewish males or more assemble for Sabbath services and holidays. Occasionally I accompanied Father to the shtibel. The Torah was read, *aliya*s were given – the honour of reading a portion of the Torah – and boys became Bar Mitzvah. I dreaded the thought of reading from the Torah. I had stopped taking Hebrew lessons at the summer break in 1939, so reading the prayers was difficult for me. I kept forgetting the sounds. Only practice could bring improvement. I had nothing to spur me on except a date somewhere in the distance, and I kept putting things off, assuming that the people believed I knew my stuff. I didn't. I wasn't going to school. I had no Hebrew tutor, and the repetition of the prayers bored me to distraction. But I did try. On Saturdays I would repeat in private the already learned portions of the Sabbath prayers. Some of it stuck. I couldn't be sure if I was pronouncing them correctly. There was no way that I could verify my pronunciation without being laughed at. Father and Mother had other matters to worry about, like how to feed us. They didn't mention Bar Mitzvah. They apparently believed that I would be ready when the time came. Why else would they never talk about it?

Aunt Bluma and Uncle Fishl were living just down the street from us, with their three sons. The boys were taking private lessons in Polish, Russian, and Hebrew. My Aunt Bluma and Uncle Fishl had been able to salvage many valuables. Though we never spoke of it, I was sure that Natek would be ready for his Bar Mitzvah. The subject was distasteful to me. Natek's Hebrew lessons were not confined to prayers, but included language, interpretations, the whole gamut. His two older brothers were taking instruction from the same tutor.

The tutor was a big-city professor who was having a hard time adjusting to life as an itinerant teacher. An older man, perhaps five feet tall, bald, with gold-rimmed glasses, he came to my aunt's house every weekday morning to teach the boys reading and writing, as well as math and science. Occasionally I would saunter in and observe. The class was held in a glassed-in veranda, where the sun would stream in. The books were spread out on a table, and my three cousins, pencils in hand, worked. A pleasant scene. Though my aunt was a kind woman, it probably never occurred to her to invite me and my sister to sit in. I believe the teacher's pay was a couple of loaves of bread for a morning's instruction – a good deal for the teacher. Anyway, I had work to do, milling and sifting.

The thought of making a fool of myself at age thirteen in front of the adults gave me many sleepless nights.

The summer ended with the Germans making a run almost into Moscow. In September Natek developed a bad cold. He was treated with sweet raspberry syrup in hot tea. Father recommended cupping as a remedy. I saw him do it once. He would take the round glass jars, or *bańki*, put a drop of alcohol in each, ignite it to create a vacuum, then quickly plop each jar onto the patient's back. For about ten to fifteen minutes the bańki would draw the blood (with the impurities of the illness, it was believed) to the surface of the skin. As the bańki were removed and the vacuum released, a popping sound was heard and red bumps would appear on the skin. A small boy like Natek would need about nine to twelve bańki. Leeches were also tried. There was no other medicine, not even aspirin. Time went by; Natek grew weaker. He had long ago stopped taking daily instruction. Dr Kirszenbaum, the only practising doctor in town, diagnosed the illness as pneumonia, for which there was no known cure. Natek was quietly buried just after the High Holy Days.

About the same time, Mother fell ill. She hadn't been well for some time. The same doctor who couldn't help Natek recommended a women's specialist in distant Kraków. Father and Mother had a series of whispered discussions. The hired driver's horse and wagon would have to take back roads in order to avoid German patrols. My parents instructed my sister and me to keep indoors and to finish grinding the batch of grain that was left in the sack. Mother and Father returned a few days later, she paler and he with a relieved look on his face. Soon Mother resumed her station at the crank of the hand mill.

My Bar Mitzvah date came and went and nothing happened. I never heard it mentioned.

12
Our Time Has Come

The winter of 1941–2 started out cold and stayed cold. The Germans had forbidden the burning of coal, and wood was expensive and hard to come by. All electric power to the ghetto was cut off. A curfew was in force. Evenings we sat or lay in dark, cold rooms. We gathered that the German armies in Russia were also suffering from the cold. Their rapid advance had stalled. Posters went up ordering all Jews to turn in their gold jewellery and fur garments. The penalty for non-compliance was death. By now very few Jews had any gold; most had swapped even their wedding bands for food. The same was true of fur coats. Only worthless, moth-eaten furs remained, worn by grandmothers in bed to keep warm.

We didn't have any gold or furs to give up, but I went along with a couple of my friends to dump their mothers' coats onto a heap in a Wehrmacht truck. A rumour was about that the furs would be taken to the eastern front to keep the soldiers warm. We derived some satisfaction from this information. The Germans were obviously suffering.

Was it possible the war would end soon? We knew it wasn't. It was only a matter of time before they would come to get us. Throughout the spring and summer of 1942, a timetable was being followed. The same squad of uniformed Ukrainians led by German officers had come to each of the shtetls and, using whips, had herded the people into cattle cars, a hundred to a wagon. They shot stragglers and the elderly who couldn't move fast enough. In every case the Judenrat and Jewish police were allowed to stay. Also allowed to stay were people working directly for the Germans in specific industries. By October there were but a handful of towns left in our area that hadn't been visited by the squad.

In the last week of October word got out that it was Staszów's turn on the coming Monday. The information came from the head of the local German police, usually a reliable source. The commandant, kept in luxurious circumstances by the Judenrat, who had been heavily taxing those who still had something to tax, had passed on the news.

By that time we were certain that the Germans were killing our people. Where, and by what method, we did not know. A lot of whispering took place among our parents, aunts, and uncles. On the Sunday night, in mid-curfew, we took a few essentials and made our way to the Myśliwieces' nearby farm. There, by the light of a kerosene lamp, we were shown inside a barn to a huge pile of sawdust through which a tunnel had been excavated. The four of us – my parents, my sister, and I – crawled into the tunnel and heard the sounds of the entrance behind us being covered up. Inside, still on our stomachs, we came to a sort of cave. The sawdust, packed tight on all sides, was held back by a few boards above our heads. It was very dark. We felt bodies and heard the voices of Aunt Bluma and Uncle Fishl, Uncle Nathan and Aunt Mania, their two children and Mania's retarded sister, Aunt Rózia and Uncle Nusyn, and our cousins Mietek, Moniek, and Geniek. They were all there, sitting cross-legged on the ground.

Uncle Fishl, ever resourceful, had paid his neighbour to prepare the cave. Just in case, Fishl had also paid a sum of money to obtain certificates for his family that showed them to be employed repairing army uniforms in the local factory – the Judenrat had set up a tailoring plant where only the rich could get work. However, there was no assurance that the Einsatzgruppe (Action Group of the Security Police) would respect the certificates. A round-up normally took a full day. As soon as the squad left town, our farmer friend, Myśliwiec, would dig us out. Just what would happen afterwards, we could not know. Our cave was as silent as a crypt. After perhaps twenty-four hours, there was a glimmer of light. Spitting and shaking out sawdust, we crawled out. Nothing had happened: it had been a false alarm.

For next time we had to find a more secure hiding place, one where we could stay hidden for a longer period – the longer the better. Uncle Fishl, we believed, was also trying to make other arrangements. It was now every family for themselves. With the exception of Aunt Bluma and Aunt Rózia we never saw the others again.

During this time, Jewish people from small towns and villages in our district were given ten minutes to leave their homes and go to Staszów, since the Einsatzgruppe apparently couldn't be bothered to collect a couple of hundred Jews from here and there. A larger town made for a more efficient job. The Judenrat opened a free soup kitchen to keep the hundreds of new arrivals from starving. I volunteered to help with ladling out the soup and cutting up potatoes. Destitute people would line up for hours before the kitchen doors opened. Some sat on the ground and just stared. One of them, a grey-haired woman, crouched on the curb with her skirt pulled up to her knees; she wore no panties. One of the kitchen's patrons, a young man who sometimes helped the cooks, entertained us daily by composing funny rhyming poems.

My friend Hershl's father had a carpentry shop next door to the soup kitchen, and I had good reason to be there, too. Casually, I fabricated a plywood cover the size of a small table. In the cover I drilled nine big holes. Later I got some cement, which I mixed with earth and straw and applied, wet, to the lid. Placed on the ground, in a weed-covered patch, it blended well with the surroundings. This was to be our air intake in the new secret hiding place, the *skrytka*.

My friend Szifra's father had come up with the idea of constructing a skrytka in the abandoned cellar of a structure close by that had burned down years ago. We could get into it by cutting a hole in the basement wall of the adjoining cottage. A family from Kraków occupied the cottage, a husband and wife with two daughters in their twenties, and they had to be included in the plan. In Staszów for about two years, they had been systematically selling every garment they had brought with them from Kraków. The Sznifers, Szifra's relatives, and my parents thought these people were daft. In no time they were wearing rags, having rid themselves of practically everything saleable. Lately, they had accelerated the process by spending whatever money they had on luxuries such as butter and eggs. Once, I overheard the man saying to Father that we were foolish in holding on to any possessions. 'I know better,' said the man, who was heavy-set, with thinning, reddish hair and gold-rimmed glasses. 'Eat while you can. Soon you'll not need anything.'

Just a couple of months before, Father and his neighbours had decided to hide anything of value so the Germans wouldn't get it. It was everyone's capital for after the war. The hiding place was ingenious – in the Sznifers' attic, the men built a matching brick wall in front of the real one. In the space thus created, Father put all the treasure we possessed – his almost new, double-breasted, dark blue overcoat purchased before the war and the three-metre piece of fine all-wool men's suiting. The neighbours brought their valuables. Father assured us that the fake wall could not be told from the real ones.

The adults, too distraught by the rapid deterioration of our situation, were not acting quickly enough on the plan for our new hiding-place. To my young mind any delay would find us unprepared. It fell to me to prepare the skrytka. I had a week at most. There were only two or three Jewish ghettos left in Kielce province. The Einsatzgruppe, whose itinerary we followed, did about two jobs a week. They probably could have done better if they'd been able to procure more cattle cars to transport Jews.

Through a two-by-two-foot, newly cut hole in the Kraków people's basement, I crawled into the ancient cellar. A mess! After a day of hauling out rubbish and wiping the brick walls by the light of a candle, it remained a damp old cellar. I punched a hole in the ceiling, just about in the middle of the room, through what had been the kitchen floor, now overgrown with weeds. This opening, covered with the lid I'd constructed, was to be our air intake: nine two-inch holes for fifteen people. There was no time to calculate our air requirements precisely. During the night we and the Sznifers carried clothes, blankets, pillows, and food into the skrytka. The Sznifers' son, Hirsch, who was in the ghetto police, was expected to help the squad round up the Jews, and he would know the exact time of the *wysiedlenie*. (The term *wysiedlenie* was yet another example of the kind of perfidy the Germans were known for: literally, it means 'resettlement,' normally denoting relocation to another place on this earth.) Hirsch would brick us up after we were in. I had a pile of the old bricks and cement ready for him.

I tried to make provision for an extended stay. A former pickle barrel was to be our water reservoir. Concerned about the water turning bad, I obtained a small bottle of arak (aniseed extract), planning to put in a few drops at a time to make the water smell fresher. Bought in the pharmacy in the town square, the arak drops were handed to me without a word by the Polish salesgirl, a vision dressed in white, with hair so blonde it too was almost white. Two buckets with makeshift lids completed the set-up. Soon Staszów was the only ghetto left in the entire province. We could feel the knife touching our throats.

On the afternoon of 10 November 1942 Jews from the village of Kurozwenki were herded into the Staszów town square. Guarded by a platoon of Ukrainians in army uniforms, they had come in on foot that fall day, carrying their belongings. They were to join the Staszów Jews for the transport east. Kurozwenki did not have a regular train station; its lifeline to the outside world was a narrow-gauge railway track.

Disregarding instructions from my distraught parents to avoid the square, which Jews were forbidden to enter, I stood gawking. Suddenly, two shots rang out. I got the message and ran home.

That evening all fifteen of us crawled into the hiding space. Hirsch's blonde sister had been sent away with forged papers to a Polish farmer. For his trouble the farmer received dozens of pairs of shoes. The sister could pass for an Aryan as long as she didn't talk much. Hirsch bricked us in, and we sat up all night, listening. In the morning, from outside, we could hear shouts of '*Raus!*' ('Out!'), then many feet running, more yelling, a couple of rifle shots, and then silence. Hirsch was supposed to tell us when to come out by dropping a note through a hole. But many days went by, and we heard nothing. Most of us just lay or sat dozing, there being insufficient room to walk about or even to stretch our legs. The toilet facilities – the two buckets covered with sand mixed with lime – were a nuisance, but the drinking water with the arak held up well. Mornings, days, and nights, it was one black, stuffy, embryonic sac where one could see nothing. We managed by groping. Little was said.

On the morning of the twelfth day I was awakened by hammering at the bricked-in crawl entrance. Soon it was open. By the light of a lamp we saw the face of Myśliwiec, our peasant neighbour. He urged us to come out quickly and to leave everything behind. On various occasions I had been told that in an emergency I was to put on as many layers of clothing as possible; these would not be confiscated, as a parcel or a valise would be. I looked around for clothes and remembered that I had little except some underwear that I didn't wear much because I had outgrown it. Nonetheless, I put it on and followed the others to the attic of the Kraków family's house. There, waiting for us, was a Polish policeman clad in navy blue.

Outside it was grey, with a fine rain falling. A cold, damp day, perfect for curling up with a book and a slice of freshly baked bread with butter. Our group of fifteen, including Sznifer's old grandmother, stood at one end of the attic, Myśliwiec and the law at the other end. Myśliwiec announced that we were not safe here, but he would undertake to move us to the forest in the evening. For his troubles he expected payment, in advance. The policeman nodded assent. Disoriented, unwashed, scared, eyes hurting in the sudden daylight, we stood huddled, not uttering a sound. The men, each in turn, counted out bills and handed them to Myśliwiec. He checked the total, asked if that was all, climbed down the ladder to the bedroom, opened the door to the street, and was gone. The policeman ordered us down to the empty and silent street. He marched us to the jail.

The local jail, meant to hold twenty at most, now held hundreds of Jews whose hiding places had been discovered. During the day we could stay in the exercise yard, but at night we were locked into the four or five cells. With so many packed together we had a problem breathing. There was not enough oxygen. This was evident the first night when a candle would not stay lit. During the day my friend Szifra and I mostly sat on the floor in the jail hallway. I didn't know what she was thinking about; for my part, I wondered whether I would ever lie with a woman and what it would be like to hold Szifra.

The warden, a Pole, demanded payment for favours such as bringing food, or getting messages to and from those still in the shrunken ghetto. To get us bread, Father parted with a gold watch that had stopped running a long time ago.

We learned that the people who had stayed in the tailoring plant had not been harmed. Neither had the boys who worked at road-building for the Omler construction company. The Judenrat and Jewish police remained in town as well. Among the people taken to the jail were some who had in their possession work certificates for the tailor shop; they were able to bribe the warden to let them go. Szifra's family and her uncle and aunt were among those who had bought the certificates and so, one morning, they left by the back door. The Sznifers presumably were in contact with Hirsch, but we did not see him again.

A couple of days later four large trucks pulled up in front of the jail's gate. The guards took us out to the street, where a couple of German officers ordered young men and women onto the open, high-sided vehicles. They told me to fall back. Father was already on board. They told my mother and sister to move back also. Minutes went by. The trucks got ready to leave. I couldn't see Mother and Anna and assumed – correctly, as it turned out – that they must have clambered up onto a truck. Some of the people had begun to shuffle back to the jail house. I climbed up the side of one of the trucks and was pulled in. The driver put the truck in gear.

I was on the truck my father had boarded. I huddled against Father's chest in the back of the open truck, an icy November rain saturating my old school jacket. Mouth sour, hands and feet numb, I surveyed the scene and our group.

The last houses of Staszów gave way to empty fields. The

trucks were heading north. They stopped briefly in the Chmielnik town square, which was deserted, as if after a plague. The thirty or so men, unshaven, bedraggled and wet, leaned on each other, pitching with each lurch of the fast-moving vehicle.

Of the people in Staszów who had paid for work certificates hardly anyone survived; neither did the members of Judenrat or the Jewish policemen. Their turn came in the early spring of 1943.

As it turned out, my nimbly climbing onto the truck in the nick of time had saved my life. We were being taken away to work, to live.

13
We Work

The hurtling truck continued on to Kielce. By 1942 the Jews of Kielce had been deported by the Einsatzgruppen. In late afternoon we arrived at a factory complex. The sign read HASAG, the Hugo Schneider Aktiengesellschaft. Herded over to the barracks, we were given a chunk of bread and told that work assignments would take place in the morning. I later learned that the factories were located in four two-storey buildings and an equal number of single-storey ones. Several smaller structures contained maintenance shops, the kitchen, the guards' quarters, and warehouses. The entire area was enclosed by a high barbed-wire fence, with tall poles bearing bright lights around the perimeter.

Previously owned by the Polish government's defence ministry, the factory had been taken over by HASAG. The output of munitions continued. The original Polish workforce was kept on, and German supervisory personnel were added. The Polish employees came in daily from the city. Production of casings and tips for rifle bullets was being stepped up, and we had been brought in to augment the existing staff. We could consider ourselves lucky.

At one end of the compound, but still within the enclosure, were newly constructed, E-shaped wooden barracks. The middle section, containing the kitchen, the delousing room, toilets, showers, and infirmary, divided the women's quarters at the upper end, where Mother and Anna were, from the men's at the bottom. The view from the open end of the structures to the outside world was cut off by a ten-foot-high wooden fence. The barracks was divided into rooms with two rows of upper and lower bunks, sleeping about fifty. In the middle of the aisle separating the rows, near the door, sat an oil drum converted into a heater and stove. The nuts and bolts were still shiny on the new, all-wood pre-fabs. I was given a thin blanket and a straw mattress, which I put next to Father's on an upper bunk.

On the first morning men and women were marched off in groups of ten or more and assigned to various German and Polish supervisors. With several other youngsters who had somehow managed to smuggle themselves in, I was sent back to the barracks. Apparently unsuitable for adult work, our fate was uncertain. Early the following day I reported for work again. Same thing. The third and fourth days I repeatedly tried to get assigned to a job. No luck.

One evening shortly thereafter a call came over the loudspeakers that everyone must leave the barracks for the factory cafeteria. At the time, while our camp kitchen was under construction, we received our soup ration there. My sixth sense told me something was not right. As a rule no one cared if you skipped the evening soup. In the cold, dark, early December evening I heard the guards methodically going through every barrack, searching for stragglers. I hid on a top bunk and waited. I remained under a blanket until I heard some of our men returning. There had been a 'selection.' The young and the old had not been permitted to go back to the barracks. Father passed inspection. Mother and Anna, who were vulnerable, fortunately managed to evade the net as well. It seems some well-wishers warned them not to enter the cafeteria as 'something strange was going on there.' The unfortunates were never heard from again. Word was they had been taken somewhere outside of town and shot.

One of the people taken away was Dov, Father's bunk neighbour. Dov was a cousin of my Uncle Nusyn, Rozia's husband. A soft-spoken, slender man of about forty-five, he wore his salt-and-pepper hair closely cropped. Under his blanket, Father found a practically new pair of trousers. Black with a prominent grey stripe, they were too small and too good for Father to wear.

Father took the pants with him one day in January 1943 when he was sent to Staszów with a work party to pick up building materials. He bribed the Polish supervisor to let him off for a short time, then pulled away the rocks he had used to cover up our hand mill. Next he went to see Myśliwiec, where he learned how the farmer had found our hiding place.

The lid I had fashioned acted as an exhaust for the combined breathing of fifteen people. Seeing steam rise from my nine holes, Myśliwiec figured we were there. He also reckoned that we had valuables with us. He consulted with his friend, the Polish policeman, and they decided to wait until there were fewer Germans around. As soon as they saw their way clear, the two of them broke the seal and made us move to the attic in the event that a German patrol showed up unexpectedly. That way, the policeman would be able to report that we had been found hiding in the attic. The Germans were unlikely to question this, and he and Myśliwiec would not have to share the spoils with them.

Father offered Myśliwiec a trade of Dov's valuable striped pants and the hand mill for a piece of cheese, a loaf of bread, and potatoes. Myśliwiec, fully aware that Father had little time on this visit, offered him only the loaf of bread and a small sack of potatoes. Father, unable to shop around for a better deal, accepted Myśliwiec's offer.

Back at the factory, I kept up my job search. One evening a call went out for six men to report immediately to Meister Milki at the 'two-centimetre marine casings' plant. In the short time I had spent at HASAG, stories had surfaced of Milki's brutality. His department employed a lot of Jewish girls. Working twelve-hour shifts, inexperienced and disoriented, the girls were easy prey for Milki, whose favourite punishment for a minor error was six lashes on the bare bottom. I didn't know what the penalty would be for a big mistake. Father was selected for that particular night shift. Anxious as I was to make myself useful, I volunteered to go instead. The group of us set off in the night to the building. There was a total blackout. Trudging, stumbling in unfamiliar surroundings, we arrived at the appointed place minutes late. Milki was waiting for us, fuming. The job we were to do couldn't wait.

Our conduct, he explained to us, was unforgivable. Disheartened, we feebly tried to explain our getting lost, the darkness, the slippery road. Milki, a youngish man with slicked-back dark hair and a good complexion, cut the discussion short and ordered us to line up and drop our trousers. We complied. Each received six lashes administered with a black, one-inch-thick rubber-and-steel hose. When my turn came Milki graciously said something about 'kleine' (small), and counted only to three. The whole ordeal took no more than ten minutes.

We trooped over to the outside of the building and were put to work pumping raw sewage. An underground connection had plugged up or frozen, and the washrooms were overflowing. Sore from the lashing, we hand-pumped the shit like hell and held our noses. That was my introduction to the German work ethic.

Later in the week I landed a job in the same marine shell-casings department, mopping up machine oil that had seeped into the electrical conduits fastened in concrete channels throughout the large plant. This in turn led to a job as the tool and supply person in the electrical maintenance department. It had been Father's job just before I got it. He had moved on to a better position as a bookbinder, and I sort of inherited the job. I was my own boss. Shortly thereafter Mother got a good job in the camp kitchen, but my sister, Anna, was unfortunately stuck in the two-centimetre shell plant, where there was no protection whatever from the acetone fumes in the degreasing department where she worked.

In a community of about twelve hundred, living literally on top of each other, there would have been a predictable range of problems; given the composition of our community, they were magnified tenfold. Wives without husbands, husbands without wives, perhaps one sister and a brother remaining out of a family of six or ten. Mostly there were single individuals, male and female, who were sure that they were the only family survivors. Their families, the populations of entire streets and towns, were gone.

Surprisingly, morale wasn't all that bad. What kept us going was the conviction that, in the end, the Germans would lose the war. Had any of us known at the time that it would be two and a half years before the Nazis capitulated, our resolve to fight it out would probably have been less firm. Speaking for myself, I took to the routine well, but six twelve-hour days of work did not leave much time or energy to make plans. If there was extra food, whether Father or I got it, we four shared it equally. Whenever an opportunity presented itself I visited Mother and Anna at work, sometimes for only a few minutes. Since my job was so much better than theirs, I felt guilty whenever I saw them slogging away. As time went on, a kind of normality set in, except that the ordinary parent-child relationships were suspended. Unable to come to each other's aid, we found that even comforting words were hard to summon.

The women's and men's sections were theoretically insulated from each other. In fact, there was a good deal of coming and going. The guards entered the camp infrequently and only for a specific purpose. Food rations were inadequate, but nearly everyone managed to scrounge additional calories, often in innovative, even fanciful, ways. We were always hungry, but no one was starving.

There were good jobs and bad jobs. A good assignment was one that allowed for 'organizing' extra victuals. The Yiddish word *organizirn* meant, for us, to get hold of food by whatever means possible – barter, theft, working for it, or stumbling upon it. Among the men, the luckiest were the teamsters (*placowy*), those who were not trained in specific factory operations but were on stand-by for odd jobs: they organized most of the extra food. The placowy team was used to load and unload boxcars, remove rubbish, move equipment, and unpack and repack goods; occasionally, they were sent into town to do work. Their possibilities for organizing were good. It follows that those who ate better also had other things on their mind besides food and survival. In order to qualify for placowy in HASAG one had to be young and strong, ideally between the ages of eighteen and thirty-five. I was fourteen, and small.

For the next two years the men were constantly jockeying for jobs that offered chances to organize. Some were stuck in dead-end positions that offered no opportunity to obtain goods. They either went hungry or found a better-off inmate for whom they could perform menial jobs, such as mending clothes or cooking, in order to earn a slice of bread or a few potatoes. The food rations consisted of bread, some margarine, sometimes jam, and soup (infrequently with horse meat), but mostly of potatoes and vegetables.

Almost none of my own 'organizing' techniques were without risk. One winter my job consisted of assisting a Polish maintenance electrician on the night shift at the plant stand-by station. From 8 P.M. to 8 A.M. we were on the ready to take care of emergencies. Occasionally, a call would go out for us from one of the plants, but most of the time we did nothing. All major electrical repairs were done during the day by a regular crew. The Polish electrician preferred to sleep while I watched out for nosy inspectors. But hardly anyone visited the basement tool shack, tucked away at the end of a corridor beside a storage room for wires, pipes, and junk. The electrician had arranged with the kitchen manager of the Polish workers' cafeteria to supply him with hot soup half way into the night shift. (The Jewish personnel had to make do with whatever they had left over from their evening rations. Soup in the barracks was at seven, just before the night shift left to replace the day shift.) The electrician would send me over just before mealtime for a pot of soup 'from the top.' Scooped from the top, the soup contained a lot of fat and chunks of meat and skin. It was the choice stuff. The rub was that we had nothing to go with it.

Everyone knew that a large cache of potatoes was stashed away in bunkers at the far end of the factory grounds. These were to last the HASAG's large labour force until the next crop in August. The spuds were sitting in makeshift huts, covered with straw to protect them against the winter cold, and were watched twenty-four hours a day by armed guards on six-hour shifts. My mission was to move into one of the potato bunkers when the guard was at the opposite end, scoop out as many potatoes as I could into a wooden tool-box, and get out. Because of the primitive storage arrangements, a lot of the potatoes were frozen. In the dark, fearing for my life, jumping at every suspicious noise, I did not manage every time to bring only good ones. You could tell the difference between a frozen and an unfrozen potato only by cutting it up. I do not recommend frozen potatoes, whether boiled or baked – they smell and taste more like sweet, rotten eggs. Still, a couple of times a week I put my life on the line for a few potatoes. It never occurred to me to refuse to take the risk for so little. After all, once I'd cooked the spuds, I also got to share some of the soup.

The following summer, I learned about a work order for the bakery in downtown Kielce that supplied us with bread. Although many electricians and helpers had vied for the job, I managed to get it. Early each morning I met the Polish electrician and, carrying his tools, followed him, accompanied by an armed guard, to the bakery. While the electrician was stringing wire, I looked around for things to organize. I struck pay dirt almost immediately. Each morning the bakery owners found loaves of bread gnawed by rats or mice. During the week that I worked there, I brought back with me at least half a dozen of these loaves. For a few days I was a great provider.

Then there was the time I wangled the job of sounding the gong. The gong was a piece of rail hanging from a rope, and the sound of it at noon signalled the start of the lunch break. The gong was in front of the Polish cafeteria, and the racket I made was heard throughout the plant area. For this distinguished service I was given a bowl of soup – soup that was superior to our evening fare. What the German soup might be like, I could only guess.

There were other benefits to being a man Friday in an electrical shop. For example, one could barter or exchange favours. Moreover, having access to equipment and tools, one could build things. At one point I gave jewellery manufacturing a try. My first creation was to be a man's signet ring. A hexagonal brass nut used for fastening high-voltage copper bars was the raw material. I placed the threaded nut in a workbench vice and filed it down to the correct size all around. I then used a rattail file to smooth off the threads until I could get it to fit loosely on my index finger. I reduced the rim to a narrow band at the bottom, leaving it wider and thicker towards the top, where I had sculpted it to a stylish gradual square. I even went to the trouble of having the ring nickel-plated at the plating unit next door. Finished, it looked every bit like a solid silver ring. However, finding a customer for it in our no-frills society wasn't easy. The ring fit Father, so I gave it to him. He wore it on the middle finger of his left hand until the plating wore off and his skin began to turn green.

Co-workers sometimes helped out. One of the Polish electricians in my unit, Pan Popławski, a dark-complexioned, Spanish-looking man, used to bring a lunch packed by his wife. She made him sandwiches of various sorts, but mostly jam on rye. He consumed six or eight at a time, but he didn't like the crusts, and would give them to me. When he worked in town, I had to go without.

Occasionally, I got half a sandwich or an apple for keeping an eye out while the electricians played poker. Often I did it for nothing, as part of my job. They played five-card stud, with small stakes. Herman, a Jewish electrician, was the only non-Pole to sit in. There was only one chair, so the game was played around a workbench. I sat at the far end of the bench facing the window and shouted if one of the German foremen happened to be walking our way.

Herman was a swarthy man in his late thirties who had a lot of blackheads on his face, owing, I suppose, to all the machine oil and grease he came into contact with, and to the lack of soap. His fingernails were black, too, and his pants and jacket were covered with oil stains. I know this because I used to sit, transfixed, watching him cheat. If he was dealt two queens, an ace, an eight, and a five, he would draw three cards. Keep the two queens? Not at all! Herman would put down the queens and the ace. If he drew an ace, a queen, and a nine, he would then put down the eight, five, and nine and take back his original two queens and ace. He got away with the stunt every time. His audacity knew no limits. If he didn't like the first two draws when he dealt, he kept taking cards until he found ones to his liking.

One of my riskier enterprises was stealing copper piping for one of the craftsmen in our shop. He made good use of it in town, where piping was very scarce, and he paid me off in bread and margarine. The copper was stored in a shed across from the administration building, in direct sight of the windows, and any movement towards the shed was easily noticed. Only daylight organizing was possible, because at night the area was locked up tight. Since our depot was nearby, I had good reason to be in the neighbourhood, but once the shortages came to light, my high visibility made me suspect, and I was called in for questioning. Playing dumb, I somehow got out of it unscathed and shortly thereafter gave up that deal. It was too dangerous. Also, my fence had enough pipe for now.

For a time Mother had an awful job tending to a dozen automatic lathes for making bullet tips. For about four weeks I was sent to the same department to do the same work, so I learned firsthand what a lousy job it was. I then got reassigned to another, better, job after I recovered from an injury to my right thumb. My thumb had got caught in the gear of a machine while I was staring at a pretty blonde doing similarly onerous work over in the next row.

HASAG was self-sufficient in many areas. It had confiscated an orchard just outside the factory, and gathered fruit for making jams and jellies. The old farmhouse at the orchard needed some electrical work, and I volunteered. While there, I stuffed my pockets and shirt with gooseberries and plums, which I intended to share with Mother and Anna. Taking this bit of fruit could have cost me my life. One of the German transport supervisors who happened to be in the area saw me. He took off after me and yelled for me to halt. Fortunately, he didn't have a pistol or rifle, so I just kept on running. Still, my heart was in my throat as I wondered if he would come to the barracks looking for me. But my luck held.

On one occasion, a quirk of fate brought me an unexpected luxury. I was walking along, on an errand, minding my own business, when I came almost face-to-face with one of the most feared of the German officers. A red-haired martinet of slight stature, he liked to hit people as he yelled at them. His habit was to strike a person over the head when least expected. Avoiding him as best I could, I kept walking. From behind me, I heard him yell '*Jude!*' in a loud voice. It was no use: I had to go back. Motioning for me to follow him, he opened the door to what I guessed were his quarters, took a piece of cake that was sitting on the table, gave it to me, and ordered me to get lost. I doubt that I thanked him. That was the only time in three years that I tasted cake. Pure white, it had layers of red preserves and a sugary topping.

My constant foraging for food often brought me to the brink of disaster, but the thought never entered my mind to slow down. One time, my goose was almost cooked. Spying a lorry loaded with potatoes, parked and apparently unattended, I scrambled aboard and filled a small wooden crate. Crouching low, I managed to get about twenty feet past the truck when I was collared by a uniformed Wehrmacht type – he was regular army rather than a guard. He had appeared out of nowhere, and he made me return the potatoes. It seemed clear that he would take me to the guardhouse, and that twenty-five lashes would be my minimum penalty. I refused to speculate as to other forms of punishment. Inexplicably, however, the soldier turned, strode away, and left me standing there. I was sorry to lose the potatoes.

Most people arrived at the camp with only the clothes on their backs. Occasionally a truck-load of confiscated clothes from one of the ghettos would show up and be distributed. Towards the end of 1943 the ghettos were no more, and our supply of old clothes came to an abrupt end. What compounded our problem was the fact that, every so often, the garments were taken for delousing. The method was simple and at least partially effective. The delousing unit was a sort of steam boiler turned on its side. The stuff was placed inside and steamed for about half an hour. After taking our monthly shower we sat huddled, naked, waiting for our entire wardrobe to come out. We gingerly sorted out and quickly put on the hot, foul-smelling garments. The lice, at some point, developed an immunity to the steam, and the hardy ones survived the inferno. The stitching didn't do as well. The seams came apart in the most conspicuous places.

At the very end of 1943 one last truck-load was dumped off.

The best goods were picked over right away by the people in charge. My turn came when there were only bedcovers and blankets left. A red velvet cover decorated with stars struck me as spiffy – and it looked to be a fabric that would last, as well. The camp tailor, a friend, offered to turn it into a pair of pantaloons. I placed the order, and was grateful to receive the trousers the very same day. Even in the difficult conditions of the HASAG, the sight of me marching smartly in my star-spangled, red plush trousers made for some amusement. The inmates may have seen my get-up as a suitable uniform for a gong striker.

Next to food and clothing, books were a necessity. Because Father had once been apprenticed to a bookbinder, he applied for an opening posted in the trade. The officer in charge asked his name. When he replied 'Drukier' he got slapped around, because *Drucker* means 'printer' in German, and the officer assumed that Father had misread the notice. Eventually they sorted things out, and Father got the job – unpaid, of course. All kinds of technical books, mostly in German, came in, but occasionally some of the Polish factory workers brought other types of books in for binding as well. These Father would bind when the manager was out. Payment was in bread, potatoes, and sometimes jam or margarine. Half a loaf of bread for doing a book was a good profit margin.

When Father found a book that he thought I might like (there were hardly any that I wouldn't), he would have me pick it up, and I would smuggle it into the barracks. Although lights out was quite early, it was possible to squeeze in an hour of reading after work. The Polish electricians I worked with in the plant didn't seem to read – at best, an old newspaper would surface from time to time – so Father was really my only source. As a rule, we were visually inspected by the guards on returning to the barracks, and any person with a bulge was searched. Bringing food was an offence subject to lashes, and the bread or potatoes were confiscated. Although lugging a heavy volume under my coat was risky, I reckoned the guards might be more puzzled than punitive if they discovered it. One of the books I smuggled in was entitled *The History of the World* – it was a gold-mine of information!

All the pretty girls in the camp had boyfriends. The only boy-friends of consequence were either in the administration or among the teamsters, because they had food to share.

I did not have a girl, nor was I looking for one. But I did notice some goings-on. When visiting Mother and Anna in the evenings or on Sundays, which was officially forbidden, I would see one or two fellows on upper bunks, holding their girls. The serious liaisons took place in the locked delousing room, the key to which was in the hands of an older chap by the name of Kornblum, a relative of the Jewish *Lagerführer*. The key had a price tag.

Some of the teamsters actually managed to acquire some money by carrying on minor black market activities with the Poles. Finding the barracks unsafe for hiding cash, they sometimes entrusted the money to their girlfriends. The women, as a rule, weren't searched as thoroughly as the men when returning from work. One woman, Felka, a short, blonde, freckled, snub-nosed girl who had a regular boyfriend, Mordechai, was also having an affair with her nightshift foreman, a thin Pole with a crew-cut. Word was out that Felka and the Pole would disappear into the spare-parts room for lengthy periods. Felka kept Mordechai's savings in a pouch that hung on a string around her neck and rested neatly between her breasts. One morning Felka returned from the nightshift and reported that she had lost the pouch. Mordechai reacted badly to the news. (These tensions notwithstanding, the two were married after the war and raised a large family together.)

Most of the women, married or single, waited patiently to be reunited with their men. It is unclear why, but a far greater proportion of the women than the men who made it past 1943 survived to see liberation. Whether it was because the men were worked harder or because they needed more food to survive the rigours of the camps, far more of them perished, some within weeks or days of the war's end.

The daily struggle to fill one's stomach left little time for other matters. News of the war and its shifting fortunes led to speculation about its likely duration. German propaganda made the Germans out to be as powerful as ever. But slowly the setbacks in the east and in North Africa became known. The Nazis termed the retreats 'regroupings.' We tried to read between the lines whenever a newspaper made one of its rare appearances in the factories.

News of the Warsaw Ghetto Uprising came to us through a new group of Jews, from the town of Nowy Korczyn, who were brought to the camp in the spring of 1943. Isolated, the group had been kept in the small town long after the entire Jewish population of the region was deported. They stayed on for months, tailoring, mending, and cleaning army uniforms shipped in from hospitals. The resistance in Warsaw did not come as a surprise, in view of the fact that the remaining residents of the depleted ghetto were said to be Judenrat administrators, Jewish policemen, and their families. We speculated that they might have felt betrayed by the Germans, who would have assured them that their safety was secure provided they rounded up 95 per cent of the ghetto population. On hearing the news that the resistance had been crushed, we said nothing.

We were certain that there were some Jews working for the German war machine in scattered areas across Poland. There were also rumours of people hiding out in the forests. A number were hidden by well-meaning, or well-paid, Poles. Others used forged papers to pass themselves off as Aryans. This was easier for women than men, who were, without exception, circumcised. We believed that, at HASAG, we were temporarily secure. The Polish world outside was hostile or at best indifferent to our fate. Most, if not all, of the ghettos were gone. What little we knew was only about western Poland. There were unconfirmed stories from Polish train conductors that Jews taken points east were not seen again. But there was nothing we could do.

Our worst premonitions were confirmed one day in early 1943, when two unfamiliar Jewish men appeared in our barracks. According to them, they were part of an Einsatzgruppe transport that had taken people east some three weeks before. Because of overcrowding and a lack of water and food, some died en route. On arrival at a place called Treblinka they were met by German and Ukrainian guards with vicious German shepherd dogs. More died in indiscriminate shootings. Everyone was ordered to undress and go into a large building, presumably to shower. The pair had managed to hide under piles of clothing, and later the same evening had stolen aboard the returning train. From their vantage point in the wagon they could see a building with a chimney belching smoke, and they noticed a peculiar smell about the place. Travelling west overnight, they got off the train somewhere near Kielce and wandered in the countryside. At some point they were reported, and either the Polish or German police – they were too dazed to be sure which – came for them and brought them to our camp. They were certain that everyone in their transport had been put to death. When we came back from work the next day, the two men were gone.

In late 1943 another two fugitives were picked up and brought to our camp. The two were young, terribly emaciated men, with yellow complexions, bordering on orange. They had made their escape from the dreaded Werk C HASAG in Skarżysko-Kamienna, also located in the Kielce province. At Werk C, inmates were dying at the rate of dozens daily. Survival was numbered in weeks because of the fatal lung disease that developed in men who did the work of assembling the floating sea mines that were produced at this HASAG plant. The material for the explosives was a highly toxic substance that turned men's skin yellow and caused their lungs to deteriorate.

Our labours helped the German war machine. Although we were hounded, beaten, and starved, and our families and friends deported and presumably killed, although we were stripped of all dignity, we performed the assigned duties diligently. Nothing was sabotaged. It just didn't occur to us, probably because we felt that it wouldn't make any difference. The Germans were all-powerful.

Holy Days came and went, but I did not see anyone praying. The first Yom Kippur in HASAG I fasted. My legs buckled under me, and I remember having to stop to rest twice when ordered to carry a small electric motor up a flight of stairs.

The one organized sport we sporadically engaged in was soccer. On a few occasions, on warm Sunday evenings during periods of relative calm, the boys picked teams and played. It was the teamsters who won, because they ate more.

During a couple of my lucky reading jags I was disturbed by the chief of the Jewish police checking the cleanliness of our feet. The men and women who worked on the production lines were the most likely to be punished for having dirty feet. They had a tough time keeping them clean, as their shoes were continually being splashed with dirty oil from the lathes and the boring machines. In fact, exposure to the endlessly recycled oil that cooled the drills gave people boils, pimples, and blackheads. We could have washed with soap and warm water, but we didn't have any. A change of shoes would have helped, but that was not available either. Those whose feet did not come up to snuff were chased out into the night to wash them in the common washroom. It happened to me more than once. To avoid the night wash and the kicks that accompanied it, I resorted to washing my feet after work. I scrubbed them with industrial solvent. My skin broke open, but my feet were clean. I also managed to acquire some strips of cloth that I wrapped around my feet to keep them neater longer. Of course, it was no use telling Mr Pisarz, the chief, that it was not possible to keep feet clean when there were no socks to put on and shoes had holes in them. Most likely Pisarz was just carrying out orders. He was shot in July 1944 while attempting to escape from the camp just before we were evacuated west. Pisarz was a tall, good-looking man with combed-back, black hair, like Tyrone Power as a pirate; he wore riding boots.

At the top of the camp hierarchy was the *Lagerführer*, a young man who became a chicken farmer in New Jersey after the war. He answered directly to the commandant, SS Obersturmbann-führer Schlicht. There was also a young lady who might, or might not, have been his wife. They occupied a small room all to themselves. Then came the chief of police and three other policemen, none of whom survived; the kitchen manager; the shower and delousing superintendent; the camp doctor and his wife, both German Jews; two medical assistants, one of whom married the old doctor's widow after the war; and a couple of minor functionaries. A lean operation. My status was at the lowest rung of the social register, but I kept hearing that I was at least lucky to have my mother, father, and sister with me.

Any complacency we might have had vanished in the summer of 1944. The Russians had broken through the German lines and captured all of eastern Poland. HASAG management decided to evacuate its equipment west. We would not be needed until the production lines and our barracks were set up at the new location.

One day a plane dropped leaflets over the camp. Fluttering down, they predicted defeat for our overlords. I tried to pick one up but was spotted by a German truck driver who went after me with a stick. Dropping the paper, I ran as fast and as far as my legs would take me. The driver was about six-foot-six and was gaining on me rapidly. As I turned my head to measure the distance separating us, I tripped over a rock, fell, and split my forehead open.

What bothered me was the fact that the driver was someone I had done a favour for only a short time earlier. His vehicle, a fuel-saving *holzgas* type, had a charcoal-filled hopper over the cab and sputtered a lot. The frequent stalling of the engine put a strain on the battery. As a precaution in the event that the battery died, a spare was lashed to the running board. One of my duties in the electrical shop was to hook up batteries brought in from the motor pool, on a first-come first-served basis, for overnight charging. I also had to add the correct amount of acid and rainwater to them. The maximum I could hook up at a time was two twelve-volt batteries. One time, not many weeks before, the truck driver in question had come to me with two dead batteries, his smoke-belching chariot blocking the guardhouse gate. I helped him out. So much for being nice!

Through luck and ingenuity I had managed again and again to avoid the 'selection' process. Periodically, the young, old, or infirm were deported. Learning of one such selection in advance and finding out that Mother was on the list, I suggested she hide out in the high-voltage transformer room, to which I had keys and access. But she was too worried about the consequences to me if our plan were to be discovered, so she refused.

In July 1944 the entire camp population was to be evacuated. Following the Jewish Lagerführer's list, Schlicht sent away the older inmates, or at least those who appeared to be older, first. Anyone who had greying hair was on the list. Mother was taken away, apparently to a nearby camp that was also being evacuated. But to where?

Just before the rest of us were to be transported out, an experienced Jewish electrician named Opatowsky was ordered to climb a pole to disconnect a wire of some sort. That hot afternoon we watched him climb, bare from the waist up. At the top, his chest accidentally made contact with the high-tension wires. His body moved slightly, then slumped, but his heels, equipped with climbing spurs, held fast. He was left there to await the Red Army. The last thing we saw as we left the HASAG was Opatowsky, a tall, heavy-set man, dangling by his feet from the top of the pole.

14
The Other Way

Cousin Meyer, the youngest grandson of my great-grandfather
Meyer, spent most of the war years in hiding. Towards the end, in
1944, he hid in a trench dug behind a manure pile. The heat gen-
erated by the compost heap kept his hide-out warm in winter,
and the stench made the curious stay away in summer. Cousin
Meyer's branch of my mother's family did not migrate to Łódź.
The German occupation in 1939 found them in Osiek, an obscure
shtetl tucked away down a dirt road east of Staszów. At that time,
Meyer's family, having accumulated considerable real estate, was
the wealthiest in the area, and likely the most frugal.

At twenty-four, Meyer became the head of the newly formed
Judenrat. With the position came certain privileges as well as an
obligation to carry out the local commandant's orders. This made
for few friends among his compatriots.

In late 1942, when he realized what the Germans were up to,
Meyer was quick to act. He got busy cajoling and bribing peasants to provide hiding places for him and his family. It was he
who made arrangements for Uncle Fishl and his boys. Aunt
Bluma was to join them as soon as they were settled in. This did
not come to pass, however. Fishl's host, discovering that Fishl and
sons were weighed down with gold bars, became greedy and
hacked them to death.

Attempting to avoid a similar fate, Meyer, his sister and
brother-in-law, and a young female neighbour were all hiding in a
nearby village. They had shrewdly placed their valuables with

the Polish reeve, a local blacksmith by the name of Blonka, from whom they withdrew money periodically for their keep. One night, as the two women made their way to his house, Blonka, apparently unhappy with the arrangement, slit their throats. Meyer and his brother-in-law moved on. No longer able to pay their way, they had to rely on the goodwill of peasants to hide and feed them.

In July 1944, using only paved roads in its hot pursuit of the fleeing Germans, the Red Army bypassed Osiek. Meyer, initially suspecting a trick when informed of this by his current host, was unwilling to give up his snug hide-out. But eventually, covered in grime, he emerged into daylight, only to be told by his jeering neighbours that the Russian advance might falter. And so it did. On orders from Stalin, the Russians advanced no farther. Without a backward glance, and fearing the worst, Meyer took off for the Ukraine, with his brother-in-law in tow. Once there, he established himself on a collective farm, where he became the middleman for a knavish management intent on diverting grain to the Kiev black market. This enterprise gave Meyer the small nest egg he would need to get started in business in North America.

I met Meyer for the first time when he arrived in Toronto in 1949. Shortly thereafter he sent for a bride, a young woman he had met in a Displaced Persons' camp in Germany. Meyer didn't waste time looking for work in factories, as most former DPs did, but took to selling household goods door-to-door. The budget plan he designed for his customers included a high rate of interest. This led Meyer to consider devoting his talents solely to becoming a lender of last resort. For some thirty years he was possibly the largest issuer of second and third mortgages in the city.

Meyer, tall, thin, and balding, was good humoured but intense. Ruthless when it came to protecting his investments, he might have been perceived as the archetypal Jewish usurer. If he was, he seemed oblivious to it. He was wealthy, but carried on in his stingy ways. Perhaps Meyer would have liked to correct this character flaw but could not find the will to overcome it.

The collapse of the real estate market in the early 1990s turned many of Meyer's risky investments into worthless paper. Accustomed to acting decisively, he might have had memories of Osiek. This time the enemy was the bank warning him that the collateral underlying his sizeable loan was being reviewed. As in Osiek, Meyer believed that his life was at stake. When I last ran into him, at a family function, he said that he had 'lost a fortune.' I could empathize – my own circumstances were not dissimilar.

Meyer became very ill; his condition was diagnosed as terminal. The exact nature of his illness eluded the doctors, and wonder drugs had no effect. Decisive as ever, Meyer asked to be taken off life-support systems. As he lay in his hospital bed he had ample time to reflect. Perhaps he was aware that his undefined illness might be traced to the shock he experienced at losing a huge sum of money.

It would be logical to assume that, in view of their experience, survivors would be attuned to the ephemeral value of money. In mid-1942, it certainly was clear to those who sought sanctuary that no amount of money would guarantee them safety. In fact, a Jew, if suspected of having money, was likely to be set upon. Others remembered that on arrival in a camp, in the short time people had to apprise themselves of the inevitable, they took to mutilating banknotes, scattering gold coins into the wind, and trampling valuable stamp collections and works of art underfoot. So, it is ironic that most survivors returned to their pre-war practices, habits, and traditions.

15
The End of the Line

We had been sent somewhere to the west of Kielce to build fortifications for the second or third fallback position against the
advancing Russians. In August 1944 we heard that the Polish
underground, on orders from the Polish government in London,
had staged an uprising in Warsaw. The Russians, not wanting to
be pre-empted, had decided not to cross the river Wisła to help
the insurrection. This had bought the Germans time to prepare a
second line of defence.

On our arrival all the men, including me and Father, were
placed in a large, two-storey barn. The women, including my sister, Anna, were put in a smaller barn. Anna, seventeen, slim, with
long, dark hair, had been ill as a result of the many twelve-hour
days she had spent inhaling fumes in the degreasing and lacquer-
ing department at the HASAG factory. She probably felt the
absence of Mother even more keenly than I did: They had been a
comfort to each other in Kielce; indeed, they had slept side by
side on an upper bunk for almost two years.

On the second day, the Todt Organization's supervisor announced that the women would be of no use to them. When the
men came back from work that evening, all the women, including
Anna, were gone, presumably to Germany.

There were several hundred men in our barn. We slept on the
floors, and an outhouse and a water-pump were our sanitary
facilities.

I liked digging infantry trenches, but I quickly found that I didn't like digging anti-tank trenches. If I wasn't hacking through a section of rock, digging my quota of infantry trenches was child's play. After breaking the earth with my pickaxe, I dug my trench to the required depth with a shovel that had a long, curved handle. Almost finished, I would take it slower until quitting time. Under normal conditions, I finished ahead of most of my colleagues.

Anti-tank trenches were a different pot of potatoes: they were about ten feet deep, eleven and a half feet wide at ground level, and cut in a 'V' to virtually nothing at the bottom. They were dug by teams of two or three. As the pit got deeper, it became impossible to fling a shovelful of earth over and out. The dirt would be tossed to a narrow ledge part-way up, from which a teammate would move it up to ground level. When the full depth of the anti-tank pit was achieved, the ledge was chopped off, and the completed trench was a smooth 'V.' The infantry trenches were laid out in a classic zigzag line and landscaped to make them inconspicuous. The anti-tank line ran straight, about a hundred feet in front of the trenches. Excess earth was removed to camouflage the fortifications. It was all straightforward, except when we ran into rock and gravel. Then, we had to break up every inch of ground with a pickaxe and weren't able to meet the quota. The Todt Organization's construction men appreciated the complications and would let us finish the next day. Because of the depth of anti-tank pits, the going was very slow. When we came up against walls of rock we just dug a row of pits to the required depth, lowered charges of dynamite, and filled the cavities with rock and earth. Wires were strung from the charges to a central point away from the line, and someone hollered 'Achtung!' and pressed the handle of a detonator. The sound of the explosion was followed by a geyser of earth and stone. I enjoyed watching it go up: it was the best part of the day. We trenched on hills and valleys, cut through roads and in front of bridges. Our section of fortifications was to be ready in time for the next Russian offensive, expected that fall. In the evening, shovels over our shoulders, we hiked back in units of fifty, singing in harmony.

Our diet consisted primarily of potatoes. The potato crop was ripe, and our bivouac was smack in the middle of the biggest potato-growing area in all of Poland. During the march to the front, as we called it, shovels and pickaxes held on shoulders, we gathered fuel for the potato bash at lunch. No fence, tree, support stick, or road sign was safe from our rampaging band. At the midday whistle everyone was out in the field scooping up spuds. The potato, I discovered, is an adaptable vegetable. It will bake nicely in hot ashes if you have the time to wait; cut up into small pieces, it will boil in a pot of water quickly; it can be cooked peeled or unpeeled; it tastes good with or without salt, nice with a dab of margarine, heavenly cut up and fried.

We did not tire of potatoes. We worked the potato deal in teams of two or four. While some of us went to get them, the others broke up the wood, built a fire, and got water. The fast-food industry could have learned a lot from our improvisations. In the evening after roll-call, we were issued rations of soup, bread, jam, and sometimes margarine. But our main diet, twice a day, was potatoes. The area around the dug trenches resembled ploughed fields where potatoes had grown.

The side effect of a steady potato diet is an urge to urinate at all hours. This was particularly annoying at night. The outhouse was some distance away, and, after considering the risk of being mistaken for a camp jumper and shot at by a guard, everyone urinated in something handier, like a can or a bucket. Packed tight as sardines in the barn, we would grope, stumble, and climb over bodies in the dark to get to the buckets. Since some kept buckets by their side, a lot of buckets were being overturned in the process. There was much cursing and swearing, especially by the chaps on the main floor, who did not appreciate having buckets of piss come down on their heads from the loft above. Such perils aside, however, I do not recall anyone getting sick. Old and young, up early, working outdoors in the summer, nourished on an 'all-you-can-eat' potato diet, we thrived. Probably no physician has ever recommended a 100 per cent potato experience. That's a pity: a spud has all the nutrients one needs to survive. Prepared any which way, potatoes will keep you awake, alert, and lean.

Out in the open, we sometimes considered escape. It would

have been relatively easy, but we had to consider the attitude of the local Polish farmers. Aside from the possibility that they were anti-Semitic, we assumed they were angry at us for denuding their fields and wrecking their fences. A further deterrent was an announcement by the commandant that if anyone was found missing from a work party, every tenth man in the unit would be shot. As I recall, only one or two were shot in retaliation for a successful escape. Father and I discussed the possibility of running away but decided against it. It was probably as good a time as any for a mass escape, but we were paralyzed with fear from the neck up. Nonetheless, getting out of the barracks and factories into the countryside did us all a lot of good. I learned to live off the land, to build a good fire quickly, not to waste matches or fuel, to keep an eye on the pot and on the guard – you never knew what would displease him – and to try to keep Father in good spirits.

One day Father spoke to a guard, a man in his forties who looked out of place and uncomfortable in uniform. He was from Vienna, he said. We asked him what he thought of the future, and he commented that silence was golden. Our digging vacation was too good to last.

My fervid imagination ran rampant. I thought of war, of winning. At my solitary work in a trench, shovelling dirt, I fantasized. It was no wonder that the trenches provided the raw material for my dreams and nightmares. One starlit August night I awakened from a dream so vivid that I would remember it ever after.

In a trench, I had concealed a heavy machine-gun with a box of ammunition, which I had stolen off a lorry after drugging its driver (I'd poured sleeping powder into his bottle of vodka). I now waited. I sat in a big tree, eating and sleeping there, waiting to see the foot soldiers come down the road. Finally, I saw them, marching, led by an officer on a black horse. They intended to occupy the newly dug trenches. The Red Army was in the forest over the hill. They would soon come down to the road unaware of the German infantry hidden in the trenches. They would be cut down.

I slid down the tree trunk and, crawling on my stomach, made for the trench and my weapon. Once there I assembled the machine-gun, made all the necessary checks, and fed a belt in. Then I sat back and waited.

I was casually munching on an apple when the first line of green uniforms came into my gunsight. I waited for another sixty seconds before opening fire. They were gone, like a puff. I didn't even use a full belt of ammunition. I moved the gun seventy feet to the right and waited. Sure enough, they opened fire and aimed at where my gun had been. As soon as they came closer, certain that they'd got me, I fired a broadside that wiped them out. A few men who had hung back were now rushing to get help. The Red Army was nowhere in sight. I could hold back infantry, but if the Germans brought tanks against me I was a goner. Strategically speaking, if I let the Germans occupy the trenches and relocated to the top of the hill, they would never suspect where I'd gone. But although I could carry the gun, heavy as it was, bringing the ammunition at the same time was not possible. I had to get help, and soon.

Out of the corner of my eye, I saw one of the soldiers whom I'd taken for dead get up and run in a lateral direction. I yelled 'Halt!' and he stopped. He was a big man. I motioned him over to my trench, made him lie down on the ground, and blindfolded him. I proceeded to place the machine-gun and belts of ammunition on his back and sternly ordered him to move forward. My transport problem was solved. Up the hill he staggered. I prodded him along with the butt of his own Luger pistol. When we got to where I figured they would not expect me to be, I told my prisoner to drop the load, and at the same time gave him a hard knock on the skull. I then tied him up neatly, with his legs and hands together behind his back, so that he couldn't wiggle free.

The place I selected for my final stand was a cemetery full of monuments made of stone, marble, and granite. These made a natural shield and, by staying low, I could leapfrog from one to the other and confuse the attackers. My plan was good, but it would be of immeasurable benefit if I had a helper to hold the ammunition belt horizontally so that it would feed easily without jamming the gun.

Suddenly, from behind, I heard a noise as if someone were

choking or sobbing. I pointed my Luger in the direction of the sounds and ordered the person, in Polish and German, to come out with hands up. I was shocked to see Szifra emerge. She wore a Polish army uniform and big army boots, and she had my old school hat on her head. I had no time to listen to her story of how she had escaped from a transport and changed into a uniform, because, just as I expected, tanks were coming at me fast.

Szifra was a quick learner, and I only had to show her a couple of times how to stretch and feed the belt. I regret to say that we weren't able to stop the tanks, but we did hold them back long enough for the Red Army to send a patrol to see what we were up to. But even the patrol was unable to fight the tanks. Together we made a tactical retreat.

I turned the prisoner over to the Russians, who had some trouble untying my clever knots. Szifra and I ran to a house set in an orchard, which we found intact but abandoned by its owner. In the kitchen there was bread, butter, salami, apples, pears, gooseberries, wine, and milk. But best of all, the house contained a room full of books. The windowless library's walls were lined with bookshelves. The door to the library was ingeniously hidden inside a clothes closet. Purely by accident I had turned the carved eagle on top of the wardrobe, thereby unlocking the door to the luxurious library.

Szifra had changed from the ugly uniform into a lacy black number that accented her white complexion. She had found some eggs and was starting to fry an omelette when I came up behind her and put my arms around her. I wanted to thank her for helping me with the gun – but I woke up, and it was all over.

Finished with digging trenches we were hauled to Częstochowa, about seventy miles west of Kielce. HASAG had moved their munitions-manufacturing equipment from Kielce into an old textile factory here, and had set up our old barracks, now reassembled. There were fewer of us. The HASAG management was setting up three or four operations in Częstochowa, and it looked as if they intended to stay. The Warsaw uprising was ending, and the Russians were still on the east side of the river, not making a move. The factory was working two shifts, making shells and other munitions. It was getting colder, and we had little in the way of winter garments. The fortification lines that we helped build were in place. The prospect of the war ending soon grew dimmer.

Most of the women had been sent elsewhere. My mother and sister were somewhere in Germany, or possibly dead. Father and I did not talk about their whereabouts. Our situation was no less precarious. Death was an everyday affair; the tragic was the norm. Rarely was there an outburst of grief. Those gone were simply dead. Filling my stomach was foremost on my mind. We were human beings reduced to fundamentals. On the whole everyone behaved decently, but to survive one had to be selfish. The luxury of giving up one's seat in the lifeboat was not available.

Father and I had an upper bunk from where we could sometimes observe people preparing and cooking potatoes or beets. The time had come to try to 'organize.' From my vantage point I once saw one of the men cook potatoes by inserting a contraption of two electrified metal rods into a pot of water. Intrigued, I examined the invention. It was relatively primitive: the water in the pot acted as the conductor, creating a short, which made the water boil. I announced that I would take orders for similar gadgets.

In the new HASAG we were given our old jobs (except for Father, whose bookbinding shop, not being considered essential to the war effort, hadn't been moved). Again in charge of tools and supplies for the electrical maintenance department, I had access to the raw material I needed. Within days I turned out a number of the pre-sold water-heating units. Business was brisk; payment was in kind. But it was too good to last. Extensive distribution led to blackouts because of the numerous illegal hook-ups. A daylight search resulted in confiscation of the gadgets.

Undaunted, I decided to make hotplates, which did not draw nearly as much electricity and which were therefore less likely to be discovered and taken away. A hotplate would not restrict one to boiling food; frying was also possible. This, I reasoned, would be a saleable product anywhere. First, I had to make a prototype. I established that some of the components could be obtained only from the outside. The wire needed to make a spiral element had to be found in the city. Insulated wire, metal cases, connectors – these I could lay my hands on. The necessary ceramic, however, was simply not available. It occurred to me that the ceramics used in manufacturing industrial ovens could be arranged in such a way as to create a hotplate. During one of my visits to the factory supply depot, I spotted a quantity of suitable ceramic pieces. They were corncob-shaped, about five inches long, and fluted. Placed three in a row and four across and fastened down, they would hold the inserted spiral element strung like Christmas lights between the ribs. The depot was under lock and key. One had to present a requisition slip to get an item.

Herr Schultz, a short, pudgy, bald-headed German past middle age, guarded his treasure house jealously. Time was of the essence. A Pole who had promised to get the wire for the element for me from the city also ordered a completed hotplate from me. The price agreed on was four pounds of white flour. Anxious to get going, I managed to obtain a requisition order for drill bits. This I presented to Schultz and followed him to the back of the factory floor and to the locked doors of the depot.

The storeroom, full of rows of shelving, contained nearly everything a modern factory needed. Schultz walked ahead, and I followed. Since I knew the inventory better than he did, he let me show him where the supplies were. As I passed and re-passed the shelf on which the ceramic pieces rested, I managed to slip a few into my pocket, in which the lining was cut. What did I need pockets for anyway? My trousers, having been tied at the ankles, held the ceramics neatly. One couldn't be too careful. Schultz was known to explode if he caught someone stealing.

My prototype turned out better than anticipated. It was a gem. My client was delighted and kept his word. I now had more than four pounds of the white stuff. I fantasized that I could turn out one hotplate a week, provided I could line up the materials. I could rely on a good living.

I discussed with Father the best way of turning our windfall into something edible. Dumplings were the obvious answer, small chunks of flour and water dropped into boiling, salted water. I remembered the taste from my miller's days in Staszów. There was enough flour for six to eight meals for two, but Father counselled against using it right away. Although he was as hungry as I was, he envisioned a barter deal, pyramiding the capital into bigger things. I suggested that perhaps we make one meal right away and decide on the balance later. He again advised against touching the principal. An irresistible trade might come. So, rolled up in my blanket, on my bunk, unknown to anyone but me and Father, was our nest egg.

Rumours had started to fly that the Polish uprising in Warsaw had been brutally quashed. Now that the Poles were defeated, the Russians were getting ready to mount their long-delayed offensive. We were sceptical. Identical rumours had been heard in September, November, and December. But something *was* up that January. A strange Wehrmacht unit took over guard duty of our factory. A special unit made up of Ukrainians wearing never-before-seen *Totenkopf*, skull insignias, on their uniforms was put in charge of the Jews, who were now being referred to as *Häftlinge* (prisoners). New rules were announced. Twice a day we were out on roll-call. We had to stand in the cold for an hour or more morning and night for head counts. More troops arrived. They were Tartars or Kalmuks in Wehrmacht uniforms who walked with heads down, looking pretty glum.

One morning they called out a list of four hundred names. Mine was among them, but not Father's. The men on the list were to go immediately to the railway siding. Within the hour we were in the cars and sealed up. The cars were, as usual, marked 'Suitable for eight horses.' There were only about fifty of us in each, so it wasn't too crowded. The trip was uneventful; we crouched and dozed. Next morning we passed Weimar and arrived in Buchenwald.

In Buchenwald we were ordered to disembark and to proceed to the shower and disinfection building. Under armed guard we were led to a snow-covered compound about 100 by 150 feet, enclosed by barbed wire. There, at one end, stood the reception building. On our way we passed a bombed-out series of brick structures. We heard later that this had formerly been a factory assembling V.1 flying bombs, like the ones that were being dropped on London. The Nazis had gambled that if the plant was situated in the middle of the camp it would not be marked for destruction from the air. They lost: pinpoint daylight bombing raids destroyed it. We would have preferred if the Americans had bombed all the lagers and the railway bridges leading to them. No matter if some of us were killed, and maybe some of the Germans, too, but it would have stopped the transports.

Buchenwald itself was unharmed. Through barbed wire, we talked to inmates wearing blue-and-grey striped clothes. They told us that all our food and belongings would be confiscated and other garments issued. If we had any food to give they would be grateful. I had half a loaf of bread and was hungry but couldn't swallow, so I handed it over. I had a bitter taste in my mouth. Around me people were tearing up banknotes and handing food over the wire. A batch of us at a time were let into the building. My turn came. We were told to disrobe and not to keep any personal things. The thought crossed my mind that it was a gas chamber that we were being led into, but it was a real shower. We undressed. All hair, including underarm and pubic, was clipped off, and a cold shower followed. We were moved into a warehouse where we were handed clothes by a group of prisoners, also in stripes.

The clothes were old, not much different from what we had just discarded. Some of the coats had cuts in them, as if they had been searched for hidden valuables. A few of us got striped jackets and pants. We were shoved into an icy loft where a number of prisoners with blankets around their shoulders against the cold took down our name, age, and occupation. My personal history was filled out by a prisoner whose cold hands held a stub of a pencil. I added two years to my age to make it eighteen. I stated that my father was a tailor rather than a businessman and that by trade I was an electrician.

The häftlinge had a red triangle sewn on their jackets over the left breast underneath their number to signify a political prisoner or Communist. Pink triangles signified homosexuals. Black meant criminal. We didn't know where we fitted in. As it turned out we didn't get a coloured triangle, only a number to go on the chest. Names were not important anymore. The Communists were the power among the inmates at Buchenwald. They accused us of having deliberately 'run off' so as not to meet the Russians. No amount of explaining that we hadn't heard of a winter offensive could placate the old-timers. We were dirt. Apparently Częstochowa had fallen.

The registration completed, we were marched through the camp to a section in the rear, past two gates, and into a compound containing three large barracks. I was led into one and assigned a spot on a bunk. The emaciated inmates, wearing a variety of garments, huddled in the cold around us and wanted to know where we had come from. They told us that the Russians had, in a matter of days, overrun all of Poland and had also taken Breslau in German Silesia. I thought Father was safe in liberated territory.

I felt somewhat relieved. Over the past two years, told by well-meaning people how fortunate I was to have parents and a sister, I took it as a slur on my ability to manage on my own. I would have preferred that Father, Mother, and Anna were away somewhere safe, so that I wouldn't have to worry about them, but also wouldn't be considered in need of them. Obviously there was little I could do for them. Now, I wanted to prove that I was okay on my own. Contrary to expectations and odds, I imagined that no harm would come to me. It was convoluted thinking at an odious time.

For reasons that may once have been more obvious, when the German armies were advancing every day, an announcer would read out through the public address system the day's military successes on the western, African, and eastern fronts. This practice, initially meant to torment the inmates, continued in the time of defeats, owing, I suspect, to the lager commandant's rigidity.

I was given a blanket and a bowl of turnip soup. I traded my portion of soup for a slice of bread, as the very smell of the soup turned my stomach. But I got to love it in a very short time. The next day we heard rumours that another transport had come from Częstochowa. I hoped it wasn't from our camp (there were two or three other HASAG factories in the city). The following morning I spoke to some of the recently arrived men. It was true: Father had arrived in Buchenwald. The men had been evacuated just hours before the Russians took the city. The Germans had abandoned everything but had taken the Jews. The new arrivals told me that they had been abused by the fellows in the registration centre, and called traitors for not hiding out and waiting for the Russians. Everyone was bitter about it. Shamefacedly, they repeated that they had had no idea that the Reds were that close. Their protestations fell on deaf ears. Our Commies were outraged.

Most of the men from the latest transport had been put in an adjoining sector that also contained three or four barracks and was segregated from ours by a wire fence with a gate. One of Father's friends told me that Lemberg, one of my former co-workers, had been shot. Nothing much surprised me in those days, but this did. Lemberg, an electrician, was a fair, tall, solidly built chap of about thirty, who always managed to stay in good spirits. He was one of those people with a perpetual grin on his face. Somehow he managed to eat a little better than most. About three weeks before, he had disappeared, and the story I heard was that he had knocked over Herr Schultz in his depot. He had apparently made a duplicate key to the storeroom and was helping himself to some supplies when Schultz walked in on him. A struggle ensued, and Lemberg made his getaway by hitting Schultz on the head. I imagined that Lemberg was after bigger game in the depot, perhaps motors or coils of wire. The Poles in the factory were willing to pay well for such material, and this would have accounted for Lemberg's cheerfulness and well-being. Schultz was keen on getting even.

Lemberg vanished, then reappeared, dirty and emaciated, trying to hop aboard the transport taking the second batch of men to Buchenwald. He was recognized and shot. Tired of hiding out in an old abandoned boiler in the plant, he was sure that in the commotion created by hundreds of men clambering on board he could sneak on without attracting attention. Had he sat in his boiler for another night, he would have been a free man.

That same day I located Father. He had been placed in the barrack sector next to ours. For now I could only speak to him through the wire fence. Father had been issued a long Hungarian army coat with a matching pointed hat. It looked a little strange on him, but it was warm. We talked briefly. I asked him whether he had had an opportunity to cook any of the white flour after I left. He hadn't.

Numbers were called out at one morning's roll-call, and these persons were ordered to report for transport to a labour camp. I had learned earlier that Buchenwald was a supply centre of slave labour to a chain of satellite lagers in the area. Orders came in for three hundred to five hundred men at a time, presumably to replace those who had died. The call-up was a lucky break for me and Father because as soon as there was space in my barracks, a group from HASAG was transferred over – Father among them.

The daily routine was simplicity itself: wake-up call at 6 A.M.; compulsory wash of face and hands in cold water at an outside shed; hurry outside wet to stand for roll-call, lasting about an hour; breakfast of unsweetened ersatz coffee; at 1 P.M., soup of carrot and beet tops and, infrequently, puréed turnips; roll-call again at 7 P.M.; and then bread rations.

The daily portion of bread was a quarter of a very small loaf of black bread. It was heavy and moist and might have contained potatoes: solid food. From day one there was a problem in dividing the loaf into four equal portions. Four very hungry people could not agree that the pieces were exactly the same size. It was a problem that one simply hoped to avoid by finding three others to split the loaf with who could be counted on not to make a fuss. To avoid a struggle that would delay the division I would, at first, agree to take the least desirable piece. But as time went on and I got hungrier, I wanted to get an even shake. Father hit on a creative idea that resolved the dilemma. Using string and bits of wood and wire, he fabricated a primitive scale. Instead of bowls there were pointed sticks, held high for everyone to see, with two pieces of bread dangling from them, perfectly level. Father had the knack of cutting the loaf into remarkably even portions, which the scale subsequently verified. The scale and Father were much in demand each evening.

The war was drawing to a close. It was only a matter of weeks before the Allies would crush the remaining German armies. We knew that in our bones. Frequently, Allied aircraft circled the camp in broad daylight, the lead plane marking the camp in a white oval of smoke. We would stand outdoors and watch the armada fly over and then turn and drop their bombs on Weimar. We could hear the distant thud of explosions and sometimes see a puff of anti-aircraft fire, but there was no Luftwaffe to take off after the intruders. The next morning the guards took groups of men to help dig through the rubble for bodies. No one minded going, because once in a while they would find scraps of food in a bombed-out home or shop. Such food was usually consumed on the spot. Those fortunate would, on their return, describe the delicacies to an attentive audience. I was never called, but Father was trucked to the city one day after a singularly heavy bombardment. His unit ran into bad luck though: they did not have much to show for twelve hours of clearing rubble. The three packages of powdered vanilla-pudding mix that Father secured weren't much good eaten dry.

Toilet facilities consisted of a shed divided into two sections by a mesh and barbed-wire partition that ran the full length of the structure. A series of long poles attached horizontally to two-foot-high stakes helped prevent an accidental trip or slide into a ditch full of excrement. A combination of untreated water and an unbalanced diet gave everyone the runs, and there was no paper of any kind. Until one's system got used to the peculiar strain of bacteria, one used up valuable reserves of energy gasping in pain, holding on to a pole.

The half of the WC that wasn't ours was used by men from the adjoining set of barracks, possibly long-serving häftlinge, who had survived because they had cigarettes to trade. The trade over the wire fence was lively: some of our people would exchange their bread ration for a couple of cigarettes. Those of us not hostage to the habit pitied the unfortunate wretches, whose life expectancy dropped from a couple of months to only days.

The dead were piled each morning in front of the barracks, naked by then, their clothes and shoes appropriated by neighbours, their serial number written by the Kapo on their chest bone in blue ink. After our masters accounted for the difference during the roll-call and correspondingly reduced food rations, the cadavers were taken away to be burned. Again and again, the bodies were those of the people who had been seen clutching poles for days on end. A medic would pop in from time to time and offer a white powdery substance that was to help cure the runs; it tasted like plaster of Paris.

Packed close on three-level, bare-board bunks, eight hundred to a barrack, we talked mostly about the kind of food we would eat after liberation. One of the men said that in France people cooked potatoes in oil, not water. It was conceded that oil-fried potatoes couldn't help but taste good, but some argued that good oil could be put to better use.

Shoes were another important item. If one didn't keep one's feet dry, any number of painful complications were possible. In Buchenwald, I had to surrender the best pair of shoes I'd ever owned. They were black ankle boots, precisely my size, converted from a pair of old shoes delivered to me by a Pole in return for a favour. They'd been stripped of their worn soles and mounted on new wooden bottoms that were reinforced with strips of heavy rubber.

The people in charge of footwear handed me an old pair of patent leather shoes. In January! Also, my feet were a bit wide, and the ballroom pair were narrow. I questioned the accuracy of the sizing. The old-timer in charge became disgruntled with me and handed me the worst shoes imaginable. For most of the winter I wore on my bare feet a pair of Dutch wooden clogs – one size fits all.

We were babes in the woods when it came to camp politics. The old-timers – the long-serving häftlinge – ran the place. The original brick lager buildings were reserved exclusively for the long-serving. That was where the action was. Red Cross parcels were rumoured to have got through, but only that far. We were on the outskirts. The red-triangle politicals had a stranglehold on the administration. The pink-triangle German homosexuals were often assigned as Kapos to various barracks where, in the back, they would usually build an enclosure. There they stored extra food and kept a boy for company. Such boys were called, in lager vernacular, *peepel* – clearly, a contemptuous label. The Kapo's boy in our barracks was quite chubby, presumably from eating a lot of bread.

One evening soon after our arrival, we were visited by a red-headed Jewish man in his mid-twenties who identified himself as Gustav. An old-timer, he wore black clothes and black leather gloves. I was fascinated by the tight-fitting gloves and pushed through the crowd to get closer to Gustav. He stated that he had come to listen to any grievances or complaints we wanted to lodge against Kapos or policemen in our previous camp. The cluster of men decided not to make it any worse for former Lager-führer Rozencwajg and his three policemen. They were bullies, but also fellow Jews.

The SS were evacuating eastern camps to Buchenwald and points west. They were obviously determined not to allow their prisoners to fall into the hands of the Reds. The Germans were using their limited rolling stock to move half-dead men and women, while leaving behind all sorts of material. Each new group of arrivals had their story to tell. Most had come from the Auschwitz satellite system. One newcomer was a novelty, though, a man who had been plucked from a front-line Wehr-macht unit. Denounced as a half-Jew, he was stripped of rank, uniform, money, watch, and documents and shipped to Buchen-wald. Here he strutted about for a couple of days sneering at everything. He was ignored, but when he said that we, meaning the German army, would win the war, it was more than his bunk-mates could take. After some serious pummelling, he got the message. From then on he kept his views to himself.

I ranged wide within our three-barrack subsection on my clog-shod feet, occasionally finding someone interesting to talk to. One time I was reassured by a stranger that my youth and the term in Buchenwald would, after the war, guarantee me a visa to the United States of America. That cheered me up a little. Another time a local celebrity was pointed out to me: With my nose close to the wire fence I gawked at my first black man, a dapper young French African who wore a little red cap.

Again at roll-call a long list of numbers was read out. Those called were to assemble out front after the evening bread distribution for transport to the Flessburg labour camp. Father's number was among those called. No one could tell us a thing about Flessburg. Father and I had to decide whether we should separate or try to stay together. I suggested that I switch numbers with someone and go on with him. A neighbour of Aunt Bluma's from Staszów, one of three brothers from whom I had borrowed Zionist books, had turned up in our barrack, and his number had been called. It didn't take much persuading for the man to agree to swap tags with me; he preferred to remain in Buchenwald. As we were hurried along by the Kapo I did the number swap on the run.

The several hundred of us spent half the night in a large hall. Past midnight, an order was shouted for everyone to line up and get ready to board the train. Halfway through the process a commotion started at the back. Someone had said that in Flessburg we would receive soup but that there were no spoons there. The same man had located a bin full of spoons, and he and others were helping themselves to them. Not wanting to be left out of a good thing, I also reached for a spoon. A guard had made his way to our side to see what the tumult was all about. Suddenly, I received an awful blow to my left shoulder. I let go of the spoon I'd managed to grasp and made quickly for the waiting cattle car. Father was already on, waiting for me.

On the way to Flessburg our train made one stop in the morning. It was in front of a water-tower in a small town somewhere in Saxony. The guards, who travelled in railway cars front and rear, came down on the gravelled side road to stretch and to wash their faces. Looking out through the little window, I saw them being approached by four elderly men who motioned in our direction as if to ask what it was they were escorting. One of the Buchenwald guards obligingly slid open the door of our wagon to show his cargo. I happened to be in front and was able to listen to what the old Germans were saying. One stated that there was little doubt that we were hardened criminals. Another nodded in agreement, pointing at me.

Presently we arrived in Flessburg. The train backed onto a siding in a young pine forest. Assembled four abreast, we were marched to the camp. The new guards were a nondescript lot, some young, others much older. The commandant was an older man, tall and pinched-faced, who spoke loudly and wielded a riding crop. He kept pace with us and would yell at us to keep our heads up: 'Keppe hoch, tzak, tzak!'

The double lines of prefabricated barracks, set in a forest clearing, looked new. Our sorry group was met by three Kapos, who assigned us to barracks and bare-board bunks. We each got a louse-infested blanket. Everyone else was at work. A briefing session gave us the camp routine and regulations:

6:00 A.M. Hot drink.
6:15 A.M. Roll-call.
7:00 A.M. Move out with work group to the day's assignment.
7:15 A.M.–12 noon Work.
12:00 noon 15-minute rest.
12:15 P.M.–6 P.M. Work.
6:00 P.M. Return to barracks. Evening meal: soup and a slice of bread.
7:30 P.M. Roll-call.
9:00 P.M. Lights out.

It was a six-and-a-half-day work week, with Sunday afternoons off. The number on our jacket had to be visible at all times. Those who wore ordinary clothes rather than the blue-grey suits were to come forward in the morning so that stripes of red could be painted on.

Dismissed!

We looked at the people returning from work in the evening and saw death in their faces. These were the Muzulmen,* men whose life expectancy could be measured in days, or perhaps

---

*A Yiddish derivation of the word Muslim, it alludes to the portrayal of Muslims in a 1930s film about the siege of Khartoum by the Mahdi and his unkempt dervishes.

weeks. Foul-smelling, with a thick growth of beard on their chins, they massed around the canister of tepid green soup, never letting the threadbare blankets off their shoulders, slurping the horrible stuff. Few used spoons. Not many had been there more than two months. We understood that we had been sent to replace the dead. The watery, tasteless soup had sand in it, possibly from unwashed turnip tops; the slice of bread was heavy and brown. Hardly a word was spoken. I saved half of my portion that night, knowing that I would not get food for another twenty-four hours. I observed a Hungarian Jew, a Muzulman, lick all the glass soup bowls stacked for washing. There was an outhouse and, next to it, a well. I climbed up to our upper bunk and moved closer to Father. There was no use talking.

At six, we were awakened by a loud bell and bright lights. Tired, scratching our bites, and rubbing our eyes, we lined up for our cup of chicory coffee, all we would get until evening. I debated whether to eat my half portion of bread now or to save it for lunch. I held on to it for another hour and then ate it dry.

The first day's roll-call took about an hour. New work teams were being formed. Father and I kept moving to the back of the line, having learned from past experience that the toughest jobs were filled first. But our manoeuvre failed: we were picked to join a team of twelve to move heavy railway ties to the site where a new siding was being constructed – possibly the worst of all the jobs. It was three men to a tie, carried on the right shoulder, so the greatest weight fell on the taller men. I, being smaller, felt little of the weight. Father was above average in height and had a horrible day. No one had had any food yet that day, and by the afternoon we could hardly move. We worked until evening, at which time we formed a squad together with another team and walked back to camp. We were met by the same officer at the gate and again ordered to hold our heads up. At about seven o'clock we had soup and bread.

The days were grey and wet, with snow but no ice. It was early March. Father was assigned to other work, and I was selected for an inside job. The work entailed manufacturing a primitive, but apparently effective, anti-tank grenade launcher. Flessburg was a

Panzerfaust factory. The Panzerfaust was a forty-inch metal tube with a firing device and a trigger. At one end was a charge of explosives. It was to be held on the shoulder by one soldier and aimed and fired by another. Together with another boy I filled tubes of powder and fastened them to the trigger mechanism. The work was done by boys my age or a bit older in a large, chilly but dry prefab hut concealed in the forest. It seemed as if I had been given a break. I could last a little longer working indoors. Sometimes when the Kapo was out, we would sit while working. I and others were sometimes even able to swipe a few white sugar beets. To cook these we ripped the insulation off an industrial hot-water pipe. Too hungry to wait for the sugar beets to cook all the way through, I ate them half-raw.

As time went by, we weren't supervised as strictly. Once or twice a day I would go out and walk around the factory grounds set in the woods, hoping to find something to eat. One morning I came up to the perimeter wire fence and saw a few civilians looking in. I didn't say anything and neither did they. Twenty-odd Italian POWs were sleeping in a hut just outside our camp. I approached them once, drawn by the fire they had built in the woods to roast something. One of them, a young man, blond and very cheerful, asked me how old I was and wanted to know what I was in for. I could give him my age but didn't have Italian to answer his second question. They didn't understand German and did not share any food with me.

In our barracks there were some Russian POWs, who were treated the same way we were. The Hungarian Jews, though they had been in extermination camps only a few months and should have had calorie reserves to draw on, were actually weaker than we were. Some of them seemed to have become deranged from hunger. A case in point was the man who snatched another's bread ration and began stuffing it in his mouth. He was pounced on by the Kapo and his assistant, who beat and kicked him but could not get the bread away from him. I watched, transfixed: though he lay on the floor taking punishment, the wretch's jaws never stopped working.

The lice were as much of a scourge as the Nazis or the hunger.

Defenceless, because we had stopped washing, at night I clutched the thin blanket, still wearing coat and pants, and scratched until I gave in from exhaustion. Awakened at 6 A.M., I was still scratching as I rushed out for roll-call. I worked my nails feverishly into the crevices of the pants and jacket, destroying the unborn lice, scratching, always scratching. In mid-March the weather turned mild. Sunday afternoons off, I carefully and painstakingly went to work checking the blanket, running my fingernails through my hair and into my scalp, groping for fat ones – fine fingercombing for lice. When I'd collected a batch, I would slowly spread them out on the hot lid of a metal drum in which a fire burned, and then I would watch them sizzle.

The lice, filth, work, and scant food were taking their toll. Daily, people who couldn't make it to work ended up in the hospital. Not one ever returned to work. I saw a former HASAG policeman being led to the hospital, a short, light-haired man who had once chased me around, administering kicks to my backside for some offence. I got no satisfaction from his misfortune. The job of a hospital orderly was much sought after. Rumour had it that the orderlies kept all the bread rations for themselves and let the sick starve to death. Every morning the dead were taken somewhere from the hospital for burial. The daily burial detail, four men pushing a large handcart, passed us as we were getting ready to go to work.

On Sunday afternoons the camp barber cut hair. It was nice to get rid of the lice, but a shaved head made me feel chilly.

Father and I didn't talk much after the time that he told me he probably wouldn't make it to the end of the war. It happened on an evening when we were sitting by an open fire, waiting for a roasted-wheat-kernel soup to come to a boil. I was unhappy, because Father had traded both our bread rations that evening for a bowlful of wheat kernels; it was my opinion that at least one piece of solid food a day was essential for survival. Father wanted it this way, believing that a big bowl of soup would be more filling. It was not a satisfactory meal, but I soon forgot about it. Father was forty-four years old at the time, and it was very hard for him. I didn't realize how hard, until it was too late.

During this period, there were overflights of U.S. aircraft. They flew low, in broad daylight, and dropped leaflets. The guards would react angrily if we picked them up, so we did so only if they landed in the camp. One afternoon the planes must have bombed something big in Leipzig, because a tall column of black smoke was visible from there for a week. We had little news from the outside world. That the Allies were closing in, there was little doubt. Further evidence of our tormentors' imminent defeat came one day when six SS men showed up in a truck and demanded all the Panzerfausts we had assembled. They proceeded to load the truck themselves while we stood by.

The soup grew even worse, which would have seemed impossible. One night we did not get our slice of bread. I went to see if I could find something in the back of the kitchen and returned with a small amount of potato peels. We cooked these on a fire outside, but they made a poor substitute for bread. The next night we got bread, but this time I decided to save half and eat it in small pieces throughout the next day. That experiment didn't work. I seemed to be even hungrier all day. I tried something else – instead of chewing the bread carefully, I swallowed it in chunks, unchewed. The idea was to give myself the illusion of being sated. When this experiment failed as well, I just ate my bread like everyone else.

Something was up. In the morning, after roll-call, we did not go to work but were dismissed. Shortly after that we were ordered to form groups according to our place of work and were marched, under guard, to the main railway siding in the forest. We were to be evacuated. They would not let us fall into the hands of the Allies. The railway cars we were to get into had delivered explosive material only a few days before. On the floors remained a heavy covering of powdery toxic stuff that got into our eyes, mouths, and noses. A few of us got on and tried to sweep it out, but it did no good.

Father was with his team, which included many Russian POWs. I tried to figure out what to do. Should I ask my Kapo to let Father join me in our wagon? For me to go with Father in his wagon was out of the question: I wanted to stay with my own group, which consisted mostly of boys who got along well together. The truth was that I couldn't decide if I wanted Father with us. He tended to complain a lot lately, and there was little I could do to help him. It would be bad in front of my peers. Possibly the thought crossed my mind that he might die in my arms, and I couldn't be sure if I could take it. Still, it was my duty and responsibility to keep Father with me. These thoughts were racing through my mind when the order was shouted to board. I tried to make a decision, but I had missed my chance to ask my Kapo to let Father into our wagon. The doors slid shut. We were on our way. It was a day in the second week of April, 1945.

The train was headed southeast. In the wagon we boys crouched or sat and talked about escaping. Leo, a Jewish boy of about eighteen who might have been chubby at one time, had a knife that he showed me in secret. His idea was to cut a square in the floor large enough for a person. In the dark, if the train stopped, we could lower ourselves to the track and make our getaway. To me the idea smacked too much of a 'saw in the cake' escapade I remembered from reading *The Count of Monte Cristo*. I told Leo so, but he managed to squeeze into the corner and, with the help of another boy, started to carve the floor. The bitter powdery substance got in our mouths. We had no water or food. We didn't need to use the toilet – if there was one – as we had not swallowed anything for many hours.

We started to make morning stops. At these we would get a slice of bread and a cup of water. We could also go down to relieve ourselves by the side of the tracks. This routine continued for about seven days, except that one day we didn't get bread. Every time we stopped, the commandant would knock on the cattle cars and ask, '*Wieviel tote?*' ('How many dead?'). A few of the older, weaker men in our wagon were talked into going to the 'hospital' car, where there was supposedly more room. From almost the first day many dead were pulled off the train and hurriedly buried by the side of the track during the stops. It became clear to us that the commandant and his men did not know where to go. We were moving in a zigzag. Many railway lines or bridges were out of commission. Once, at a provincial railway station, our convoy was parked near wagons loaded with sugar. Soldiers, Ukrainians in German army uniforms, were looting them. We gestured to the soldiers to give us some. A small paper bag of sugar came flying at the window, broke on the barbed wire, and spilled onto the floor inside. There, on all fours, we licked the sweet, bitter stuff off the floor.

The Americans were bombing the tracks ahead. Our convoy stopped dead near a farm. They let us off, perhaps hoping that if the aircraft saw who we were they wouldn't strafe us. The planes came close, but not close enough. We didn't care if bombs fell – the commandant and his men would get it too. It gave me a chance to run down the line of wagons yelling my father's name at the top of my voice. Too weak to move, few of our men had come down. I didn't get a response until I reached the hospital car. There, a man with a big head of ginger hair who worked with Father answered me through the high window. He shouted, 'Your father died on the tenth day after Passover.'

What had happened back in the dark of my father's railway car? Father might have died of starvation, the usual cause. The ginger-haired man had given me only a date. A date to observe for the rest of my life, to say Kaddish, the prayer for the dead – if I lived.

I was sixteen, alone in the world, but still alive. The grass in April was young and green. I sat by the side of the track and pulled it up, one blade at a time, then sucked the sweet nectar of its succulent roots. Soon, a whistle sounded to get back on the train. While I was out, Leo got a beating from the commandant. Someone had leaned on the almost cut-through panel, and it had dropped to the track. The hole was plugged, and the train moved on again.

Now, nothing held us: 25 April had passed. Leaflets had been dropped back at the lager stating that the victorious United Nations would meet in San Francisco on that day. We were hoping this would mean the end of the war, but we didn't know how it was going to happen.

As we rode on, I learned from Jurek, a thin, blond boy in my wagon who was slightly younger than I, that his father, who had been in the same car with mine, was also dead. This sounded suspicious: Jurek's father was a big man who had appeared to be in fair shape. Jurek said that there was talk that the Russian POWs had made more room in the wagon by choking some of the Jewish men in the dark of night. The next two or three days we made frequent and longer stops, during which we talked to people in the other cars and found out that our wagon was by far in the best shape. Not one of us had died.

I blamed myself for Father's death. If only I had taken him in, or at least tried. I had a bit of authority among the boys, perhaps because I didn't give in to depression. Father had not been the only person to say that it was not possible to survive. My wagonmate Izidor Wierzbinski had said it also, and on one occasion, I had succeeded in calming him down when he started to weep. I knew of only one suicide during the time I'd been in the camps, and its cause wasn't clear: a short, nearly bald, bespectacled man I knew in Kielce HASAG had thrown himself in front of a locomotive. I remembered his wife, statuesque and a head taller than her husband. The man's bunk-mate said that his friend had been jealous of his absent wife.

I calculated the days since we left Flessburg and the stops we made, trying to fit in the date of Father's death to the locations where big burials had taken place. I came up with the name Schwarzwald as the likeliest place that his body would have been put in a mass grave. That was the name that stuck in my head, a name I'd read on a sign that I saw from the little window. More likely it was Schwarzenburg, which is half way between Chemnitz and the Czechoslovakian border.

We had entered the Sudetenland. Czech-sounding names appeared at railway stations. We hadn't dreamt of escape in Germany: the odds of being helped by someone there were hardly in our favour. In Czechoslovakia, we could count on sympathy. During the night a few of the boys lifted themselves over the window and jumped. Shots were fired by the guards in the caboose next to us. Two or three more boys got away. We didn't know if they'd been hit. Out of fifteen hundred men that got on in Flessburg, fewer than nine hundred were alive. There was no time to lose.

The ration was still one slice of bread. We had now been twelve days en route.

Izidor, from the Poznań area, was also sixteen and alone. We decided to pair up and jump out the window nearest to us. It was risky, because it was only about eight feet from the guard in the caboose. I figured that as soon as the train went around a curve, possibly where an embankment dropped down a bit, we would jump. I would go first, Izidor would follow. He was to walk back and I forward along the track, and we would meet. The guard in the caboose, I was positive, was watching the window farthest from him on the opposite side of the car, from which the other boys had dropped. This window, ours, was so close to him that he probably thought we wouldn't dare. Jurek also wanted to jump with us, but three wasn't practical. I had to suggest that he find another partner.

Four or six people had already jumped from the other side of the car when we made our move. It was night, and we were passing through forests, which were excellent to hide in. We were in a Czech-populated area. I had to get some food in me.

I tried to raise myself to the window but was too weak. Two boys pushed me out, and as I fell I saw the guard in the caboose staring at me. I don't know whether he fired at me or not – I was busy falling head first down a steep embankment. I came to sometime later. Izidor was dragging me into the woods. It was almost dawn, and it was getting light. Everything smelled fresh and clean. I was babbling incoherently.

16
Auschwitz, 1991

Half a century after the Second World War we subscribe to the notion that the retreating Germans insisted on dragging any remaining Jews with them in order to do away with witnesses to the 'final solution,' that a denial of the Holocaust was in their plans all along. On the Flessburg train all we knew was that they hated us too much to let us live.

Freda and I took the train from Warsaw to Kraków, a pleasant three-and-a-half-hour trip. Until the 1600s Kraków was the capital of Poland. It had 105 churches, a castle, many palaces, and the second-oldest university in Eastern Europe, after Prague. Its industries include a large steel complex and tourism. From Kraków, Auschwitz is about a half-hour by car. Mother had been in Auschwitz. Her tattooed number was prominent on her forearm until the day she died, in 1985.

In Kraków we visited the state-run Jewish museum, the synagogue, and the Jewish cemetery. The Jewish community in Kraków was possibly the oldest in Poland. It went back to the 1400s, when Kazimierz the Great invited Jews to settle there. The king needed tradesmen and merchants to service the court, since the Polish population was engaged mainly in agriculture. Bringing in Jews and Germans to settle seemed like a good idea. Soon the city became German-speaking, and it remained so for more than a hundred years. The Jews eventually moved to a nearby area known as Kazimierz, which the king hoped would be Polish in character. In 1941, this area became the site of the ghetto. Ulica

Podgórska, the street in Kazimierz that runs along the river Wisła, was not made part of the ghetto so as to deny the Jews access to running water.

Some German students were just leaving the shul and cemetery as Freda and I arrived. An elderly Jewish woman, with the voice and appearance of a market woman of old, greeted us at the door. Approaching us aggressively, she clutched her harvest of donations in bills of small denominations. We promised to return shortly.

We went on to the Jewish museum, which is located in an old, renovated synagogue. The exhibits are arranged well, and the museum is institutional in every respect. The Polish staff is polite and unobtrusive. A young female attendant volunteered that she had an aunt who had married an Israeli and was living in Holon, near Tel Aviv. She had visited her aunt the previous year, and, as she put it, she had left 'half her heart' in Israel. Looking at her dark red hair and brown eyes I inquired if she was Jewish. Not by blood, she said, but in her soul (*dusza*).

Returning to the older shul Freda and I encountered two groups of students, one German, the other Israeli, accompanied by guides. One of the guides, an old man, detached himself from them and accompanied us through the synagogue and into the cemetery. Restoration was in progress, the work being done by a dozen or so Polish students from the archaeology department of the university. The oldest monuments were being chemically washed and sanded. Broken pieces were being recemented and in most cases missing pieces were being replaced with identical material. Judging by the size of the cemetery, the project would take many years. Our guide, limping from a shrapnel wound he said he received in the Russian-Finnish war of 1940, was contemptuous of the work. He became upset when I suggested that this was the only Jewish cemetery where work was being done to maintain the gravestones. The reason for his distress became apparent when he mentioned that the shul and the cemetery would eventually be taken over by the Kraków Heritage Foundation, and he would be out of a job.

Our guide justified a huge pile of earth, overgrown with weeds and obviously covering graves, as an attempt by the Jews in 1938 (one year before the war) to hide the graves in the event the Germans invaded the city. That, he expounded, would prevent the Nazis from ever finding the old tombstones. I pointed out that there were a lot of untouched stones dating back to the 1600s and wondered what had saved them from destruction. He told us that in the case of a small area of gravestones encircled by a wrought-iron fence, an attempt by the Germans to cut the fence down failed when sparks from their welding torch blinded one of the welders. The man took us for ignorant North Americans for whom any logic-defying story would do.

The guide seemed in a great hurry to show us the far side of the cemetery, where he said a great rabbi lay buried. At this point it became obvious that his only objective was to get me to give him a large tip, preferably out of sight of his partners, so that he would not have to share it. He said that he was relying on us to give him money for his sick mother-in-law. She had returned from hospital but was still bedridden. His wife had died thirteen years ago. After I handed him some money and we were on our way back to the synagogue, he repeatedly asked me not to tell his friends that I had given him cash. It got a little embarrassing. Predictably, the others in the shul also demanded money. I paid again and said good-bye, feeling that perhaps the sooner the Heritage Foundation took over, the better.

At the exit another old man was blocking the way of a Scandinavian student who was searching through his pockets for change. The man's female companion, the market woman, said that she was from Lwów. Perhaps, but her accent was Russian.

Exploring the streets off the main square, Freda and I came across a building displaying a plaque with Hebrew lettering. Curious, we went inside and were greeted by Henryk, the secretary of the Jewish cultural club of Kraków. A scholarly, balding, bearded man of about forty who spoke with a stutter, he said, with a sardonic grin, that the only difference between the old Jews in East Bronx and those in the old shul in Kraków was that the Bronx Jews were poor, apparently a local joke. He said that a similar situation prevailed at the Warsaw synagogue. According to Henryk, the Jews of Kraków were steeped in Polish history and leaned towards the side of the Catholic Church in Polish politics. The situation in Warsaw was the exact opposite – the Jews there had been staunch Communists and hence were foes of the church.

The cultural club's future is uncertain. In 1946, after the war, about thirteen thousand Jews returned to the city. But because of the anti-Semitism and the lack of opportunity for advancement in a stagnant economy, they emigrated to Israel and the West. There were now only about a hundred Jews left.

The Polish writer Tadeusz Borowski once read in Kraków from *This Way to the Gas, Ladies and Gentlemen*, a novella about Jews becoming obsessed with the legacy of the gas chambers. In 1951 Borowski committed suicide by kneeling beside an open gas oven with his head inside, the jets turned full on. Jerzy Kosinski had come to the city to speak about his work. In Henryk's opinion, Jerzy Kosinski had taken his own life because he feared failure.

Excursions to Auschwitz are a steady business in Kraków. Signs offering guided bus tours are plastered all over town. In the shops figurines of Jews in various poses of prayer are a popular souvenir. Over dishes of ice cream, Henryk expounded on Kraków's history, telling of how the 1794 revolutionary Tadeusz Kosciusko asked the Jews to rise against the tsar, of how the former aristocracy lived and how their palaces had since been turned into museums. Kraków, he declared, had never been the location of a pogrom. As it happens, Henryk was wrong – there had been a minor pogrom in 1946, and a bigger one in Kielce the same year.

At the turn of the century Oświęcim was a sleepy town about twenty-four miles west of Kraków in the southwestern part of Poland where a number of railway lines converged. This might have been the reason why the largest Jewish travel agency in Galicia had located there. Jews fleeing pogroms in the Ukraine, Moldavia, and Belarus booked steamship passage to America or Argentina through this agency. The countryside in this part of Poland is pretty. The roads follow the natural contours of the land, the hills are covered with pine and birch trees, picturesque farmhouses and barns overlook ponds and streams, cows and horses graze on the hillsides.

Rudolf Höss must have liked his assignment. It was surely a plum: to arrange for the construction of a concentration camp where enemies of the Third Reich would receive instruction and be persuaded to mend their ways. Höss took to his job with alacrity, and did his work with zeal and dedication. It beat going to the front, and, since it was part of a growth industry, it came with a few perks. Next to the Auschwitz camp, on the other side of the railway tracks, Höss built the Birkenau complex. For his own comfort, he erected a two-storey house nearby. Giving his macabre sense of humour free rein, he placed a sign at the entrance to the camp that read *Arbeit macht frei* ('Work makes one free'). Höss's successor was still enlarging and improving the death facility when the Red Army broke through German lines on 18 January 1945. Unable to save the real estate, the Germans decided to move the inventory west. In the January snow and ice, twenty-six thousand emaciated prisoners were ordered out on a march. Anyone not able to keep up the forced pace was shot, the body left by the roadside as a warning to others. The Germans would have preferred to slaughter their charges, but time did not permit it.

At his trial in 1947, Höss disputed the number of deaths his organization was accused of causing. He insisted that it was one and a half million at most, far fewer than the four million victims claimed by the prosecution. Sentenced by a Polish court to death by hanging, Höss was executed in the lager he had built and loved.

Originally designed to hold Poles whom the Nazis considered potential troublemakers, Auschwitz kept expanding and became the first concentration camp to test the effects on humans of the gas cyclon B.

Freda and I had hoped to go to Auschwitz with the group of visiting Israeli students. We had first noticed them at the cemetery, then later at the Holiday Inn in Kraków, and again on Saturday morning at the Wavel Castle, where we tagged along and made friends with them. Aged seventeen or eighteen, they were a wild-looking bunch. Most of them with long, dark, curly hair, they stood out from among the almost all-blond Polish visitors. When I asked Moishe, one of their teachers, a tall, muscular young man, if we could go along with them to Auschwitz, he eyed me suspiciously and suggested I speak to Yacov, the group's leader. The kids seemed to take to us, but their teachers were aloof and undecided. Yacov said he would be in touch.

Mystified, we spoke to him and Hali, the school psychologist, that evening at the hotel, and they told us that they could not be too careful with strangers. I explained that I wanted to join them so we would be among youngsters not unlike our own children in age. After a brief run-through we passed the test. They asked me if I would be willing to give the kids a first-hand report on war-time conditions in the camp. When I said that many in Israel could do so, Yacov replied that their group was not interested in listening to 'professional survivors.' I accepted on the condition that I would only answer questions put by the students. I was curious about the kinds of questions they would ask.

Next day on the bus I sketched out for Hali an account of my survival, which she offered to relate to the group in Hebrew, as an introduction. I now had a chance to take a closer look at the students. There were three times as many girls as boys. These youngsters, I was told, would be in the Israeli army soon. The girls, mostly with dark hair, were animated; the boys, tall and slim, with blond or dark hair, seemed shy and subdued.

Yacov directed the bus to take us first to see the movie showing the liberation of Auschwitz by the Red Army, and then on to Birkenau. From Mother, I had some idea of what to expect there. She had occasionally mentioned the crematoria ovens spewing smoke day and night. It remains a mystery to me how my mother, who would jump at the sound of a dropped spoon, and who was so unassuming that her life's philosophy had been to be nice no matter what the provocation, was able to survive the horrors of Birkenau.

One of the boys located and led us to Blok 20, in which Moishe's late mother had been in 1944. The *Bloks*, or barracks, had been left as found. Similar to the ones I had been in at about the same time in Buchenwald, here the uprights between the bunk-beds were of brick rather than wood. Here, also, the prisoner appointed to head a barrack, the Kapo, often a criminal, had his room at the front rather than the back. The old, sloped roofs had been replaced, and skylights installed. Sunlight streamed into the shabby interior, exposing dust and the roughness of the boards. Undisturbed, spiders had woven their webs in corners. In the distant past small, barred windows let in little light, and at night four low-wattage electric bulbs were all that lit the interior. The Israeli kids were uneasy and a little jumpy.

We walked across the green to the rail line where men, women, and children disembarked and the 'selection' took place. We saw the ruins of the gas chamber and crematorium where one day in October, 1944, the incongruously named '*Kanada*' *Sonderkommando* had staged a short-lived uprising. The commando was composed of several hundred Jews from Greece, France, Poland, Hungary, and Russia whose job was to remove and cremate the corpses of gassed Jews and Gypsies after wrenching out their gold teeth and shearing off the women's hair. In the uprising, they used explosives smuggled in by women working in the *Pulwer* (powder) pavilion to blow up a gas chamber and a crematorium. Three SS men died before machine-guns cut the rebels down. Several young Jewish women were tortured by Höss for their involvement. No participant in the struggle survived.

My mother had limped off at this same siding a little more than forty-seven years before. The day was probably sunny and warm, but the smell, rather than of trees and green grass, was of acrid, protein-rich smoke. Mother had been selected out at Kielce as being unsuited for work. She had been included in a group of Jews from the neighbouring Hendryków camp, all destined for Auschwitz. In 1944 Birkenau was slaughtering thousands of Hungarian Jews daily. There was little time for selections. Consequently when Mother's transport arrived full of what appeared to be healthy people suitable for work, no selection took place. The men went straight to Auschwitz, and the women across the railway tracks to Birkenau.

Mother once tried to deal for a sweater there. Another inmate had a thick sweater that she was willing to trade for three bread rations – three thick slices of black bread. Mother began to save her daily ration in anticipation of the trade. The early winter of 1944–5 was a cold one, and the prospect of a sweater made the sacrifice worthwhile. Clutching her three pieces of bread Mother wrapped herself in her blanket and went to sleep, no doubt dreaming about the splendid sweater. Ready to do business in the morning, she woke up to find the bread gone. The punishment for stealing rations was severe, but Mother was too timid a person to report the theft. And anyway, the bread would have been eaten by then.

From Birkenau, Freda and I and our group were bussed over to Auschwitz. The Bloks there were in neat, even rows. Poplar trees had recently been planted on both sides of the area once used for roll-call (*Appel*). There were also concrete sidewalks. The red brick buildings gave the appearance of a large, well-kept boys' school.

Inside the Bloks, displayed behind glass, were heaps of hair and samples of cloth fabricated from human hair. On display was a letter from an SS treasurer advising other similar camps that human hair could become a source of revenue. It quoted prices in Reichsmarks and gave the shipping address of a German textile company. In another unit were displayed thousands of shoes, with children's shoes in a separate bin; there were also a small exhibit of baby clothes, a bin of eyeglasses, and a bin of suitcases and bags with the names of the owners crudely hand-lettered on them. The children's bags were clearly marked with their name and date of birth. A huge bin contained shaving brushes, hairbrushes, and toothbrushes. One compartment was devoted exclusively to artificial limbs, back supports, and neck braces.

Perhaps it was the Teutonic refusal to let anything go to waste that made the Germans hold on to these things.

Looking around, I saw the German passion for order in the many personal information documents on display. Inmates who were not gassed immediately were required to fill out a card stating name, age, occupation, names of parents, mother's maiden name, father's occupation, nationality, most recent address, and so on.

There were more horrors to see. One punishment for minor infractions was a stay in an individual, standing-room-only cell – a punishment that invariably meant death. But those on whom it was inflicted were the lucky ones – they were not gassed immediately on arrival. At each grisly Blok we lost one or two students. Some had tears in their eyes, some clutched their stomachs, and others just sat outside, staring.

We regrouped in the courtyard where, in Höss's time, executions took place. Against a brick wall about twelve feet high, prisoners sentenced to death by firing squad were made to disrobe. Naked, summer or winter, usually at daybreak, they lined up waiting their turn. Some sort of tribunal sentenced them. No records showed that charges were ever dismissed, nor was there evidence of verdicts other than death.

Visitors had placed flowers and lit candles at the foot of the wall. Above hung a vertical banner of blue and white stripes, the pattern of prisoners' clothes and also of the prayer shawl. On it was sewn a blood-red triangle, the ID of a political prisoner. A chill went down my spine.

Moishe put on his tallit and began reciting Kaddish, the prayer for the dead. Moishe broke down, and Yacov continued for him. A few tourists walked by, watching us with interest, but not wishing to intrude. I wiped my eyes and passed my handkerchief around. For us, at this moment, it was as if the Holocaust was happening all over again, and all we could do was weep helplessly and silently.

When it was all over, away from the Bloks but in sight of them, the kids sat down on the grass in a semicircle, and I stood in front of them. Hali outlined my history in Hebrew. The first question was unexpected. 'Did you believe in God?' I hesitated, then temporized. 'Sometimes I did, and other times I didn't.'

Other questions followed. I told them what I believed, and what I knew of.

The Jews did not go to their death like lambs to slaughter. The Germans were successful in keeping everybody in the dark as to their plans. As a fourteen-year-old, I had not wanted to believe that these horrible things were happening; perhaps we were all fooling ourselves. We sensed that something bad was taking place. People were being sent east – into Russia, to work, presumably. In Mielec, a little town northeast of Auschwitz, the Germans rounded up everyone in the spring of 1942 and sent them away. It was the first ghetto in our area to be deported. The Germans waited nearly two months before repeating this experiment elsewhere. Maybe they had been expecting a backlash of some sort and were waiting to see what would happen. But they had nothing to worry about. Less than sixty miles away, unsuspecting, we wondered whether it was possible that the people in the Mielec ghetto had offended the Nazis in some way and, as punishment, been sent to the eastern front to do hard work.

We did not know the truth until the late summer of 1942. Even then, we didn't know that in eastern Poland and Russia the Germans were machine-gunning entire ghettos. But as the transports increased through the summer of 1942, we watched with dread as a pattern emerged. The people in the Warsaw ghetto went because they were too weak to resist – they had been starving for a long time. The people in the smaller towns like ours tried to hide rather than fight – the only alternative possible. Maybe the deportations would stop, or maybe the war would end. The thousands that did go didn't have a choice – they were forced to go, and they didn't know what awaited them. In 1943 and 1944, the French, the Dutch, and the Greek Jews surely had no idea where they were being sent. Even the Hungarian Jews I met in the camps in 1945 claimed they didn't know what was happening when they were deported in 1944. By that time the Polish Jews were all gone, as were the Lithuanian, Latvian, German, and Belgian Jews. Even the Allies, when the information got to them in 1942, refused to believe that the Germans were systematically killing millions of people.

As to why more people didn't fight, the answer is simple: With what? We had no weapons, and the Poles around us could not be depended on to help. Moreover, by the time we realized that people were being sent to their death, we still didn't know about the gassings or the massive nature of the extermination. That they were being killed – yes, we finally knew that. Deep down we knew. But it wasn't as if my mother and father sat us down and said, 'Listen, children, we're all going to be killed next week.' In the spring of 1943 we were in a camp making munitions for the Germans, and we heard that in the Warsaw ghetto there had been an uprising. We did not exactly sympathize with the uprising, since we weren't sure who had taken part in it. We thought it must have been the Jewish police and the Judenrat, who had helped the Germans round up thousands of Jews every day. We didn't have all the facts. The men who should have been our leaders had let us down badly. Members of the Judenrat in every town were often people of poor character: anyone who was honest didn't want to do the Germans' dirty work for them, and resigned. Many people just wanted to save their own skin.

The Israelis naturally wanted to know why I didn't take my family to Israel to live. I told them my youngest child was twenty-one. As adults, our four children could go where they wished. As to why I personally hadn't chosen to move there earlier, I said I felt, perhaps more so in Canada, that I was free to live as I pleased. Though I had been to Israel several times, I had never really learned Hebrew.

There were other questions, which I attempted as best I could to answer. It had been an exhausting hour on top of a draining day. It was now after four, and no one had eaten since morning.

Later, I was to be asked how I felt after seeing Auschwitz and Majdanek. My answer was that I wanted to scream and smash things. I could see and hear mothers clutching small children to their breasts, using soothing words to try to comfort them as the Germans loosed their dogs on them. I could see old men and children tripping over their useless bundles and valises as they were kicked and whipped and ordered to strip naked and run in snow or mud to the showers. The Germans had found that the idea of showering gave the doomed a feeling of hope that perhaps they would be put to work. Together, men and women, covering their genitalia with their hands, marched to be gassed.

Upset and confused, Freda and I said goodbye to the students, who were going on to visit Łódź. We got the only taxi available, and the driver, a young man with a beard and an ingratiating manner, gave us a tour of the construction site of the new Carmelite convent. The existing one, built after the war inside the confines of the camp, had been strenuously objected to by religious Jews. Most of the victims at Auschwitz had been Jews, and it was, they claimed, highly improper for the Carmelites to appropriate the site. The Catholic Church felt justified in resisting the attempts of Rabbi Weiss and his followers to picket and obstruct entry to the convent. In a sermon he gave in 1989 Cardinal Glemp, the Primate of Poland, went so far as to state that the rabbi had attempted to injure or kill the nuns, that the Jews controlled the world media, that it was the Jews who had brought Communism to Poland, and that it was the Jews who, by forcing alcohol on the Poles, had turned them into drunkards. The dispute wouldn't die. Eventually the church gave way by moving the old concrete and barbed-wire fence to make it appear as if the original convent was outside the camp.

The semi-final round of this struggle was being played out just about then in Albany, New York, where, during a visit to the United States, Cardinal Glemp, on leaving the cathedral, was handed a writ to answer charges of having defamed Rabbi Weiss two years earlier. The cardinal had declared recently that his statements were matters of historical fact and that he was merely repeating what was common knowledge.

The Polish press gave the incident in Albany wide coverage, without commenting on the merits of the accusation. Citing U.S. law, the papers pointed out that the cardinal was caught in a peculiar dilemma. He was free to leave the United States but, if he chose not to defend the action and was convicted on the charge of slander, he would be barred from ever returning to the country. Rabbi Weiss declared that an admission of error and an apology from the primate were all that he sought.

The taxi driver, on learning that we were from Canada, said that many people from all over the world come to visit Auschwitz. Recently seven thousand French students had camped there. He also pointed out several dormitories built by the Germans to house students coming to Auschwitz to restore the camp; the project was as a form of expiation. A party from Chile had been his passengers recently. When I enquired if they were Jews or Poles, he carefully refrained from answering the question directly by saying that the woman in the party had been born in Palestine, of parents from the area who had left Poland in wartime through Romania and Turkey. From Palestine they had emigrated to Argentina and then on to Chile.

The driver obviously couldn't make up his mind whether we were Jews or Poles. He began telling us about the misfortunes of his family and countrymen. His two sisters had spent time in the camps at Bergen-Belsen and Ravensbrück for political crimes committed under the occupation. Judging the driver to be about thirty-five years old, and even assuming that the sisters were ten or fifteen years older, they would have been infants in 1944 when convicted of political crimes. His sisters received awards and pensions for incarceration, he said, but his mother couldn't prove her case, as the Russians, who liberated Auschwitz, where she had been held, had destroyed or carted away most of the records. There were many people, he told us, who had lived through the war in comfort, then forged documents and managed to obtain two sworn statements by 'witnesses' in order to receive huge pensions for alleged mistreatment by the Germans. A Communist mafia, as he put it, organized this fake documentation, while deserving folk who had suffered and needed help most were left to live out their years in misery.

I recognized the driver as a particular type, a person who tries to ingratiate himself to get a larger tip or just to get people to like him. Many survivors visited Auschwitz, some with their children. He had obviously taken in the stories of the survivors' wartime experiences and had gone on to fabricate a family history for himself. Running a shuttle service between the lager and the city, he had plenty of opportunity to practise.

17
The Kindness of Strangers

Czechoslovakia, 28 April 1945. Aided by morning's first light Izidor and I made our way to the nearest house. *'Chleb'* ('bread'), we said. Giving us some bread and milk, an elderly couple and their daughter, themselves poor refugees from the Sudetenland, advised us to keep on going. The Germans patrolled the area constantly. Dressed as we were in grey with three-inch-wide red stripes on the back, sleeves, chest, and pant legs, there was no mistaking us for anything but escaped häftlinge. Having made it this far, I was not keen on risking a bullet in the head now. Promising to come back after the war was over so that we could thank our gentle hosts properly, we left.

Emaciation would poorly describe our condition. We had eaten hardly at all for the past three weeks and very little for the past three years. Struggling up the wooded hills we saw from the rise a cluster of homes below, a village called Žichovice.

Smoke coming out of the chimneys reminded us that we were still very hungry. There was no road traffic. Cautiously, we moved towards the village. Peering from behind the house on the edge we watched for movement. Nothing. Voices could be heard from inside. The street was deserted. It occurred to us that it was Sunday, a day of rest. Cap in hand, I knocked on the door and politely asked for food. We were handed bread, cheese, and a dish of what seemed to be dumplings in butter, with sour cream and chives. It was a good start. Moving along, Izidor rattled the doorknob on a prosperous-looking cottage. A motion to the mouth, a palm down to the stomach – and, like magic – food appeared. Bread, cheese, apples, plates full of dumplings in sour cream. We had never had it so good. It was time to move on to the next spot. Practically falling over the threshold of the adjoining house I had my routine down pat. Bread, cheese, dumplings in sour cream. Loaded down with victuals we decided to try one more farm-house, unable to accept that we could ever get our fill. Here we were asked to sit down and eat. More dumplings and sour cream. Hauling our booty, we beat it out as fast as etiquette allowed. My digestive system, accustomed to nothing, or at best a diet of black bread, turnips, and watery soup was in total revolt. I moved as fast as I could, stealing a glance at Izidor. I noticed that he was holding his stomach and gasping for breath. We made for a hay-stack out at the base of the hills.

The haystack was our headquarters over the next two days. Sleep and eat was all we did, coming out only to relieve our-selves. We had severe cramps and diarrhea. Fuelling our condi-tion was our steady diet of apples, bread, and cheese. We were racked with pain, but still ravenous. Our provisions gone, we had to forage for more; we also needed to check on the status of the war. Barely able to walk, at sunrise we were back at the door of our last benefactor.

The previous Sunday we had taken a stab at proclaiming that we were refugees, Polish Catholics down on our luck, but honest and ready to do any kind of work. Encouraged by the farmer's interest, we now returned to his house. The farmer, wife, son, and daughter remembered us well. Right away, nothing would do but we must go to the hospital. Were they mad? We resisted the farmer's urging, pleading fear of the Nazis. He replied that he had it all figured out. We'd be travelling in his horse-drawn wagon and should we be stopped by a patrol, his story would be that he had picked us up at a train that was hit by an American bomb nearby: we were being taken to the hospital, suffering from shell-shock. Covered to our chins, my stomach rumbling out of rhythm with the wagon wheels, I stared up at the blue heavens and thought of nothing. At the city limits of Sušice I heard the guard challenging us in German. Our benefactor's story was air-tight. The same for admittance at the hospital. We were admitted wearing our pants and jackets inside out to hide the red stripes. The jacket was a giveaway though, the paint visible on the reverse side as well. The clothes were taken away by a nun in a black and white habit. I was hoping that the nuns would burn our clothes, but when I stumbled to the toilet the next day I noticed them being folded clean. Sušice was undoubtedly off the beaten track and nowhere near a camp, but surely the military were trained to spot escapees, and we would be shot on sight, stripes and all.

We were given a hot bath and had our heads shaved. I attempted to hide my tell-tale penis between my legs. I was weighed: eighty-eight pounds. I was getting the full treatment, nightgown and all. Our deliverer had disappeared. We were marched into a ward and put into beds with white sheets and feather pillows. Our condition had obviously been diagnosed because the food we got was mush. We were reeling with hunger but kept quiet. There were ten beds, five on each side of the room. All except two were occupied by men who looked pretty healthy. Only German was spoken. My optimism faded quickly. Every one of the German patients was a military type. One flame-headed brute, in a bed by the window, immediately started haranguing the nun to have us ejected. Something about us being unfit to share the ward with the heroic soldiers of the Fatherland. The nursing sister pretended not to understand and moved on. Across the aisle, a young boy whose black Hitler Youth uniform was draped over his chair muttered something unpleasant. I tried to ignore him. Izidor feigned sleep. Bored, the bullies left us alone.

The next morning after breakfast, our nun led in a man wearing a priest's cassock. He was light-haired, blue-eyed, and a bit paunchy. He sat down beside my bed and without as much as a how-do-you-do told me that he had come to take my confession. I quickly decided to try to make out that I didn't understand Czech and maybe he would leave me alone. My luck, the priest spoke excellent Polish. Now I was truly worried. There was no escape. Debilitated as I was, I racked my brain to find the right words. I confessed to stealing and lying. True enough. Frantically, I went through the motions of making a cross. It's possible that I started at the forehead, but it might easily have been the chest or even the shoulder. My Hebrew teacher could not have foreseen this emergency. The priest said little but placed a wafer in my mouth and strode over to Izidor's bed. Too scared to watch, I shut my eyes. I then decided to brazen it out and stole a glance at the priest. He had stood up and was staring at me strangely. The Nazis were at this point sitting up and taking notice. Our priest impassively took it all in, said something to the nun in an undertone and, from what I could see, left. After his departure Izidor and I held a hurried conference. Would the priest hand us over to the Germans? Did we get away with our mime? Most unlikely. But nothing happened.

The following day was just as uneventful except that the Germans were restless. A couple of them got dressed and left. Throughout the night we had heard noises and whispers. In the morning we heard strange voices in the corridor, and the last two Germans left. We had the entire ward to ourselves. The head nursing sister came in with our priest in tow. They brought two brand-new, black Hitler Youth uniforms. We were informed that the U.S. army was entering the town. The German armies had surrendered. We were free to go. The day was 8 May 1945. We were liberated on the last day of the war. Watching through the second-storey window, we noted passing tanks and trucks in green with a prominent white five-pointed star. Could it be the Russians and not the Americans? We said goodbye and took our leave. Near an American tank we found a half-eaten can of Spam.

The very first call we made was on the people who had helped us that first morning. Their daughter photographed us. In the picture Izidor and I are dressed in Hitlerjugend black, looking thin and holding on to a parcel. The back of the photo reads, 'Chmelna 8/5/1945.'

The parcel contained our concentration camp clothes, laundered, carefully folded, and wrapped by the nuns. We later abandoned it behind a barn.

Much later, I thought about the hospital. Like chicken soup, the confession and absolutions couldn't have hurt. It was possible that divine Providence had watched over us. I will never know. Mentioning the episode for the first time to my wife of thirty years, I remarked that my impersonation must have been convincing. 'I doubt it,' Freda said. In her view, the farmer knew our identity from the start. He confided in the nuns, who in turn consulted with the priest. To save us from the Germans, the priest had gone through the charade of taking our confessions.

The Japanese soldiers who, many years after Japan's surrender, were lured out of their jungle hide-outs, still ready to fight on, were much like us. Conditioning can make you believe anything. Izidor and I, walking out of the Catholic hospital in Sušice, were not certain that we were free and out of danger. We were not exhilarated that at last the war had ended. There was nothing to go back to, no family or home. We were sure that our continued survival depended on cunning. Surrounded by enemies, conceivably the only two of our faith for hundreds of miles around, doubtful if there were any other Jews left in all of Europe, we decided that posing as Polish Catholics was a plausible way to elude enemies.

On foot, we continued our journey to Žichovice. Our farmer friend, who had delivered us to the hospital, was glad to see us. Moreover, he made good on his promise to give us work. Exchanging congratulatory winks and smiles, we clambered up to the hayloft over the barn that was to be our sleeping quarters, certainly for the summer.

Below us were two horses, three cows, and a sow with piglets. The hayloft was filled with straw and last season's hay. Chickens moved about in and out of the barn, noisy roosters chasing after them. Facing the large yard were two sheds. One contained a fancy horse-drawn cart, to be pulled by a single horse, and a large utility wagon equipped to haul the crops, a two-horse affair. Near the barn was the other shed and a huge compost pile. The single-storey farmhouse, white with a sloping roof, faced the village lane. A gate at the side was usually kept locked except to let the wagons and animals in and out. A sense of prosperity and well-being oozed out of every corner of the large kitchen. Several big round loaves of bread were cooling on the sideboard and table.

The aroma of fresh bread was overpowering. We'd landed with both feet in heaven.

Work started early. There was a lot to do. The wife did the milking, fed the chickens, and did the household chores. The son, in his early twenties, shovelled out the manure, put down fresh straw for the horses, fed the pigs, and put out chopped straw and hay in a trough for the horses, and straw and fresh-cut grass for the cows. The father got equipment and the wagon ready for the day's work. Breakfast was early. Disappointingly, Izidor and I first had to finish off the previous week's bread before moving on to the newly baked loaves. However, the family ate the same food we did. As time went on I discovered that, as the bread was baked only once a week, stale bread was the norm. No matter.

The farm property consisted of many small parcels accumulated through shrewd purchases over the years. Some were planted with barley, others with wheat, a few had potatoes, and some were in hay. May was haying time, and a month later, hay was cut again. Father and son sharpened their scythes, put them over their shoulders, and marched off early to cut hay in a particular spot. Izidor and I followed shortly after, led by the wife who would also bring with her a basketful of bread, cheese, and coffee with milk and sugar for our lunch. Using rakes, we flipped the rows of cut hay so it would dry evenly, spread out in the sun. In good weather, after twenty-four hours, we gathered the hay and loaded it into the wagon. We tossed it up to the barn loft, making our bedchamber even more aromatic. Occasionally, when clouds threatened rain, we rushed out to the meadow and quickly raked up the not-quite-dry hay into piles. Then we waited for it to rain, in which case we got wet. As soon as the clouds passed or the rain stopped, we would spread out the hay again to dry. And if the rain started again we repeated the exercise.

The lunch menu never varied. The chores were not onerous. The days were sunny and long. Ever cautious, whenever we passed a holy statue or cross at the roadside on the way to rake or weed, our hats came off. The farmer eyed us questioningly, but said little and kept his own hat on. It didn't surprise me, as he told us that he was a Communist. But one could not be too careful.

The word was obviously out that two Polish fellows had been taken on by our farmer friend and that we would help with the harvest in late summer. This became evident one afternoon when another farmer, leading a gaggle of geese to feed on a low patch of green, stopped us on our way to move some hay around and suggested that we switch jobs. The geese needed handling, he explained. The work was much easier; we would only have to take the birds out in the morning and bring them back in the evening. A small sum of money was mentioned, as well as room and board. I'm proud to say that we turned him down. Money was not a factor, since our farmer had promised us a sum of money at harvest time. Besides, how could we be so ungrateful? However, what really tipped the scale against the goose man was the very idea of leading a pack of dumb geese every day. In a village short of labour, we were a hot property.

My stomach was still not back to normal. As well, my ankles and feet had swollen up. I wasn't too alarmed, as I had seen a lot of men with the same symptoms in the camps. What made it embarrassing was that I couldn't get to the outhouse fast enough to relieve myself. One morning our farmer discovered my not particularly well-concealed pile of evidence in the hay that was meant for his horses. He justly pointed out to me that the horses would reject it when it was mixed in with their fodder. I apologized and promised not to let it happen again. Soon enough, my stomach and feet were fine.

Izidor and I were sought out by a Polish couple with an infant daughter who had been in the village since the 1944 Warsaw Uprising. He, a tall, handsome man who spoke in an educated idiom, was a high-wire circus performer, at present unemployed. His wife, a pretty, petite, blonde woman, was also an artist. They had managed to hoodwink the German police by registering as Galicians. Under the Habsburgs, Galicia was the name of the southwestern section of Poland, including Kraków. The couple were delighted to meet two of their countrymen. If they suspected, or cared, that we might not be authentic Poles, they showed no sign.

Work went on. We were getting our strength back. The relations with our farmer were formal. Sometimes their daughter, a girl of fifteen or sixteen, would make snide remarks about my being Jewish. Two weeks went by. One Saturday, our farmer insisted that we accompany him in his horse-drawn wagon to a neighbouring town. Assuming that he wanted us to help him push the wagon uphill, which was often the case, we agreed. But he had other reasons. In town, a farmers' market was taking place when we arrived, but the three of us proceeded directly to a house facing the town square. After our farmer knocked on the door we entered a whitewashed room where there were a few chairs and a table. A man sat at the table. Our host explained to us that the man was a local Jew, and he felt that we would like to meet a fellow religionist. It seemed like some kind of a trick, to what purpose we had no idea. We were not going to be taken in. Danger lurked everywhere.

The possibly Jewish man had said nothing so far. We vehemently denied our Jewishness. Our farmer, obviously disappointed, suggested to the man that he take us into the next room and examine our penises. It sure looked like a set-up. The emotionless man perfunctorily asked us if we were Jewish. We said no. Without another word, our farmer took us back to the village. The matter was apparently closed. No more was said.

The personnel of B Battery of the 17th Field Artillery Observation Battalion, of the 8th Corps, attached to General George Patton's 3rd Army, was quartered outside the village. Their tents were pitched on a rise overlooking a stream. The troopers were young and friendly. Among the village kids Izidor and I stood out. We were older and thinner, and our scalps showed through where the hair was just beginning to grow in on our shaved heads.

Patton's 3rd U.S. Army had swept through southern Germany and into Czechoslovakia ahead of the main force. The soldiers had been through Buchenwald after it was liberated. Patton had stopped at Pilsen, having apparently agreed to let the Russians take Prague. Although our war experience was of a different sort, we had an immediate rapport with the soldiers. Soon we were trading fresh eggs for cigarettes. The GIs had watches that they had swiped from the Germans, and also German cameras that they were willing to offer in trade, but of such lofty financial heights we could only dream. We had precious little to trade. It was easy to make friends with the GIs. Soon we were spending more time hanging around the camp than working. Izidor and I became a fixture there. Cigarettes were accumulating in our loft, perhaps fifteen or twenty packs, substantial capital in those days. Our employer was good about it. We had been getting eggs from him for cigarettes and managed a profit in the trade. The cigarettes were to be our travel fund.

The American army was moving on, perhaps to France and then back to America. Our friends were gone, just as suddenly as they had come. After their departure, we began to see that farming was a dead-end occupation for us. We told our host that we wanted to try to get back home to Poland. He didn't try to persuade us to stay, although it must have been a blow to his plans for bringing in the crops. Early the next morning we bid the family goodbye and marched off to Sušice.

Arriving in Sušice at midday, we found the town square full of parked U.S. army trucks and armoured personnel carriers. GIs were moving about everywhere, eating, lounging on top of vehicles, walking down to the river to shave, wash, or do laundry. We now determined to declare our Jewishness and take our chances. The plan was simple. We would find an American soldier who looked Jewish, reveal our identity, and try to get him to let us travel with the army westward, into France. From there we planned to go on to Marseilles and across the sea to Palestine. Spotting a trooper who was definitely Jewish, we waited until he started walking, a towel around his neck, towards the river. We cautiously approached him and, pointing at ourselves, said 'Juif.' The man looked interested, but we got no further. He kept on walking. At no time did it occur to me to speak to him in Yiddish.

We gave up after this single attempt to come clean. We would make it to Palestine on our own. We were healthy, alert, and prepared for any emergency. We had a little money, enough to purchase railway tickets to get us out of Czechoslovakia, where the railway was actually running. Our easily barterable goods consisted of two or three cartons of Camels, Chesterfields, Sir Walter Raleighs, and Lucky Strikes. Bread and hard-boiled eggs complemented our arsenal. But we still wore the black Hitler Youth uniforms, which made us stand out among the locals.

At the railway station we purchased tickets to Klatovy, the next town west. Beyond Klatovy was Germany. The road to Palestine was either via Austria or Germany. First things first.

We met with catastrophe in Klatovy – or so it seemed at first. Getting off the train, we were arrested by the Czech police. They advised us that a transport was being assembled in Pilsen of stranded Poles who wished to return to their homeland. The train for Pilsen was leaving immediately, and it was our good fortune, we were told, to be in time for it. The message was clear: we were not welcome in Czechoslovakia. A soldier carrying a rifle led us back to the train. Going home with an armed escort! The whole thing smacked too much of everything we feared. They were sending us home, fare paid.

But was Poland home? There was nothing there for me. The ghetto population of Łódź had been sent to Auschwitz. Staszów was *Judenrein*, most likely. I was the only survivor in the family. Taking the train to Pilsen was out of the question. Once there, under heavy guard, it might be difficult to get out. Our escort was chatting up a girl passenger and had turned his back on us. We were the only ones inside the passenger car – the guard, Izidor, and I. The guard was blocking the door, and the girl was on the pavement outside. They were getting on well; he was making some headway. His uniform was nice and clean (I couldn't figure out how the Czech army had managed to get hold of first-rate uniforms so soon). It didn't take us long to discover that the passenger cars had doors on both sides. As the girl came up the car's steps, we quietly slipped out the opposite side. We crossed the tracks into town and freedom.

The affair had made us hungry. As it was time for lunch we headed for the city park. We hoped to buy some bottled water to go with our provisions. Whatever happened, we were free again.

Crossing the Klatovy town square on the way to a vacant

bench, we noticed a familiar vehicle parked nearby. We could hardly believe our eyes: it was a B Battery truck, and on it were our friends. Nothing would do but we must return with our buddies, they insisted, to their new lodgings. These turned out to be some eighteen miles distant. It had been sheer luck that the bored men had decided to take a run into town. While they got to rounding up their friends I happened to notice a familiar face staring at us. Meeting the man halfway, we rejoiced in the fact that we had jumped safely from the same Flessburg train. None of us were keen on returning to Poland. His plans were to stay put in Czechoslovakia for the time being. He told us he had heard that the Flessburg train had made it to the Mauthausen camp in Austria. We were glad we had jumped.

In the evening, we got to B Battery's new quarters and were assigned two army cots and blankets in one of the tents.

Battery B of the 17th Field Artillery Observation Battalion was billeted in a small inn near Klatovy. This area in the western part of Czechoslovakia was within the U.S. zone of occupation; Pilsen was its largest city. The Russians occupied the eastern part of the country, including Prague, the capital, and Slovakia. All this was on a temporary basis. It was understood that foreign troops would leave as soon as the Czechs got organized. Some Czechoslovakian military units wearing British uniforms with patches on their left shoulder saying 'Czechoslovakia' had begun to appear in our sector. They were part of the British and Canadian invasion forces and had fought their way through Holland and Germany. Czech police were around, and a civilian administration was in place. The country seemed untouched by the war.

The few rooms of the inn, above the bar-and-game room, dining room, and kitchen, were taken by the officers and NCOs. The GIs pitched their tents on the grounds. Everyone had settled in.

I'm not sure who spoke up for us, but we were taken into the bosom of the outfit. The captain agreed that we stay and help out in the mess. First Lieutenant Lis, who was Jewish, at our urgent request sometime later had the company clerk issue us a piece of paper verifying our existence. The paper read:

TO WHOM IT MAY CONCERN

This is to certify that the following person

MANYAK DRUKIER

is working now as a helper in our battery mess, and therefore is wearing the uniform of the U. S. Army.

He is awaiting a visa from the American consulate to be shipped to the United States.

Signed: Arnold Lis

30 July 1945

Affixed was a rubber stamp that read '17th FOB.' I now had an ID, an important item in a foreign land.

A mystique surrounded us 'Polacks' from the time we made contact with B Battery in Žichovice. The men had seen the conditions in Buchenwald first-hand. Possibly they felt sorry for Izidor and me, two Polish boys stranded in Czechoslovakia. After a while they had convinced themselves that their contribution to the war effort had been the liberation of Buchenwald. Though it hadn't – their duties were in the rear, to plot and advise the artillery – our presence testified to their version of events. A bit of harmless fiction that made everyone feel good and which Izidor and I did not feel inclined to dispute.

The unit had been conscripted and assembled from the greater New York, New Jersey, and Boston areas. There were only three or four career soldiers among them. The captain and the 'top kick' were positively army men. The Japanese were fighting on, and there were rumours that some of the men would go on to the Pacific theatre. However, there was general agreement that long-serving personnel and married men would be demobilized.

I got to know the GIs better and discovered that there were a few Jews in the outfit. I was befriended by the head cook, Milton Zeldis, a strapping, six-foot twenty-four-year-old, with curly hair and a sunny disposition. He had an enormous capacity for drinking and for finding women in the most unlikely places. In the evening after chow we would sometimes sit, and Milton would tell me about how he and his sister, orphaned at a young age, were raised by grandparents and an aunt, and about his love for his wife, Yetta, who had been his childhood sweetheart. Yetta had given birth to a daughter as Milton's ship was steaming towards England. Milton showed me pictures and regaled me with tales about the wondrous world of Brooklyn. A shoe-leather cutter by trade, Milton hoped to go into business on his own one day. Our conversation was in pidgin English, Yiddish, and German.

I asked Milton about stowing away on a ship sailing to America and what my chances were of not being caught and deported. I could hide out in Brooklyn forever, Milton assured me. He explained that the population density made one invisible. I thought about letting Milton in on our secret, and one evening I confessed that we were Jewish. Milton was pleased with the information, but perplexed about my insistence that he continue to address us as 'Polacks.' Hitler was dead, Germany had lost the war, yet we were still suspicious. Izidor had become friends with another GI, Milt Freeman, a Kosher butcher from Boston. Milt became another confidant.

Our job was ostensibly in the mess, but all the jobs there were taken. Even KP, washing up after meals, was done by GIs in rotation. The food was plentiful and good, all shipped in from the United States. We tasted, for the first time in six years, real coffee, oranges, cocoa, bananas, rice, and many other fine treats. The men, however, grumbled about the food. They did not like the powdered milk and eggs, frozen meat, and dehydrated potatoes. They demanded fresh vegetables. For the first time we came face to face with the phenomenon of the ethnic melting pot. The normal big-city mix was there, the groups, playfully referred to as 'Wops,' 'Micks,' and 'Hebes.' There was even one Chinese, who, however, kept to himself.

The men had a lot of time on their hands. On pay-days poker games would last until one or two GIs wound up with all the money. My Milton was either very good at it or just lucky. To avoid the temptation of gambling his winnings away, he sent them home to Yetta.

Although the inn was in a lovely setting, it was a bit isolated, and the distance to town made meeting girls something of a hit-and-miss affair for the men. Nonetheless, romances soon flared up. The girls were extremely pretty and well behaved, but communication was a bit of a problem. Thus, I took on another much-heralded function – that of interpreting – and acquired another piece of paper, which read:

BTRY "B" 17th. FA. OBSN. BN.
APO 403   U.S. ARMY
21 November 1945.

To whom it may concern:

Maniek Drukier, has been associated with the 17th. F.O.B. for the past six months, having been taken from Buchenwald.

This person speaks Polish, Czechis [sic], German, and English. He has served well interpreting and working in the Mess.

He has been clothed and fed by this organization. It will greatly be appreciated if consideration be given him for a job.

EDWARD J. BANNON CAPT.

I was often requested to write or translate love notes. Reading the girls' notes was seldom difficult. Anyway, I could extrapolate at will. Writing was another matter. Just what these notes said, dictated in English, translated and written in my own Polish/ Czech, I can only imagine. I hoped I didn't break up too many liaisons.

New uniforms or shoes were issued in exchange for worn items. Izidor and I obtained two changes of U.S. army-issue clothes. A local seamstress made alterations. I put on some weight and started to look presentable. A couple of the younger local girls took an interest in me. I became friendly with one, a blue-eyed, dark-haired beauty whose older sister had a boyfriend in B Battery, and I visited their home once. The other was a younger, light-haired girl, who dropped over every afternoon. The girls obviously wanted to be friends, but I was unsure how to handle this development.

Near our inn were houses abandoned in an apparent hurry by their German occupants. Looking through the junk strewn about I found a copy of *Mein Kampf* signed by the author. I thought of keeping it, but, on reflection, decided to burn it. I also found a satchel full of old Reichsmarks, photographs, dishes, pots and pans – all stuff we couldn't use. A small box containing various foreign coins appealed to me and I brought it back to my tent.

On a trip into Klatovy I learned about a Jewish family there. We visited the people in their home. There were four of them, the parents and two gorgeous teenage daughters. There was nothing the matter with my taste; all the girls I met were beautiful. I asked how they had survived the war and got an unsatisfactory explanation. They showed me yellow Stars of David that they had had to wear, and gave me one. I suspected that the mother was Christian – perhaps that made a difference in Klatovy. I wanted to stay longer, but the situation got awkward when two boys showed up to take the girls to a party. We said goodbye. On reflection, I was a hybrid – not a GI, not a Czech – too young, crude, and clumsy. Not much of a catch.

Izidor and I gold-bricked, boxed, played catch baseball, and helped dole out food at meal times. Some dishes were more popular than others. Spinach was hard to sell. One day, when canned spinach happened to be on the menu, two Nazis awaiting trial at the local jail were brought in to clean out a garbage dump. When their turn came to eat, I dropped enormous dollops of spinach on their plates. What was intended as punishment was interpreted by them as an act of sympathy – a look of surprise and appreciation came over the men's faces at the size of their portions.

Weeks passed. In August we learned about Hiroshima and, thereafter, the surrender of Japan. The men were overjoyed. The spectre of fighting another war had disappeared. Three officers left for home, but there was insufficient sea transport to return the millions of troops to America at once. In September, the two Milts, Izidor, I, and two others drove to Pilsen for High Holy Day services. A U.S. chaplain officiated. The services were brief, and no one paid the slightest attention to us. It hadn't occurred to the Milts to introduce us to the army chaplain, who might have helped us in some way.

I was unaware of it then, but time was rapidly running out for me to make up for my lost school years. Temporarily safe with the GIs, I knew that it was only a matter of weeks before our good friends went home. Soon it was Milton's turn to go. He promised to send for me and gave me a five-dollar bill. It was, he said, for me to hold on to to pay for the bottle of spirits we'd share when we celebrated my arrival in America. Some months later in Germany, I received an affidavit sworn out by Milton Zeldis sponsoring my immigration to the United States. It stated that he was employed by the Phoenix Slipper Company and that his earnings were fifty-five dollars per week.

Just before the atomic bomb was dropped, I got a taste of real army life. The battalion went on manoeuvres. We moved out in full battle gear and joined up with an artillery unit. No shots were fired, but a lot of instrument-plotting took place. We slept in tents and got our meals from a field kitchen. A persistent rain broke up what the men called a 'picnic.' I tasted Jell-O for the first time in my life, one of the boys having received a packet of it by mail from his mother. In October orders came in to pack up for Marienbad. B Battery was assigned to the Florida Hotel. Two to a room, we were in the lap of luxury. In the heyday of the Austro-Hungarian Empire, Marienbad was a water-cure centre of some renown. I sampled the water and found it distasteful, so it must have been other pleasures that Marienbad had to offer that brought the rich and wasteful.

More GIs were leaving. To bring the battery up to strength, men from another unit joined us. We were hosts now to the new mess sergeants, Italian fellows from St Louis who were interested in a good time. Our recruits hailed from Kentucky, Arkansas, Missouri, and Washington state and were a slightly wilder lot than our former mates. I had little to do in the mess. Because of the rapid depletion of personnel, a few cooks and waitresses were taken on. I guess the brass figured that since we stayed in a hotel we might as well live like it. The new help were Sudeten Germans; their days were numbered, too, as the Czechs wanted them out.

In the fall of 1945 the entire hotel strip was taken over by a jubilant U.S. force. But it was a fact that the 8th Corps would be disbanded and that Patton was up to his neck in trouble. The other news was that B Battery was ordered to arrange for a nightclub to entertain the weary army of occupation. The sergeant in charge of the detail sought me out to help get it organized. I volunteered to obtain samples of supplies from the depot. My English had progressed to the point where I could rapidly spout entire lines of army slang. Overconfidence was my undoing here. Misreading the list, I brought soup instead of soap to the nightclub. I resigned from my supply-requisitioning job.

The cabaret turned out to be a lot of fun. Music blared – Bing Crosby, Glenn Miller, Duke Ellington, and Hoagy Carmichael. Posted at the door, where admission was free to enlisted men and restricted only by the number of persons the place would hold (a lot), I fastidiously and arbitrarily directed traffic. One busy night I refused a lone soldier entry by laconically saying, 'Can't see it,' a favourite expression in 17 FOB. The boy said something uncomplimentary about my English, and that soured me on door duty. My decision the following night to join the revellers was not something I enjoyed thinking about afterwards. I got very drunk and argumentative and had to be carried to our hotel. Waking in the morning in a pool of vomit, I decided never to get drunk again. I had just turned seventeen.

In town there were a lot of girls and women, and the GIs told me that some had not had the pleasures of a man's company for years. Their boyfriends and husbands were in POW camps, or they may have been dead. Pretty well all of them were Sudeten German. The set-up in the hotel made meeting them more *gemütlich*. One or two of the boys even got rooms in a small hotel across the street, for total privacy. Our waitresses tried to learn to speak English, but the chaps taught them only swear words.

The Rest and Recreation department also took over an enemy riding academy. I made use of it too. The itch to travel persisted. Every week a truck would go up to the main supply depot, a two-hour drive. The depot and its large fleet of trucks were manned by an all-black company of soldiers. On one trip I spotted a young refugee, obviously Jewish, walking about the compound in an army shirt and pants. Although I tried to make eye contact with him and jumped off the truck, the boy avoided me and walked off. Seeing him made me realize there were other survivors, boys like us among them. On the return trip a vehicle passed us; in it were Russian soldiers. I had no idea what they were doing in an American-controlled area. As we passed them I tossed a bunch of bananas into the open truck. In return I got a salute.

The truck full of Russians made me reflect on how close we were to Łódź. For about six months Izidor and I had led a sheltered, isolated existence. Our everyday contacts were with the GIs; we ate American and conversed American. Of the world around us, we had no news. There was only one radio, located in the mess, and it was tuned to the Armed Forces station, Radio Luxembourg; I was able to understand only some of the English. The GIs talked almost exclusively about going home. The newspapers were in Czech and hardly of interest.

To protect the civilian population from starvation, the U.S. expeditionary force was forbidden to acquire food locally. One day, however, tired of eating powdered eggs for breakfast, our master sergeant decided to go out and see if we could barter cigarettes for fresh eggs. I went along, as interpreter. We drove into the country, stopping at farmhouses, picking up half a dozen eggs here and there. It was November. The leaves had fallen, and the birds were flying south in great flocks. As we drove through the countryside, we flushed all sorts of fowl. We even spotted a deer standing calmly in a clearing, head down, nibbling on the grass. My companion carefully took the army rifle out of the weapons' carrier, took aim, and shot. We loaded the deer onto the truck and covered it with leaves and branches. The animal's eyes stayed open, big and brown. A select few of us had tough venison for dinner.

Just before dark, the truck had a mechanical problem. I wasn't much help. I couldn't ride a bicycle, which we could have borrowed to get help, and there were no horses to ride. The sergeant stayed with the vehicle and eggs, while I walked off to look for help. Somehow, I found a U.S. army post. The guard was suspicious. I offered my recently acquired ID. He read it, and I explained our dilemma. I must have made a case because the next thing I knew, I was in a jeep with a mechanic. The sergeant and I arrived back late, but the men had fresh eggs for breakfast. No one asked questions.

My predilection for innovation landed me in trouble. Our storeroom was full of cocoa, rice, and other unpopular supplies. On my recommendation we served hot chocolate instead of coffee one morning. A near-riot ensued. Pleading ignorance, I was forgiven.

On Thanksgiving we had turkeys and cakes baked in big pans. I suggested and helped make *brezelech* to put on top: years earlier, I had seen my mother make a mixture of butter, sugar, and flour into crumbs. It was my favourite part of the cake, and we even baked the leftovers separately. The turkeys and cakes with crumble were consumed without comment.

I made many new friends among the GIs who joined us in Marienbad. One of them was an aspiring policeman from the Bronx, by the name of Banks. He was Jewish and offered to act as an intermediary in locating my Aunt Frieda in Toronto, my mother's younger sister who had been in Canada since 1928. Together, Banks and I wrote a letter to the Canadian Jewish Congress in Toronto. I also visited the office of the Red Cross and addressed a letter via them to the janitor of number 6 Gdańska in Łódź, inquiring if any of my family had been back to our apartment. The international mail was still not functioning, but I was able to use the U.S. army postal service. I had no idea whether my mother or sister were alive, and I had no way of finding out.

At last I met some Jewish people in Marienbad. First, there were a father and daughter, survivors from Hungary. The girl, Ruth, was a stunning redhead of about twenty. The father convinced me that I would need money once the troops left. (So far Izidor and I had managed well without it.) Their apartment was a few doors away from the hotel, and one dark night I hauled over one of the bags of cocoa and one of rice. I gratefully pocketed their money, but I never did it again, even though cocoa and rice were piling up in the storeroom. The other encounter was with two men, a father and son, Polish Jews who were stranded in Marienbad. They wanted to rejoin their friends in the U.S. zone in Germany and hoped to enlist my help in smuggling them across the border. I was offered thirty dollars to find room for them on an army truck going west, but I declined. In talking to them, I learned that there were Jewish survivors in both Germany and Poland.

In December we got news that the battalion would be demobilized. Izidor and I discussed the future with our friends. Our options were few. There was no doubt that the U.S. Army of Occupation would stay on in Germany for a long time and that Zeldis's affidavit would reach me eventually. Also, Milt Freeman had promised to sponsor Izidor. Some of the girls left behind by our boys came to bid a tearful goodbye. Early one morning our convoy pulled out.

The notice to pack and leave had been posted a few days before. It had to come sooner or later, but it was a shock to Izidor and me just the same. What to do? Go with B Company as far as France and take our chances trying to stow away on a Liberty Ship destined for the United States? Security was reportedly tight. Stay on in Czechoslovakia and risk deportation to Poland? Go a certain distance with the men and let ourselves be dropped off somewhere in Germany? Lulled into a sense of false security, we had forgotten how precarious our position was. Hardly anyone showed concern for our plight – after all, we were strangers to these new men. Our friends from Sušice and Klatovy were back in America. We decided to leave with the convoy.

On the night before departure I visited Ruth and her father to say goodbye. The father was out, but Ruth, the remarkable redhead, was in, reclining on the couch. It was late. The two of us talked a bit. I was nervous in the company of a real woman. We agreed that the chances of seeing each other again were slim. I'm not sure how it came about. I leaned over, or she raised herself, and we kissed fully on the mouth. Astonished at my audacity, savouring the surprisingly sweet taste of the girl's lips, I made for the door, where I hesitated. Returning to the again-reclining Ruth, I stopped, leaned over, and received her partially opened lips. What to do next I didn't know. Confused, I retreated, and made for the door.

We soon passed the Czech border post, still within the U.S. zone of occupation, which stretched from Pilsen to Mannheim. The 17th FOB, the entire batallion, was travelling in about forty army trucks and jeeps. Destination – the French coast for embarkation to the United States.

The convoy reached Bamberg and proceeded to Würzburg. It was cold. A fine icing of snow covered the fields and trees. We passed bombed-out towns. To refuel, the drivers used the cans of gasoline stored on the rear of their vehicles. Provisions were C rations. We were wheeling non-stop to Calais. At Mannheim, on the Rhine, the bridges were down, and a rickety pontoon bridge was the only way across.

Slowly, the vehicles made it to the other side, to the ruins of Ludwigshafen, in the French zone of occupation. Around us were moonlike craters of desolation. There was not a single undamaged building in the whole city. People, mostly women, pushed carriages or wheelbarrows containing clothing or household articles. They came out of basements or holes in the ground. There was no traffic. All was quiet, very quiet.

Our cavalcade motored into this scene, the lead vehicles waiting on the west side for the balance to catch up. I had come off the truck to stretch my legs, joining other men already on the ground. A discussion ensued about our uncertain future. At this moment one of the lieutenants came by. Seeing Izidor and me beside the truck he expressed surprise that we had not disembarked somewhere along the way. He explained that it was against regulations to have us on board, and he would not risk taking us across the border into France. Unceremoniously, our duffle bags were dumped on the roadway. The trucks pulled away and were gone. And so, duffle bags on our shoulders, we made our way back to the pontoon bridge.

Both ends of the bridge were guarded by armed Polish troops wearing American uniforms dyed black. They were young, not much older than we were. Our U.S. uniforms were our pass across the river and to the ruined railway station on the other side. We took stock of the situation and agreed that somehow we had to make it to Frankfurt. Back in Marienbad, I had learned that some surviving Jews had turned up in Frankfurt as well as in Munich. The war had ended seven months ago, but around us was a wasteland. Late that same evening a long train pulled into the station and immediately filled with men and women dressed, or rather wrapped, in civilian and military articles of clothing. Some, unable to get in, hung onto the doors. Many lay or sat on top of the passenger cars. A few tried to climb in through the windows. The roofless station was crowded with refugees, all waiting to go anywhere where there was food and shelter.

The car reserved for the U.S. military was full, too, but we made our way into it. Sitting on our duffle bags in the forward vestibule, we ignored the enlisted men's suspicious stares. Into the cold night, puffing white smoke from the coal-fired engine, the train pulled out of Mannheim. We were on our way to Frankfurt.

Our half-year sojourn with the 17th FOB in Czechoslovakia, where GIs dated local girls and where some sort of peacetime normalcy reigned, did not prepare Izidor and me for what happened next: A female train conductor gave us only a sidelong glance as she passed to enter the car full of soldiers. At first we heard squeals and laughter, then silence. The conductor remained with the soldiers for several hours, emerging only when the train pulled into a bombed-out Frankfurt *Bahnhof* in the early morning.

Frankfurt was no better than Mannheim. Levelled houses, gaping holes, walls without roofs, rubble everywhere. On enquiring, we learned the location of a Jewish home for refugees and orphans. It was a house on a residential street, one of the few buildings left standing. We paid off the elderly German who led us there, pulling our duffle bags along on a dolly. A father and daughter, German Jews, were in charge. After Marienbad, a room full of rows of bunkbeds was not an appealing prospect. Izidor and I stayed the night and left on the morning train for Nuremberg.

Personally, I was sorry to leave so abruptly. The night before I had exchanged a few words with the daughter, a freckle-faced girl about my age whom I found appraising me with her large green eyes. She said little. I would have liked to get to know her. But we were young men on the move.

We chose Nuremberg on the advice of two fellows sharing our room. These men, actually boys in their late teens, were involved in the black market. They had brought sugar and bacon to sell in Frankfurt and, having completed the deal, were on their way back east.

The railway station in Fürth, sister city to Nuremberg, was amazingly intact, but full of people who had made it their temporary 'permanent' home. We followed our new-found friends to their hostel in a small apartment owned by a German lady who rented floor space in exchange for food or goods. The place was not far from the station and warm. The landlady made coffee.

We kicked around the topic of what to do next. There was obviously a thriving black market in food, clothing, dollars, and cigarettes. Reichsmarks were circulating. I was dismayed. In Czechoslovakia the GIs were being paid in money called 'script' issued by the U.S. High Command, and I was under the impression that it was the only legal currency. However, it turned out that in order not to disrupt the fragile economy the authorities permitted the circulation of Hitler's currency. Unaware of this anomalous situation I had discarded as worthless a suitcase filled with Reichsmarks in large denominations. I had found the valise in the summer in the loft of an abandoned house in a small town in Czechoslovakia.

I rejected the idea of becoming involved in the black market. I wanted secure employment with a unit of the U.S. army. Izidor agreed.

Regensburg and Schwandorf were supposed to be in relatively good shape, and this was where our friends advised us to go. We rose early to make the train. We followed the street that ended at the square in front of the railway station. There was rubble here too. Suddenly, I remembered that I had in my army coat pocket a pistol I'd found in some abandoned house and had unthinkingly picked up. That cold morning it occurred to me that the penalty for carrying a concealed weapon was severe. Martial law was still in force. I dropped the gun into a charred hole in a burned-out bank building.

18
In the Orphanage

Neuburg, just south of Regensburg, had a few things going for it in January 1946. It had been untouched by the war. A sleepy fifteenth-century walled town with quaint crooked streets and only one tavern open for business, it became the locale where I again hooked up with the U.S. army.

Second Lieutenant Boyd Burton of Company F, 405th Infantry, interviewed Izidor and me, and, shaking his head in wonder at our stated proficiency in four languages, took us on. It meant three meals a day and a room with two cots. Marienbad it wasn't.

At the outskirts of the town the Americans had taken over three low buildings. The company, a unit that came over after the fighting had stopped, was to be the garrison for the area. Company F had been moved a couple of times before they found a permanent home here.

In Neuburg there was nothing for GIs to do. The district had been pacified long ago. Anyway, there were no German males here under sixty who were not crippled. But there were lots of women, women hungry for food, and for men.

The GIs received a lot of attention from the girls. At night they would come and rap on the windowpanes. What could one do but let them in from the cold? Soon every man in the outfit had one or two sweethearts. Ten years of National Socialist indoctrination making relations with foreigners *verboten* was now clearly out the window. Soon the problem became how to keep the company mess functioning with so many more mouths to feed. In double-quick time Izidor and I became redundant. There was little to interpret, as the couples got along well with sign language. The natives were so friendly that the men wondered why it had taken so long to win the war. The captain and lieutenant rarely left their cots.

What made me quit without giving notice was that one afternoon while we were out getting haircuts, one or two GIs broke into our room and ransacked it, taking only some gold coins from a coin collection. I wasn't particularly attached to the collection, as I had found it only about two or three months before. However, I was peeved at the intrusion and walked out in disgust, leaving the balance of the coins for the rip-off artists to choke on for all I cared.

We trooped up to the *Bürgermeister*'s office and made a demand for accommodations and double-ration cards, our entitlement as ex-camp inmates as decreed by the U.S. Army High Command. The accommodations turned out to be a room in the house of a Nazi, an older man with a wife and daughter, who, needless to say, was not enraptured by our intrusion into his peace-loving home. As for the food ration cards, they were a joke. The coupons offered at controlled prices larger portions of black bread, margarine, and chopped meat, or your choice of smaller quantities of white buns, butter, and sausages. Growing boy that I was, and having developed an appetite for better things, I chose sausages, buns, and butter. A month's coupons netted me about four or five decent lunches.

Everyone who was someone among the DPs in town hung around the tavern, which offered coloured soda water, a thin soup, and ersatz coffee. But it was a place to see and be seen. Ivan, a former Russian captain, asked to be called Irek and spoke only in Polish. He said that he had been taken prisoner in the Crimea and had spent time in a German POW camp. He was liberated by the U.S. army and went home, only to be arrested and accused of being a traitor for having surrendered to the enemy. Calculating his chances of clearing himself to be not very good, he fled and returned to Germany. Once burned by his own, he decided to be of Polish nationality and had the ID to prove it. He was strong and could bend nails with his fingers.

Henryk was a skinny, sex-obsessed Pole who came in every

morning when the tavern opened and spent the entire day at a corner table. He was on a day pass from the local jail, where he awaited trial for killing a German, because, Henryk said, the German had given him 'fishy' looks. His sexual bragging usually involved a count of his recent orgasms. He had me convinced he was telling the truth until I remembered that he spent all his nights in jail.

There was also Władek, who hung around Jewish boys and wanted to be circumcised. I think I made a good case for him not to go through with it when I pointed out that sometimes the knife slipped. Besides, there were no *Mohels* left.

Jan was the only Gypsy left in the world, or so he claimed. He was punched sometimes for grabbing people's hats and trying them on. Adam, the 405th Infantry's barber, had a Ukrainian girlfriend who was lovely to look at, and he earned real money giving haircuts. Shmuel would drop in, and we would admire his polished riding boots. Wladek's roommate Icik was tolerated because Wladek was a regular guy. I talked to Pincus, or Paul, as he preferred to be called, who liked girls and did some black-market trafficking.

Girls dropped into the tavern now and then. For over four years – a crucial four years for a teenager – I had not exchanged more than a few words with any female, let alone carry on a conversation with one my own age. I don't think the fact that the girls were German had anything to do with the brash and arrogant stance I now affected. My coarse attitude and audacious manner, learned partly through my exposure to the world of soldiers, helped mask a great deal of fear, curiosity, longing, and shyness. The tavern, run by a Nazi woman well past her prime, closed at seven, so we saw the girls only in daylight, without benefit of the forgiving shadows of evening. We consequently found them less than attractive, and they were hardly scintillating conversationalists – they were too preoccupied with hunger to bother. One girl, though, I quite liked. She was flat-chested and had long, straight blonde hair. She told me right off that she was the oldest child in a family of seven who had been driven out of East Prussia and were now lodged in a nearby village, where they were cold and starving. I couldn't summon much sympathy, since practically everyone not lucky enough to have settled in somewhere was in the same situation. Nonetheless, I listened to her with rapt attention, as I was fascinated by her huge, solemn, luminous brown eyes set in a small, thin face. One time she wanted to go home with me, but we were overheard by the Nazi woman, who managed to put her two pfennigs in and kill the plan. Sometime later, at the communal bathhouse, I met a Polish *Volksdeutsch* girl with whom I didn't have to speak German; we became friends.

There wasn't much to buy in town, and we didn't have much money. But there was a shoemaker who did a thriving business making riding boots. A carry-over from the fashion-conscious Prussian officer corps, boots were popular with the crowd that met at the tavern. Izidor wanted a pair of riding boots. We counted out our money and agreed that with careful handling it would do for about five weeks of black market grocery shopping, or a sharp pair of boots. Izidor wanted the boots. We agreed to postpone the decision.

Black marketeering didn't appeal to me, but smuggling on a grand scale did. I still had the five-dollar bill that Milton had given me in Klatovy, and with this capital ready, I approached Pincus and suggested that we take American cigarettes to Prague. There they would fetch a premium price. On the strength of my knowledge of Czech and my ability to read railway timetables, Pincus assented to form a partnership. On the black market we bought twenty cartons of Lucky Strikes and Camels and two mornings later we took the train to the Czech border. A heavy snow had fallen. The little station we got off at was snowed in. Our inquiries about hiring a guide to lead us across the border brought the response that new footprints left in the snow were easy for the Czech border guards to spot and that it would be better if we waited. It got dark. We spread our coats on the station floor and rested.

Two Sudeten women beside us had just come from the Czech side. They were waiting for the morning train to take them west. We talked a bit and tried, all four of us, to stay close together for warmth. One of the women, who appeared to be an albino, was married, with a husband at home – a rarity. She had nice hands. I didn't like the gist of the conversation. The women told us that the Czechs were starting to get nasty with smugglers – something to the effect that those who were caught were being sent to work in the coal mines. I wasn't even aware that the Czechs had coal mines. The women kept giggling, making it impossible to get a peaceful night's rest. We had arranged for a tracker/guide to take us across in the morning; instead, we took the same train back.

For Pincus the exercise wasn't a total loss, as it turned out to be for me. Halfway home we met two ladies on the train, but when Pincus picked the younger one I went to sulk in another car. Paul sold the cigarettes back in Neuburg at a small profit, as a temporary scarcity had driven the prices up. Since he would have to convert the marks he received for the cigarettes into dollars on the underground market, I had to wait for the return of my five-dollar bill.

My only business venture a fiasco, I gave up. Two or three days later I said goodbye to my Polish Volksdeutsch friend and took the train to investigate the UNRRA (United Nations Relief and Rehabilitation Administration) children's home in Indersdorf, near Dachau in Bavaria. Two weeks later I was back to see Paul and to retrieve my five dollars. Paul was pleasant about it and counted out five singles. I put in an objection and demanded a five-dollar bill. The matter got no further, as he had only singles, or so he claimed. But as far as I was concerned I was getting less than I had put in. Dollar bills were, at that time, considered inferior to fives or tens. I told him I would be back in town in two weeks and would see him then and would he please have the five dollars for me in one piece. I heard a little later that Pincus had gone off to Palestine – with my five dollars.

In 1946 UNRRA provided funds and personnel to set up its Indersdorf children's home in a convent. We learned about the home's existence via the DP grapevine. The money we had brought with us from Marienbad was running out. It made excellent sense to find a place where we would get meals and a bed for free. There was also talk that it was possible to get visas to America through this UNRRA-run place.

We slept six or eight to a room, had three meals a day and, infrequently, lessons in auto mechanics, Hebrew, arithmetic, and how to love thy neighbour. Nuns did the housekeeping without undue resentment. We were an exotic lot. Group A included infants up to one year old. Where they came from and who their parents were we never learned. Group B comprised boys and girls aged eight to seventeen and was divided into subgroups: Polish youngsters; Jewish boys age sixteen to eighteen from Poland, Czechoslovakia, Ukraine, Hungary, and Germany, and four Jewish girls; and a few Christian boys and girls from places like Estonia and Yugoslavia.

The Jewish youngsters, with few exceptions, had made it through the camps and were orphans. I didn't know what the Christians' status was. Not counting the babies, we added up to about ninety.

Aside from the usual friction among diverse personalities, there was general harmony. I suppose we were so happy at having at last a roof over our heads and regular meals that the best of our natures came to the fore. The routine revolved around meals, which were nourishing but nearly devoid of meat, desserts, or good bread. The food was mostly mush.

Classroom instruction was intermittent and haphazard, because of the lack of pencils, paper, textbooks, and a curriculum. Some, like me, hadn't attended school in seven years. Our common language was German. Another problem was the absence of qualified instructors. Not for a moment did we think the situation strange. The Polish kids received a fair amount of instruction in Polish: we didn't participate, because we did not consider ourselves Polish nationals any longer. There was no personal animosity; in fact, we often got along better with the Poles than with the Hungarian Jews. But with our families wiped out, we did not look back. Our eyes were focused on the United States, Canada, or Palestine.

At times we were told to sit in a classroom and listen to a lecture on musical notes and scales. Other times we copied letters of the Hebrew alphabet from the blackboard. We got lessons in auto mechanics from an engineer, a particularly handsome, light-complexioned Jewish man in his early thirties who had, with his pretty and similarly light-skinned wife, made it through the occupation on Aryan papers. Well educated, they both hailed from Kraków, where 'high' Polish is spoken. The wife was also going to teach a subject at the home, but the pair left to go back to Poland before she could start. Some days before their departure they were visited by the wife's brother, a lieutenant in the Polish army. Perhaps he had talked the teachers into returning. I had an opportunity to discuss with them the disadvantages of a Jewish identity. Under no circumstances would they bring children into the world, the husband said, but if they were to change their mind and have a son, circumcision was out of the question.

The Hebrew teacher taught us pioneer Zionist marching songs, which we sang lustily, if off-key. For calisthenics we had an Estonian teacher who, some said, had competed in the Olympics. Arithmetic was a hit-and-miss affair. It was spring, then summer. Our desires and ideas ranged from getting extra food and more clothing to finding a way to make a few marks, to girls, to figuring out how to get out of Indersdorf.

For more reasons than one could think of, Europe was a write-off. Almost daily, new kids arrived. No recruiting drive was in progress; they had simply heard somewhere, just as I had, that in Indersdorf, if you were under eighteen, lost, and not German, you could get shelter, food, and maybe a ticket out.

Everyone had a story to tell and, if permitted, would tell it. We listened patiently to many lurid tales. One afternoon two sisters and a brother reported in. They were of mixed parentage (*mischlunge*), from Berlin. The three had managed to remain at home throughout the war. Their Jewish father had been taken away and not heard from since. We gave them the once-over and found them dull. Later we learned that the older sister had been raped by members of the victorious Red Army.

Once, two brothers, one fifteen and the other seventeen, checked in, claiming to be Belgians. Blue-eyed, blond, with good haircuts, decent clothes and shoes, and speaking an excellent idiomatic German, they showed up for lunch one day. Handling their forks and knives correctly and saying, 'Please pass the salt,' they made a poor impression on us. I decided to test them on their knowledge of French. I knew no French, and neither did anyone else. The first question I posed was, 'How do you say "boy" in French?' The older one looked perplexed and said 'Jacques,' which I marked as incorrect. From that point on we called all their definitions wrong. After lunch the boys packed up, and clutching their valises, left. The audacity of the Germans hoping to get a free ticket to America riled us.

A Hungarian Jew, who was marvellous on the piano and who could sing, too, joined our select group. Claiming to be seventeen, he looked about twenty-seven. Another pair of Hungarian brothers, actually from Ruthenia in the Carpathian Mountains, which had gone from Czech to Hungarian control, had decided that the older one would sign in as being the younger. No matter. The older boy liked to jump. Tall and slender, he considered himself an athlete and took ever-longer leaps. One evening he jumped out of a second-storey window to our applause, and sprained both ankles.

A Romanian Jewish boy found himself a German girlfriend in town and said that he might marry her, as she had an uncle in Chicago. The few Jewish girls in our group were possibly older than I was. On paper, it was a good idea to be young. The cut-off age for the special U.S. visas was eighteen. In any event, I was tolerated, possibly even liked, but I was not a contender. The Polish girls were younger, but there was a sort of unwritten rule that we didn't pester them, and, in return, the Gentile boys would keep to themselves. Likely, there was little in the way of amours going on. Certainly, we lacked experience.

Red Cross parcels started to arrive. Two Polish and two Jewish boys were assigned to unpack and sort out the stuff. I was one of the four. Canned meat, cheese, tuna, powdered eggs and milk, soap, sugar, macaroni, crackers, chocolates, and cigarettes made up the contents. The last two items were of interest, and the four of us tied our pants at the ankles to hold them. Every afternoon for over a week we came out of the kitchen where the unpacking took place, walking like astronauts.

Yosel and I didn't smoke, and our stash was getting too big to store under our beds. Besides, we risked discovery and disgrace, or worse. Fortunately, on a visit to neighbouring Dachau – the town, not the infamous camp – I met a man I knew from the Kielce HASAG. He had survived with his wife and four-year-old son. The three of them had been brought into the camp in 1943 with a group of adults. The German guards, noticing a baby among them, didn't react as expected. The baby stayed. I had lost track of the family but here they were, settled in a fine apartment in Dachau. Mr Szlafsztajn, the husband, was a clever business-man. He offered to buy our hoard and even pick us up in his automobile. He met us down the street at the agreed time, and Yosel and I, struggling with the bundles of loose cigarette packs, got into the car. Yosel at this juncture had an attack of the shakes and kept blabbering that we were being followed. White as a sheet, he wrung his hands and kept repeating that it was curtains for us. My nerves were in relatively good order. We had to wait for the pay-off as our fence had an appointment with a Dachau barber who, we learned, came to his apartment every day to give him a shave and light trim. Our fence had style.

With money in my pocket, I debated ways of spending it. First I tried to buy a small lamb from a farmer, but he wouldn't part with it. Just as well. I had not thought the thing through, like who would slaughter, skin, and cook it? But I could almost taste the meat as I kept staring at the lamb and offering the anti-Semitic German any reasonable sum of money. He wouldn't be budged. I moved on to other deals. The lamb said 'beh.'

A certain lady in the village raised pigeons. A friend and I had one each for lunch one bright day. Small, bony, sad, they looked as if someone had run them over with a truck. The taste was below my expectations.

A suit of clothes. Definitely, I needed a suit. A made-to-measure kind of a suit. Because one day I would go to America and to get off the ship not wearing a suit would cause me shame. The only working German tailor in Indersdorf had a limited selection of cloth. Measurements taken, I closed my eyes and with index finger pointed at a bolt of cloth. A heavy, grey ersatz wool, it would have to do.

In late summer, 1946, our population had outgrown the convent's fifteen or so rooms. We moved on to Prien am Chiemsee. All the Jewish kids went into one lakeshore hotel, the Poles and the rest into another about two miles down the road. Chiemsee, a calm lake bordered on one side by the Austrian Alps and on our side by the pine-covered rolling hills of Bavaria, was beautiful. On lovely grounds, right on the water, the hotel was in the four-star range, and even had a few rowboats. We barely gave it a passing grade and concentrated instead on getting the hell out.

The setting was great for picture taking, though. We all knew that we would soon go our separate ways, as our periodic visits to the U.S. consulate in Munich for examinations gave us reason to believe, and so we went on a picture-taking binge. A cigar box full of black and white photos taken with little box cameras testified to our desire for immortality. Group pictures, pictures on backs of trucks, pictures behind wheels of other people's cars, posed pictures, pictures with inscriptions in Polish, German, and Yiddish. They stated without exception that the memories of an extraordinary place and time would remain with us, and that I had been a true and loyal comrade.

Smack in the centre of the lake was an island on which Mad King Ludwig of Bavaria had built a palace. He had all the rooms mirrored – walls, ceilings, the works. We went there but weren't impressed. We made faces in the mirrored walls and columns. Perhaps there are studies on the effects of early trauma and arrested development on adolescents that would explain our juvenile behaviour. One of the symptoms we shared was crying when hurt or distressed. Seventeen- and eighteen-year-old boys, we would often be seen with tears running down our cheeks, sniffling and generally behaving like babies. Some of us hadn't cried for many years.

Our hotel had a large ballroom, and dances were held there. The Poles came over, but somehow the groups didn't mix. We seldom asked the Polish girls to dance, perhaps because we were shy. My excuse was that I just didn't know how to dance. After a while they stopped coming. Jadwiga, possibly the most mature of the Polish girls, was kind of sweet on me. She was certainly the most interesting of the girls to talk to. One day we just sat on the pier and talked. Next thing I knew, she was looking at me strangely. She had very long brown hair, brown eyes, and, oddly for a Slav, a dusky complexion. She was tall and slim and had some schooling. A couple of times at dances I had said hello and taken some steps with her, just as the music was coming to a halt. I fantasized about asking her to take a ride to the island with me in a rowboat, and letting her take the lead from there.

By that summer two distinct groups had emerged among the hundred or so Jewish kids: those who were preparing to go to the United States and those whose choice was Palestine. The first batch of visas was to be issued shortly. I had passed all the preliminaries and was scheduled to leave on the very first available postwar vessel taking immigrants to America. The boys and girls who picked Palestine as their destination were unsure how they would get there. For the time being, the British were keeping the ports off-limits to Jews, presumably to please the Arabs.

Passing through Munich one day, I met a man whose girlfriend had been in the same barrack in Kielce as my mother and sister. He asked if I had had mail from my mother. Incredulous, I wanted to know more, but all he could tell me was that Mother and Anna were alive and in Sweden. I returned to Prien telling everyone of my good fortune. No one expressed surprise. There were far too many improbable things happening to us. The Red Cross office in Munich took a letter that I wrote to my mother and promised to forward it to their counterpart in Stockholm. I waited for a time, but heard nothing further. In the meantime, the UNRRA office informed me that my visa to the United States was being held up because the organization's aim was to reunite families rather than disperse them further. Anyway, orphans had first call on the few precious berths. This was not good news, since my eighteenth birthday was coming up in three months, and then I would become ineligible under the 'war waifs' program.

I decided to visit the fellow's girlfriend in the small Bavarian town of Türkheim. She and other women had been liberated there when the train they were on ran out of coal to fire the locomotive, and the guards deserted. The U.S. army arrived soon after. The girls were lucky. By order of the U.S. military commander they were assigned to rooms in the little town, mostly in the homes of Nazis. They had remained there ever since – a total of fifteen months now. Some had sent for their husbands; others, widows, had nowhere to go. Girls whose boyfriends had survived made the boys join them.

On the way to Türkheim, I learned that the Zionists had called for day-long demonstrations in Munich and Frankfurt to protest the British blockade of the ports at Haifa and Tel Aviv. The Americans were cooperating with their allies and were determined to prevent the demonstrations from taking place. They had cordoned off the Munich railway station with the intention of stopping potential demonstrators from reaching the city. As I was changing trains at Munich, I got into an argument in English with the sergeant in charge, who tried to tell me that his job was to screen all incoming non-Germans. In disgust, I said to him, 'Well, that is just tough shit.' I wasn't sure what this meant, but back at the 17th FOB it was a favourite expression signifying an impasse. That didn't sit well with the non-com. He put me in the paddy wagon, behind a locked door with a barred window. When I was let out, my train had already left.

Arriving in Türkheim the next morning, I met eight or ten girls from the Kielce camp. One of them handed me a six-month-old letter from Mother. The girl had received it through the International Red Cross post. Mother was asking for assistance in locating her 'Moniutek.' Apparently she and Anna had met up in the Ravensbrück camp in the early winter of 1945. From there, more dead than alive, they were taken to Sweden by Swedish Red Cross bus-ambulances just days before the war officially ended.

Mother had learned that I was alive from Aunt Frieda in Toronto, who had my note of October 1945, addressed to the Canadian Jewish Congress there. My return address had been: Prvt. Banks, Army P.O. Box 403, the 17th FOB, U.S. Expeditionary Forces, Europe. Of course, the 17th FOB had since demobilized. It was now July 1946.

I posted a letter to Mother and Anna using the return address on the letter the girl had given me. The Red Cross must have improved their service, because within a month I got two letters from Mother, saying that she and my sister expected to leave Sweden soon for the United States or Canada. These letters convinced the UNRRA people that the best place for me was out of their hair, and persuaded the U.S. consul in Munich to issue me a visa.

My train back to Prien was not until evening. I did some sightseeing. Munich had been damaged in the Allied bombings, but the zoo was intact. Someone in Germany had the animals' interests at heart. There were few cages: the wild beasts had roomy pits, caves, and hills. On this warm day in late summer I walked about, not a care in the world. One of the largest set-ups in the zoo was a pit for the baboons. They sure were having a good time, lots of food and play room. I noticed that they had the knack of delousing down pat – taking turns picking the tiny bugs off each other and then smacking their lips as they swallowed them.

After a while I got hungry and decided to go into town. In 1946 there were no restaurants or grocery stores aside from those honouring ration coupons. Only one place in Munich that I knew of offered soup without demanding coupons. The 'one item menu' soup kitchen was one street over from the railway station and next door to the continuous-newsreel movie-house. I would have preferred not to eat fish, especially fish pieces that I couldn't identify, floating in a soup. But on trips to the city, this was where we all had soup, with the bread we had brought with us.

The streetcar was the only mode of transportation. Changing trams downtown during rush hour, I had an accident. There were no buses, not many autos, few bicycles, and no traffic jams. After letting a few crowded trams go by, I boarded one by getting on the step and hanging on to the bar. We were moving along briskly when another streetcar came out of an intersection and headed towards me fast on the rails running alongside ours. I saw the monster closing in but my options were limited. The two vehicles moving in opposite directions turned my body into a kind of ball-bearing. It flashed through my mind that this was the end. I had my U.S. visa and a bright future – and now my mother would never find out what had happened to me. My struggle to survive had been for naught. As I pondered the irony, the trams pulled and whacked me, but the pain didn't register. It was over in a few seconds, and I rode on to my stop. I lost my appetite for soup and, after checking my bruised body for broken bones, I went to the newsreel place and sat in the dark, still checking for damage.

After the rooster came out to announce the newsreel, the show began. The Nuremberg trials were popular just then. They showed the accused standing at attention with earphones on, listening to the verdict being handed down by the judges. The German announcer lamely explained that a couple of the criminals hadn't made it to the finals: it turned out that they had swallowed poison.

Within a few weeks I was on a train taking me to Bremen, en route to America.

In Bremen we were put up in a former school, twelve to a classroom. We were the second group of immigrants that autumn to be sailing to America. One group, including kids from Prien, with Izidor among them, had sailed in early September, I believe to some press attention on the other side of the Atlantic. They were the first batch of concentration camp survivors to land in the New World.

Scheduled to occur within days, the sailing was delayed until mid-December because of a maritime strike. Learning that the length of the strike was unpredictable, I decided to make the best of it. Our building, a three-storey affair, was guarded day and night by a platoon of Polish ex-soldiers wearing U.S. issue uniforms in black. What they were watching was unclear, but accustomed as we were to being regimented and ordered around, we didn't question it. The guards did not permit us to bring food into the building and enforced a curfew. The no-food rule was not for any reasons of hygiene that I could see, but rather stemmed from the prerogative of the stronger to push around the weaker. I suspected that the Poles were as poorly fed as we were and resented the fact that we could lay our hands on extra food.

In Bremen the shelves in the stores were empty, the same as in the south, which made shopping irksome. There were no restaurants. However, bartering or paying cash, we did manage to occasionally obtain a piece of salted bacon, a loaf of white bread, or a blood-and-cereal salami. Any of those had to be cut up into chunks, stuffed in pockets, and smuggled into the building.

The Poles had been part of the Home Army irregulars (AK) who would ambush the Germans from their hide-outs in forests. Under orders from the Polish government-in-exile in London, they were a thorn in the side of the Germans but distrusted by the Russian-led partisans who worked the same forests. One of our boys remembered a run-in he'd had with a unit in the northeast region of Poland. He and his brother were fortunate to escape from a ghetto and join up with a small party of partisans led by a Russian officer who had been dropped into the forest. The group co-existed warily with a battalion-strength AK unit camped a mile or two away. One morning they were aroused by shouts. It was the Home Army demanding that the Reds surrender to them all the Jews in the group, or else they would open fire and destroy the smaller unit. The Russians negotiated their way out of the dilemma, and the Jews were not given up. In 1945, fearing incarceration by the Red Army, many of the AK units had crossed over to Czechoslovakia. There they gave themselves up to Patton's troops. The Americans found them useful for various guard duties, as this relieved the U.S. infantrymen, who were being rapidly demobilized. The Poles were expected to leave the U.S. zone as soon as things got back to normal at home. In the meantime, they were being nasty.

Reports had also begun to filter through that many Russian POWs, released from German prisoner-of-war camps and forced to return to the Soviet Union, had been deported to Siberia, or worse.

Bremen, shell-shocked, was wet and cold. The locals went about their business paying little attention to us, speaking in a harsh form of German. I tried to kill time reading German books from the school library, or going to the movies. *Going My Way,* with Bing Crosby, was a big hit. I went to a barber for my first shave: he humoured me. At our residence, we received parcels from America: I got one addressed to 'anyone in Europe,' from a little girl in Yonkers, New York, containing crayons, colouring books, and a dime fastened with scotch tape to a book. Crossing a soccer field, I ripped the pants of my new, custom-made suit on some rusted barbed wire.

Of the fifty of us, at least twenty were girls. For reasons best known to themselves, the girls wanted to form liaisons with the boys, but the guys resisted. The men didn't want to pledge their future carelessly. However, girl-watching was okay. This was easy. Open seams in the partition separating the men's and women's shower sections gave us a good view of the girls soaping. Actually, it was impossible *not* to see into the girls' shower, since the open cracks were so obvious. A few of the boys would perch on a beam near the ceiling to get a better view, as well as to be out of the way of others who were glued to the cracks, or who might actually be taking a shower. Since the girls seemed to be fastidiously clean and showered often, some of the boys, not having much else to do, only came down for meals, making sure to take in the complete show. A Czech boy held the record for an uninterrupted watch. He developed a rash on his face that Abe, our resident medical hopeful, explained as 'turbulence of the blood.' The girls were undoubtedly lovely. I had made it a point of honour to peek only when I was actually taking a shower.

At last the day came when the strikers decided to give me a break. A Liberty ship took me aboard. It was 19 December 1946.

The accommodations were strictly navy – hammocks hung two or three high, in cabins holding at least fifty. Dining room and food were regulation army – bacon, eggs, real coffee, apples, bananas, oranges, cakes, and pies. Ice cream! It sure looked and tasted good but was hard to stabilize on plates and in the stomach. Encountering big waves, the ship gave in and rolled with them. Soon most of us were seasick. I couldn't wait to recover in order to get back to the good chow. I was also anxious to get back to my duties as the ship's interpreter. It was an unpaid position, but it gave me a chance to practise my English and impress the girls. The many ship regulations, posted in English, had to be translated and explained to our group in Polish, Yiddish, or German. Hungarian was beyond my abilities. Whether I understood and interpreted what I read correctly will remain unknown. Some ideas were conveyed to me verbally by the people in charge. I was chosen, obviously, as the best of an indifferent lot. At the time I noted that the girls showed a lot more resistance to the effects of the sea voyage than the boys and were mostly still interested in adventure.

We docked somewhere outside New York harbour on the evening of 25 December, just missing the Christmas rush. I stayed up late on board ship watching the skyscraper lights and the traffic moving over highways, streets, and bridges. To one who had seen only desolation, darkness, cold, and misery, it was pure magic. I had no idea what I expected in the 'land of opportunity.' I knew, though, that I was lucky beyond my wildest dreams.

To make myself presentable, I went down to the washroom and, making sure that there was no one around to mock me, tried to shave. It went well, except for a few nicks and cuts.

In the early morning light a little boat pulled alongside our ship, and one of the officers climbed down the rope ladder and boarded it. Wearing a splendid blue uniform, attaché case in hand, he was tall, ramrod-straight, with dark hair and steel-blue eyes. A hero sailor, like in the movies. For a moment I thought of joining the navy, but decided against it, as my sea legs were none too good and I was only five-foot-eight.

Down the gangplank we scampered onto the pier. A number of longshoremen had gathered at the foot. One made waving motions to me and hollered 'Italiano.' I waved back and ran my fingers through my uncut, dark curly hair. Great pains were taken to sort our luggage alphabetically (in fact, they could have put all our luggage in one large pushcart). What happened next caught me off guard. Standing beside our boxes and bags was a group of New York Yeshiva students holding prayer books and tefillin, two little leather boxes containing brief biblical extracts to be fastened with leather thongs to the forehead and the left arm for morning prayers every day but Saturday. The students urged us to put on the phylacteries, there and then. It would be, they said, a mitzvah, an exceptionally good deed, the score being kept in heaven.

The incident confounded me. A religious ritual the very moment I stepped into the land of freedom and opportunity? It wasn't at all what I had expected. I felt that what was due me was a word of sympathy, of kindness, a willingness to hear me out. I had so much to tell. Perhaps I even saw myself as something of a returning hero, but the compassionate and curious for news were nowhere in sight. Even among relatives, later on, there were no questions or gentle prodding regarding my experiences. I thought it strange, but then, the world was a tough place, and gracious-ness was not something I had much experience with.

What the Yeshiva students hadn't grasped was that not one of the group that came down the gangplank that December morning believed that the Almighty had earned our gratitude.

As I learned later, my mother's sister Frieda had come down from Toronto to New York to await my arrival in mid-October, when it was originally scheduled. Since she had small children at home, she couldn't try again. In letters from Sweden Mother had possibly prodded Aunt Frieda to make sure that I was taken care of by a relative, no matter how distantly related. In a letter to Mother I had mentioned that a group of us from the children's home were getting visas and free passage to America. From this bit of information she and Anna got the notion that, as I was arriving with a group of orphans, I would be snatched off the dock by strangers, possibly a childless couple, and be adopted on the spot.

19
That Side Jordan

The America of my imagination had been created by the carefree soldiers of the 17th FOB. These boys talked about jobs, left food to spoil on their plates, put out half-smoked cigarettes, played poker for money, were unconcerned about the state and cost of clothes, called sergeants by their first names, and said that the United States was the land of plenty. But I also had more sombre thoughts, a wariness and suspicion that for me, life would not be easy.

It was sixteen months since Hiroshima. America had fought and won a global war, during which time a horrid ten-year depression had ended. Businesses earned profits; the unemployed found work. In the Nuremberg trials, the wicked had been punished. The evil-doers were humbled. Having contributed so much to the Allied victory, few U.S. civilians felt uncomfortable about having sat out the war in safety.

On the morning of 26 December 1946, our group was bussed into New York City. The streets were wet and cold. There was little traffic. We were deposited in front of a narrow, grey, three-storey building whose sign included the word 'shelter.' I tried to get my bearings: we were somewhere in the Bronx. To the right of the building, down a few steps, was a small shop that offered cigarettes, newspapers, candy, and, according to the poster, ice-cream. The rest of the street looked to be a series of three- or four-storey apartment houses.

I wondered if my dime, still sticky from the scotch tape that had fastened it to the gift book from the little girl in Yonkers, would be enough to buy an ice-cream. If allowed, I wanted to walk around a bit to get a sense of the area.

Once inside the shelter I was given a zippered, grey wool jacket with slash pockets, then shown to one of the many identical rooms that held three or four cots and had a wall of hooks for hanging clothes. I placed my valise under a bed and stealthily made my way out onto the street. No one stopped me, or even asked where I was going. Clutching my dime, I entered the little shop, mentioned the ice-cream on the poster, and exchanged my ten cents for an Eskimo bar. The fact that I was now penniless did not bother me in the least. What did gnaw at me was that I was unable to produce the five-dollar bill that Milton had given me back in Klatovy for our celebratory bottle of whisky. As I was buying my ice-cream, I wondered what sort of impression I was making on the elderly Jewish shopkeeper. Although I correctly identified the item and asked for it in proper American English, did I not give away my fresh-off-the-boat ignorance by selecting a summer novelty in winter? I stopped myself: I was just being silly. I had to start thinking of the bigger picture.

The day was overcast and chilly, with a light drizzle. I walked up and down the street, and then returned to the shelter. A couple of the boys loitering in the lobby shoved me over towards two girls of about sixteen or seventeen who were standing to one side. They introduced themselves to me as friends of Izidor, who had come to say hello to me. Izidor, during his extended stay at the shelter that fall, had become friends with the girls, who lived nearby. Betty was petite, dark haired, and vivacious. Sandra was taller, slim, with blonde hair and blue eyes, and silent. My unspoken question was which of the two could I claim? Simply on looks, I preferred Sandra. I felt a pang of envy. Izidor had preceded me to America by three or four months. He had by now overtaken me and managed to have at least one girlfriend (with whom he was surely at ease), and here I was, tongue-tied, green – a simpleton.

No school today, the girls excitedly explained. Izidor had instructed them to keep a look-out for me as I was expected to

show up from the next shipload out of Bremerhafen. I followed
the girls out the door as we made our way to Betty's. I was unable
to come up with the necessary small talk; I felt terrible. My GI
English hadn't supplied me with vocabulary for conversation
with the opposite sex. Words eluded me. Fortunately, we were
soon going up several flights of stairs and into an apartment.
Betty's parents weren't in. Whether this was intentional or not
was my immediate concern.

I looked around the crowded dwelling of normal people. This
was the first home I'd seen in seven years. I was perplexed, I
wondered whether I wasn't missing a cue. It seemed that the next
move was up to me. There was an air of expectancy, as if something was about to happen. I was speechless; I felt I would never
live this disaster down. The girls twittered between themselves
for a time and then simultaneously announced that we would
return to the shelter. I felt that I had missed a chance for establish-
ing my credentials, but I was relieved, too, that the impasse had
been broken, albeit by default.

Keeping my head down to keep the rain out of my face also
conveniently hindered my taking part in conversation on the
way back. The three of us force-marched back to the shelter.
Walking in with two attractive ladies practically on my arm, I was
led to a middle-aged couple who said they were Ben and Edith,
my cousins.

Having made the grand entrance, I read approval in the eyes of
my new-found family. However, in truth, I was totally disoriented. Ben clapped me on the back and said something that
sounded like 'Atta boy!' Edith then proceeded to tell me that my
Aunt Frieda, my mother's sister in Toronto, had arranged for me
to stay with them in the Bronx. Ben owned a kosher butcher store
there and was the president-elect of the New York Kosher Butch-
ers' Association. Their middle son, Harry, was getting married to
someone named Sarah in January; the youngest, Irving, was
studying at a university in Pittsburgh; and the oldest, Herman,
was an artist.

The paperwork done, I fetched my valise, bade a brief goodbye
to Betty and Sandra, who didn't seem particularly upset over my

early departure, and then, fanning my free hand to my gawking shipmates, I walked out a free man.

I couldn't stop thinking about my inability to speak, the total verbal paralysis that overcame me when I met the girls. Certainly, the subjects I was acquainted with – military lore, an ocean voyage, farming, milling, electrical work, cooking, fancy tricks like placing one's trousers neatly under one's bedsheets and finding them perfectly ironed in the morning – were things I could have talked about with Sandra and Betty, and possibly made a better first impression on them. Alas, it was too late. Would I meet other girls soon and get a chance to recoup? I thought I had better not speculate, but concentrate on the trip I was taking with Ben and Edith.

Ben led us to a maroon Chevrolet. I sat in the back; Cousin Ben drove, and Edith sat beside him. They explained to me that Cousin Edith was my mother's cousin, once removed: she was the daughter of my Great-grandmother Faigele's youngest sister. Somewhat bewildered, I rested against the back of the seat, taking in the sights. The buildings were unharmed, no signs of bombs or fire. Ben turned to me and, in man-to-man talk, enlightened me on the difficulty of purchasing a new vehicle. The Detroit automobile plants had yet to retool after the wartime production of tanks and trucks; consequently, there was a temporary shortage of passenger cars. However, as soon as more cars became available, Ben would purchase one right away. It would definitely be a model by General Motors.

Edith told me that sugar was still being rationed, the last item on a list that had originally included foods like canned salmon and tuna. But extra black market sugar was available for those with a sweet tooth, she added. I felt like making light of these difficulties, but thought better of it. I decided I had better get used to this new mentality.

As we stepped out of the car that Ben had parked at the corner of Lydig and Cruger Avenues, he pointed out to me their kosher butcher shop, closed at this hour. I followed my cousins around the side of the building, through a double glass door, and into an elevator. We got out at the third floor and walked along a corridor lined with doors. Edith used two keys to unlock their door and invited me into a hallway lined on one side with waist-high shelving containing books. To my left was a room with a patterned red carpet – a floral design – red, flecked wallpaper, little tables holding lamps with silk shades, and a sofa and chairs covered in a shiny striped fabric. At the window was a brown radio and gramophone cabinet. There were large and small framed pictures on the walls, and on one of the tables I spotted a porcelain dish full of candies and nuts.

I passed a white painted kitchen and was shown the white bathroom, where the walls were tiled halfway up. I was to share a bedroom with Herman, the artist, as Harry would only be there for another three weeks before his wedding. Irving had been home for Christmas – or Hanukkah, they corrected themselves – and would not be back until the school term was over. I was assigned to one of three beds in the room, at the head of which was a radiator on which sat an ivory-coloured mantel radio. Herman worked evenings as a make-up artist in the theatre; the radio was mine to do with as I wished. By force of habit formed in the war, I decoded and filtered information in terms of how it would affect me and, especially, the benefit I would derive from it. A dresser drawer was pulled out for me to place my extra shirt, pants, and socks in. My German-made shoes displeased Cousin Edith, and I was given a pair of light brown ones to try on. They belonged to Harry, but since they fit me, I was told to keep them.

At this point, Harry, a pleasant young man with a large shock of wavy brown hair, came in. We were introduced, and Harry promptly reached for his billfold, withdrawing a five-dollar note, which he handed to me, remarking that he was happy to make my acquaintance and that since we were cousins, would I accept the money. I saw no reason not to. Harry then proceeded to tell me that he had come home to change clothes and that he was on his way to pick up his fiancée, Sarah; they were going to see a movie. Afterwards, they planned to come back to the apartment so that I could meet her.

Cousin Edith remarked that her parents had been neighbours with my grandparents in Łódź and that she remembered my mother well. It seemed that Edith had been in the United States for twenty years. I was pondering how to respond to questions about how members of my mother's family had met their deaths. But nobody asked such a question. Aunt Frieda had brought Edith up to date on the family: my mother had apparently met up with my sister in the Ravensbrück concentration camp. They, and Aunt Bluma, who had also been in the lager, were taken from Germany to Sweden by the Red Cross. They had been in Sweden for about twenty months and were impatient to leave for the United States or Canada. At that moment a Canadian entry visa looked the more promising. Should they go to Toronto, I was expected to join them there.

Aunt Frieda had also been corresponding with her sister, my Aunt Rózia, who was somewhere in West Germany and had remarried, again to a cousin. Edith said no more, so I had to assume that that was *it* as far as survivors on Mother's side were concerned. I was sure Father's family had been wiped out.

I asked if I could use the telephone to call Milton Zeldis, and Benny obligingly got him on the line. Milt told me how to get to Kings Highway in Brooklyn by subway, and I promised to make it there the following evening.

That night we had tuna fish salad, and then it was time to take a walk around the neighbourhood. By now, the evening had turned colder. Stores were still open, brightly decorated for Christmas and full of merchandise. Coloured signs read 'Sale,' an unfamiliar term to me. We strolled by a shoe repair store, and here Edith purchased a set of shoe trees. These, she explained, were necessary items that would keep my nearly new shoes in shape. We continued our walk over to Pelham Parkway, a wide shop-lined street with an elevated transit line in the centre. At one of the metal staircases I read a sign saying 'I.R.T.' My cousins exchanged greetings with passers-by, presumably out shopping, as they were carrying parcels. One, a Jewish man, engaged the cousins in a lengthy conversation. On learning that I had just arrived and was a great-grandson of Faigele, he insisted that I visit his father. The father had, at the turn of the century, been an admirer of Faigele's. He lived on Washington Avenue, also in the Bronx. I promised to visit the gentleman as soon as I could.

The cousins also exchanged greetings with a shop owner and his red-headed wife. A mass of ladies' undergarments layered the shelves and hung all over the store. I followed closely their discussion about the serious shortage of ladies' nylon stockings. I also overheard them say that because of wartime shortages of cars and appliances, the public's surplus funds were invested in liberty bonds, or else spent on fur coats. In fact, Benny said, most women, given the choice, would prefer to be married to a furrier. The excessive prices that the fur manufacturers charged could be described as war profiteering. Ben, in an aside, also said that during the war choice steaks fetched a high price.

How odd, it seemed to me, that these people, though Jewish, were apparently untouched by the war. It was if it had never happened. I decided I'd better keep my mouth shut or I'd stand out like a sore thumb. I felt that I mustn't speak any language but English, even to my shipmate friends. As soon as the holidays were over I would enrol in a night course to see if I could fill in the gaps in my formal education. I would also get a job so that I would not have to depend on hand-outs. There was no time to lose.

On returning to the apartment, we found Herman waiting for us. He embraced me and declared that his stint in uniform had been no fun. His army engineering unit had taken part in the invasion of Normandy. On D-Day plus one, his ship struck a mine and sank. Many of the men drowned; Herman was one of those fortunate enough to be rescued by a destroyer. They made it to Utah Beach, which was a minefield and where they came under artillery fire from German emplacements above them. Wet, and minus all gear, they were told to dig in with their bare hands. My future roommate was a war hero! This was exciting. Herman complimented me on my English, and told me that I would do well in America.

Harry and Sarah came in shaking snowflakes from their coats and hair. They were laughing and repeating lines from the movie that they had just seen, starring Betty Grable; it was, according to them, a 'must' for me to see.

Sarah was dark-haired and in her early twenties. She and I

took to each other immediately. 'Heck, how opportune,' she exclaimed, the wedding party was short an usher and, since I had turned up, I would be paired with someone by the name of Marlene. I was to go downtown as soon as possible to get fitted for tails and a top hat. I was not to be concerned about the cost of the rental, as that would be taken care of.

To keep the momentum going, I asked about registering for night school. Sarah was quite certain that the Theodore Roosevelt High School on Fordham Road and Grand Concourse had such a program. It was a short bus ride away, and I was to be sure to ask the bus driver to let me know where to get off. Sarah soon took her leave, Harry accompanying her home.

Herman had been in and out. At last I was alone in the bedroom. Before getting into bed, I examined the radio. Tuning it to CBS, I heard the announcer state unequivocally that it was the network's key station. The programs that followed were extraordinary: *The Henry Morgan Show*, in which Henry met his squeaky-voiced sidekick, Gerrard, at a corner cigar store; *It Pays to Be Ignorant*, with male and female comedians exchanging wisecracks; and *The Thin Man*, a scary detective yarn.

Agitated, I didn't think I could fall asleep, but when I woke up in the middle of the night, it was with severe stomach cramps. Rushing to the bathroom, I found it occupied, apparently by Herman, whose bed was in disarray. Holding on to the borrowed pajama bottoms, I ran out into the corridor, but there was no outhouse there. Unable to hold off any longer, I squatted down in front of the incinerator chute. I then sauntered back to the apartment. I wondered what the neighbours would think of this messy deposit. I knew then that I had to move on to accepted standards of behaviour. I had to overcome my rude past.

Morning, day two. I ate breakfast alone. Herman was asleep. The cousins were in the store, and Harry had gone off to business. At a loss as to what to do next, I went down to the butcher shop. Ben had come back earlier from the slaughterhouse, bringing sides of beef, slabs of liver, and dozens of dead chickens with brown and white feathers. A Jewish man wearing a hat was seated on a low stool, methodically plucking the chickens. Edith greeted me and, taking me aside, spoke about the hard work that butchering entailed. Being young, I could probably learn a better trade. However, one must know a trade because no matter how bad things get, anywhere in America, one could always fall back on a trade. This refrain I heard a number of times over the next few weeks. Edith also said that my Aunt Frieda, whom I was yet to meet, had been very explicit about this matter: Ben and Edith were to teach me the kosher butcher trade. Reluctantly, not wanting to offend Aunt Frieda, I sat on the other low stool and joined the silent man in the hat, both of us now plucking chickens.

I wasn't totally unfamiliar with this exertion as I had watched Mother pluck chickens back in Staszów. I tired of it soon though, as the fowl had fleas that got into my hair, ears, and nose.

I was next shown how to band-saw big bones into smaller pieces, cut up chops, open a chicken and remove the entrails, and cut a large turkey into four quarters. Then it was time to go up for lunch. The cousins were not really keen, I thought, on having me underfoot in the shop. I would tell them that I wasn't thinking of becoming a butcher.

I didn't return to the shop, because Izidor showed up. Having spoken to Milton Zeldis the night before, he had learned of my whereabouts. Izidor was mastering the butcher business in the shop of Milton Freeman, in Boston. He asked me to feel his biceps, and he showed me a couple of healed cuts on his left hand where the butcher knife had slipped. Asked if I had any ideas about finding work, I replied that I had none. Izidor's formula for employment was that it was far better to start at any job than wait around for an attractive one. He was thoroughly American in his insistence that 'any job is better than no job.' I decided to heed Izidor's counsel and accept the first position I was offered. However, he cautioned me, demobilized GIs had first crack at the scarce jobs.

Since Izidor was in from Boston for the whole day, we could take in a show. After perusing the *Daily Mirror*, which happened to be sitting on the kitchen table, he offered to treat me to see a re-release of the 'greatest movie ever made': *Gone with the Wind*.

The tickets were cheaper because the movie was playing in a secondary theatre. With an expertise that I began to envy, Izidor made the necessary El connections and transfers that had us arrive at our destination in time for the start of the afternoon picture show.

At bustling Lennox Avenue, where there was a row of movie theatres, the faces on the street were all black. Izidor had landed us in Harlem. He muttered something incomprehensible and suggested that instead of going to the movie we should visit Private Banks. Banks had joined the New York police force, and, since he worked nights, we were sure to find him home. Back we went to the IRT Lennox Station and, after a short ride, emerged on a street not unlike Ben and Edith's.

We found Patrolman Banks just getting dressed. After we had reminisced about our time together in Marienbad, Banks told us that he wasn't happy with his current assignment in a predominantly Irish neighbourhood. Night duty involved breaking up drunken brawls in which women, he asserted, disgracefully kicked and screamed at the men, and at each other. I promised to visit Banks on the job as soon as he graduated to day duty.

Izidor had to catch the train back to Boston, and I went home to the cousins who were waiting with news for me: A customer in the butcher store had offered to recommend me for a job at his brother-in-law's factory. The nature of the product being manufactured was unknown at the moment. The address, though, was clear. It was in an area of the city called Soho.

Buoyed by the prospects of a job for which I would receive American dollars, I quickly downed some food and set out for Brooklyn. Following Milton's directions, I had no trouble finding the apartment building on Kings Highway. There, I was warmly received by Milt and his pretty wife, Yetta. Arrangements had been made for a babysitter (a new term for me), who turned out to be Milt's sister. Very attractive, she was single and suggested that we go to the pictures one day. I was definitely drawn to her. But, at eighteen, and with barely the prospect of a job, I could not see why she would want to bother with me. Nonetheless, not hesitating, I agreed to be taken to a movie.

Milton and Yetta had a similar idea for the evening. They had been dying to see *The Jolson Story.* There was still time before the next show, so they suggested that we sit down and I could tell them what I had been up to since my arrival. In no time, the conversation turned to my attire, which, in their eyes, needed upgrading. Milton suggested that I take the black dress-suit that his recently departed grandfather had worn only a couple of times. It was sure to fit me, as grandpa had been about my height and weight. Out of a jam-packed closet, Yetta removed the pants, jacket, and vest for my inspection. I demurred at taking it immediately, since we were going out to the movie. In fact, I was aghast at the thought of wearing a dead person's clothes, as I had had to do in the camps. Why would Milton suggest such a thing? I thought about Milton: he seemed tired and bedraggled. What happened to the forward-looking twenty-four-year-old, the merry staff sargeant Zeldis?

The evening was lovely, not too cold, with light snow flurries. The movie left a lasting impression on me. In it a cantor at a synagogue leads the choir; the leading vocalist is the cantor's son. The boy, over his father's objections, graduates to the theatre and becomes a star. (The fine-looking young man playing Jolson was not Jewish, Milton whispered.) The cantor's son falls in love with a nice, blonde, Gentile woman, and she with him. The cantor-father eventually reconciles himself to his son's new lifestyle and invites the couple for a Friday, Sabbath dinner. There, given horseradish with the gefilte fish, the woman makes a wry face, thereby endearing herself to us all. Jolson sings wonderful tunes, everyone applauds, the couple get married, and the Jewish ethos prevails.

Although I found it hard to believe, given my experience, Milton assured me that anything Yiddish was extremely popular in America. I thanked them for a lovely evening, and we parted.

The next morning, Friday, I arrived at the Heatproof Pad Company, located on the fourth floor of a doleful, red-brick building, and accessible only by a freight elevator. The operator was a slim black man with close-cropped salt-and-pepper hair. Friendly, he joked with me, while another man unloaded cartons of merchandise. We went up the clanging elevator to the fourth floor.

I was interviewed by a glum gentleman who wanted me to spend the morning trying out for the job. I was turned over to an equally sorrowful Jewish man who explained to me the nature of the business: Heat-resistant dining-table covers were manufactured to customers' patterns. The American people seemed to value their possessions and wished to protect them from spills, scratches, and burns indefinitely, it seemed. How curious. As highly polished mahogany tabletops were particularly vulnerable, the protective covers were made of heavy cardboard, the top side covered in white plastic and the underside in brown felt. The pads were designed so that they could be folded neatly for storage. My job would consist of cleaning off any excess glue, packing the pads, labelling the cartons, delivering them to the post office on a four-wheeled cart once a day for mailing, sweeping the factory floor, and any other miscellaneous duties that needed to be done.

At the end of the tour, my guide scolded me for leaving my grey jacket on the floor in the corner. 'Garments,' he admonished me, 'should be taken care of.' After lunch I was to be shown how to work the gum-paper machine, the stapler, and other pieces of equipment. The lunch bell went off, and I took the elevator down.

This time the operator was even friendlier. He wanted to know if I'd got the job, how long I had been in New York, my name, and so on. I bought a Danish from the stand in the lobby, and walked up the street to where a number of men were parading in front of a factory, holding placards that read 'On Strike.' I went closer in the mistaken belief that I had spotted a GI from the 17th FOB among them. A few of the men wore parts of army uniforms and GI-issue shoes.

When I got back to the plant at half past twelve, I was given instructions about equipment and told to report for work at 8:00 A.M. a week from Monday. I had nine days to do whatever I wanted. I wasn't sure whether I should be jubilant or not. As Izidor had said, a job was a job. Also, twenty-five dollars a week was nothing to look down on. Back in Germany, anyone with a hundred dollars was rich. I rang for the elevator, and when it came I told the operator the good news. He closed the wire-mesh gate but didn't put the car in motion. Instead, he came up close to me and stretched out his hand. Assuming he wanted to shake mine, I extended my right hand, over which he laid his and guided it to the area of his crotch. I quickly withdrew my hand. The elevator started moving, and the man said something inaudible under his breath. Whew! I had to be careful not to get too friendly with strangers.

On my way to the subway station, I passed a Horn and Hardatt Automat. It turned out to be a truly amazing place. Two walls were lined with little metal-framed glass doors, behind which, on small carousels, were an array of sandwiches, pies, drinks, and more elegant dishes. All one had to do was drop a nickel or a dime in the slot, and, presto, the door sprung open. There was never any guesswork as to what one would get for one's money; it was there for all to see.

A stern-faced lady sat in a booth ready to exchange bills for nickels, dimes, or quarters. I bought a chocolate cupcake for a nickel and sat down to eat it at a table by the window. From there I could observe the line of wet strikers, shorter now that it had started to rain. Only three or four of the men had umbrellas. Some of them were conceivably members of the 8th Corps that had liberated us, I thought. How sad that they now had to stay out in the rain.

Unerringly, I made my connections to the Lexington Avenue line, but was so lost in thought that I was two stops out of my way before I noticed. Back at the apartment a letter from my Aunt Frieda awaited me. It contained sixteen dollars for return train fare, New York–Toronto, plus a little extra for expenses. Milton's sister, Sara, had left a message that she would pick me up at half past six. I checked in a mirror to see if I needed to shave, but there was hardly any stubble on my chin.

It looked as though things were out of my hands. There were relatives in Toronto, also my Grandmother Hudys's youngest sister, Brancia (which would make her my great-aunt), and a great-uncle, too. These were the ones who had sponsored Aunt Frieda. I didn't recall that Mother had ever mentioned any cousins, but Edith said that there were many in Toronto. I wondered how long the train ride was and how far away Toronto was.

Herman volunteered to find out the train schedule for me. He reported that the train to Toronto left every evening from Grand Central Station, arriving in Toronto the next morning. The cousins suggested that I leave the following night, Saturday. In the meantime, Benny had come up from the shop. It being Friday, he closed early for the Sabbath. He invited me to accompany him to the bank. At the Manufacturer's Bank, located near the El station on Pelham Parkway and White Plains Road, he introduced me to the manager. Here I made my first big mistake. The friendly bank manager asked me what I thought of America. In my English, which had markedly improved over the last couple of days, I replied in an off-hand manner, 'It's pretty good.' (At the 17th FOB, mild praise of this nature had been acceptable for nearly every occasion.) It must have been my tone, because the manager lectured me about ungrateful persons who do not appreciate the wonderful country that has welcomed them. Crestfallen, I left the bank. The last thing I heard was Ben telling the manager that I was just learning to speak English. That was adding insult to injury. Still, he may have been right. I needed to speak more slowly and to think before I spoke.

This Friday evening the faces and comportment of the people on the street were unmistakably Jewish. Many were going in and out of stores, from which music could be heard. The El rumbled overhead, and the roadway was full of cars. I had not seen such gaiety among Jewish people in many years, if ever. It disoriented me: What could Jews have to be happy about? How could they be so light-hearted? I had to remind myself that this was the United States of America, that there had been no war here. I had better get used to it, I thought, and start thinking like a normal person. I had better keep my mouth shut about the camps and the brutality. These people didn't want to know about it, or perhaps they had already heard too much. Still, I was one of the first to cross the Atlantic after Germany gave up.

Milton's sister and I met that evening. We took the 7th Avenue line to Radio City Music Hall. I was a lot more relaxed with her this time, but we didn't talk much. We sat beside each other in the trembling subway car. I wondered why she wasn't married. She was old – at least twenty-nine – pretty, a schoolteacher, with nice eyes and dark, shiny hair. (Observing her surreptitiously, I wondered if she could possibly be unaware of the dandruff on her coat collar.) She treated me like a schoolboy: I'd been miffed when she told Edith that she would take care of me and return me at a reasonable hour. But I told myself not to dwell on these minor details. Why should I feel I had to assert myself all the time? She could take charge. What did I know anyway? As we rode, my thoughts raced: I should get serious and try to catch up on my schooling. Perhaps I should ask Sara to advise me. I wondered whether I should tell her that my formal schooling had ended at grade 4, in Polish, yet, and that even that was almost eight years ago. I had better make some money soon and start night school before I made any long-term plans. Nobody was going to support me while I went through public school, high school, and, later, university. Who was I kidding? It was impossible! When Mother and Anna came we would need to rent an apartment. I didn't think Mother should work. The only thing I could do right then was to keep my eyes and ears open. Returning to the present, I realized I wasn't at all sure what this Radio City could be.

The Rockettes, Sara explained, were performing in a dance extravaganza at Radio City Music Hall, and there was also a film showing. 'It's the highlight of the holiday season,' she said. (I'd never heard the word 'highlight' before.) She talked about the new plays on Broadway – live theatre, in case I didn't know – and said there was one in particular that I might want to see, called *Skipper Next to God*. Before she had a chance to explain, Rockefeller Center station came into sight, and it was time to get off.

At the theatre a long line of people waited to get in. Sara tried, unsuccessfully, to talk the policeman on duty into letting us in. She made a good case about my having just arrived, but to no avail.

My English was improving by the hour. Still, I wondered if I'd be able to follow involved dialogue. *The Jolson Story* had been easy, but that may have been a fluke.

We walked a couple of blocks to another movie-house, where a big lit-up marquee read, '*The Razor's Edge* – Tyrone Power and

Gene Tierney.' I knew Tyrone Power – he was in a pirate film that I'd seen in Łódź, and here he was playing a monk or something. I had difficulty with the dialogue, but I didn't admit that I couldn't quite follow the story, or understand why Tyrone gave up the good life for Tierney, who looked Chinese, but wasn't.

The trouble with going to a movie was that we didn't talk. I had wanted to find things out from Sara, and here we were, the evening over. What's more, in the brief time we did have to chat, Sara addressed me in Yiddish. She couldn't have known of my recent resolution: I responded in English.

I found out the next day that *Skipper Next to God*, with John Garfield, was playing in a theatre on 48th Street, the area that I had become familiar with the night before. The afternoon show was only $1.75 and the return subway fare twenty cents, still under two dollars in total. Since I would be making five dollars a day, I decided I could swing it. I had never seen live theatre before. Mother used to talk about going to see Yiddish theatre when she was single. She would go into raptures when she talked about Molly Picon.

When I told Edith I was off to see a Broadway play before I left for Toronto, she gave me a quizzical look. She suggested that, instead, I should see the man who'd been a friend of my legendary great-grandmother, Faigele. She thought the man would give me some money. I hated to go for hand-outs, but since I'd promised, I had to. Faigele was Edith's aunt. She said it was possible that the old gentleman had had more than a passing fancy for my impressive ancestor, and that, as I was a blood relative, he might have a soft spot in his heart for me. I could see the man first and then go to the play.

I found the address after taking the El to Washington Avenue. I knocked a few times, and a voice said, 'Come in.' I introduced myself to a man seated in the semi-darkness of a room full of overstuffed chairs. He asked me, in Yiddish, to stand in the light at the window, and then said, '*Gut, di kans gayn*' ('Good, you can go'), and I left. The visit has always puzzled me. What had the man expected to see in me?

The view from the second balcony at *Skipper Next to God* was just fine. The plot had to do with a wartime shipload of Jewish refugees from Germany brought by an idealistic captain into New York harbour. The ship is not allowed to dock, and there is a long scene in which John Garfield and an immigration official argue the matter. In the background the wailing of the men, women, and children is audible. The official talks about visas, quotas, papers, and so forth. Garfield scuttles the ship and gathers the passengers into life-boats (all this occurs offstage), and the coast guard rescues them. The refugees land in America, but the heroic skipper loses his licence. I thought, 'This is good fiction. If it were only true.' This time I understood the entire plot and all the dialogue.

In the evening I took the IRT to Grand Central Station and bought a return ticket to Toronto. I found an unoccupied bench in the train compartment where I hoped to stretch out for the night. The wooden slats reminded me of the bunks I used to sleep on. The train ride was uneventful until we got to Buffalo in the morning. There, the train stopped, and a new conductor got on, along with some Canadian officials. The man who interrogated me wore a dark blue uniform and a cap bearing the words 'Dominion of Canada Immigration.' After examining my landing card, he suggested that I obtain a proper American ID card with my picture on it or else I might have trouble getting back to New York and my new job. Since the train would be in Buffalo for only a quarter of an hour, I had better get off, get my papers in order, and board the next one.

Bag in hand, I sought out the U.S. immigration office. There I was told that since all photography studios were closed Sundays, I would have to wait until morning. I asked the immigration officer whether I could use a photo from the photo machine in the penny arcade, but he wouldn't hear of it. Too late, I saw my mistake. If I hadn't asked him about the photo machine and had simply handed him the pictures, he might have accepted them. What had become of the cunning that survival in Europe had taught me? Why was I suddenly following rules? Was it because the Canadian had been so polite?

The Genesee Hotel advertised single rooms at three dollars a night. I checked in and went to sleep. I spent the rest of the day and night munching potato chips and reading the Bible that the Gideon Society had providentially placed in the night-table drawer. There, I found passages appropriate to my situation.

20
Greetings

In the late 1960s, Freda, our children, and I visited the Zeldises in Long Island. The apartment they lived in was in the path of airplanes taking off and landing at La Guardia. Our conversation was interrupted constantly by screaming jets. This wasn't the Milton I had known; his business had recently failed, and his life savings were lost. Not long after, we returned to Long Island for Milt's funeral. He had succumbed to a massive coronary. A few months later Yetta committed suicide.

The other night I started reading *Koniec świata (End of the World)*, the diary of Baruch Milcha. It deals with the particularly cruel murder of the Jewish population in the Lwów area. Cold shivers ran down my spine, and my hands were unsteady. I got as far as page 18 when I had to put the slim volume down. Swallowing whisky in gulps, I managed to control the shakes. I went to bed but woke up within an hour and took another swig. This episode brought home to me vividly how vulnerable I was. Reading the diary in the original Polish made Baruch's experiences more immediate and horrific. I cannot easily explain why my family's suffering pales in comparison with that of Milcha's. Certainly I did not have it easy, and I might easily not have made it. My father starved to death, to the best of my knowledge, in a transport similar to the ones described by Milcha; the difference is that the train wasn't taking him to the gas chamber and the crematorium. I believe that the Jews were so inured to cruelty that we behaved like pack animals moving forward when whipped. I

believe also that although we could somehow grasp the impersonal brutality of the state, it was the cruelty of individuals, of
certain guards or of people whom we had got to know a little,
that denied God. That was the end of human dignity, ours and
theirs.

In Flessburg during the final weeks of the war, some very young
German guards came on duty. One fellow, chubby, with rosy
cheeks and a mop of blond hair, asked me one day how old I was.
'Sixteen,' I answered. So was he, he said. He seemed sympathetic.
That day, our group was out working, shovelling stones off open
railway cars. There was snow in the pine woods, but, luckily for us,
it wasn't cold out. I was wearing a jacket and pants made out of
thin, grey fabric and a filthy, torn overcoat. I had tied my shoes,
which had come from a cadaver, with string to hold the soles in
place. I weighed seventy or eighty pounds and hadn't washed in
months. The young man wore a new uniform, beautiful boots, and
a long army coat, and had a gleaming rifle slung over his shoulder.
In his right hand he held a heavy stick. The guard paused on the
ledge of my car as he moved from one car to the next; I continued
shovelling. Suddenly he was near me, and, bending over, he hit me
with full force with the stick. Meant for my head, the blow caught
me on the elbow. I kept my eyes on the gravel pile and shovelled
faster. Luckily the guard had not broken my arm. Had I been
unable to work, my fate would have been sealed.

People who live at what is considered the poverty level or who
work below minimum wage are to be pitied. So are the old and
infirm who must subsist on their old age pensions. At the bottom
of the social ladder are the homeless, who stand in line daily for
soup and bread and look for room in a different shelter every
night or sleep under culverts or in bank-machine cubicles. We feel
sorry for people who have lost their businesses or their jobs, and
their dignity, or who have lost the use of one or more of their
faculties. We sympathize with victims of robbery or extortion,
assault or rape, and thank God we're not one of them.

Imagine for a moment that you are hit with all these problems
at once, but, for a kicker, all your belongings except the clothes on
your back are taken away, you are allowed only two hundred

calories a day, and a death sentence has been passed on you, to be carried out at the whim and will of the overseer. In the meantime, the overseer routinely abuses you. This goes on for several years as you contemplate your fate.

Sanity is a precious gift. Holding on to it while you are being tested becomes your top priority. The luxury of dropping out is not available. There is no safety net, only the abyss. Still, your lot is better than that of the ones whose death sentence has been carried out. You have a chance.

Visiting Majdanek, I found myself idiotically comparing the conditions there to my experience in Buchenwald. The small portions of marmalade, margarine, and cheese the prisoners received twice a week were more than we had got. Straw-filled burlap-bag mattresses on three-tier bunk beds were also an improvement over our sleeping arrangements.

Back home after our trip to Poland, I felt lost in a sea of indifference. Memories of another time and place were etched in my brain. People went about their daily business; nothing had changed except for my inability to return to relative normalcy. Throughout my adult life I had felt that my accomplishments were temporary, that the real test was still to come. Those who have not experienced war are afforded the luxury of feeling comfortable in the apparent permanence of their society.

Making money for its own sake was never my goal. I felt that the point was to conduct business in an efficient manner, and that generating money would simply be a useful by-product. In the heyday of land speculation and development, when others bought and sold acres and tracts, laughing all the way to the bank, I laboured on ingenious but difficult projects. My aim was to replace imports with domestic products, to fabricate, redesign, manufacture, and reproduce. I considered these to be noble endeavours, and they brought both profit and heartache. More to the point, however, the work satisfied my craving to accomplish the extraordinary. It was perhaps a similar craving that drove Kosinski, Morgentaler, and Edelman: it was likely the historical Jewish-Polish need for self-fulfilment that could be satisfied only by some form of heroics.

Anyone of my era and of similar background who ignores his or her past and lives entirely in the present, making plans for the future, is surely a pragmatist. The downside of this approach is that it limits our ability to cope with any harm that might come to us and those closest to us. But must one remind oneself constantly of the tragedy? Is it a matter of personal choice? Armenians, three-quarters of a century after the massacres of their people, grieve for relatives whom they have never known. This doesn't surprise me at all.

As I get older, the feeling of loss and pain, paradoxically, grows sharper. At business or social gatherings, 'survivors' discuss anything but shared experiences. Business, financial matters, holiday trips, families, current politics, new homes, clothes, theatre, but never the past. Their preoccupation with financial security, particularly for the children, seems to have superseded all other concerns. It would make more sense for us to reconcile ourselves to the fact that peace of mind can come only when we accept that there is no security. There is a dossier in the files of my mind that tells me that security, a goal nearly everyone strives for, is a mirage.

Many years ago Freda and I were approached by an estate-planning consultant who suggested, quite seriously, that we make provisions for our grandchildren. Astonished, I observed that our oldest child was only in his teens. 'That,' he said, 'doesn't matter. You must plan for the future now.' I did not agree. Was it possible that, having abandoned the hope of attaining security, I had found a greater peace?

I believe that mysterious forces direct our lives, that we have only limited influence and control over what happens to us. Although it helps to believe that things happen for reasons, reasons that we cannot know immediately, but that will reveal themselves at an appropriate time, this theory founders on the reasons for the annihilation of European Jewry.

I pinpoint my habit of making hair-trigger decisions to that critical morning in 1942, that day in Staszów when indecision would have been fatal. What awaited the children and the aged who were left behind could not be in doubt. Those who by chance or by choice have ever found their lives on the line probably find decision making in normal circumstances a piece of cake. The stakes are far smaller. This is not to suggest that only quick decisions are desirable; if time allows, sleeping on a decision is usually a good idea. What is unacceptable is procrastination resulting from irresolution and misgivings. A huge proportion of men and women cannot and will not make swift, intelligent, businesslike decisions. Errors must be recognized, analysed, and stored away in memory, but dwelling on miscalculations is soul-corroding. That way lies depression, illness, death.

My agenda in life is full of such do's and don'ts. When I have money in the bank I want to dispose of it, preferably spend it or at least invest it. I will not collect objects, ever. I do not associate with people who flaunt their wealth. I won't drive a flashy car, wear jewellery, or live in an exclusive neighbourhood. I reject the idea of a second home, winter or summer. A closet full of clothes makes me uncomfortable. I opt out of discussions about delectable meals or fine restaurants; gourmets I find only mildly amusing. I cannot suffer bores. Business dealings can be unpleasant because too often they are taken too seriously. By treating business as a game, a challenge, I can get through the day. Finally, I have little patience for people who are self-centred: their love of themselves and their attitude of looking after Number One nauseate me.

When I first started in business, with all its problems, I tried to imagine how Father would have dealt with the decision-making dilemmas that confronted me. Starting with little capital, I had it rough. Father, the consummate businessman, would have found Eden in North America.

I have found throughout my adult years that I hold back from enjoying life to the fullest. Although 'survivor's guilt' may be involved, that is too pat an answer. Can I explain the need for self-denial, the need to share bounty, or my ever-present awareness of mortality without being morbid? Other habits that persist are to take food along on even the shortest trips and to bring a gift of food when visiting, rather than something frivolous, like flowers. I also know for certain the truth that when you're gone, you're gone, and soon forgotten. In a way, it is a comforting thought. No matter how you knock yourself out, determined to leave a piece of yourself on this planet, it makes no difference to the one who really cares – you.

The Germans have a saying: '*Hoffnung verloren, alles verloren*' ('When you've lost hope, you've lost everything').

Clinging to life by a thread, we never lost hope. Despair sometimes set in later, when things had returned to normal.

Two men of letters who resisted the evil designs of Hitler and lived to tell about it have called it quits. The Polish Jew, Jerzy Kosinski, and the Italian, Primo Levi, have written their final chapters. The methods they employed to end their lives are beside the point. We will never know for certain, but likely they died of broken hearts.

For about forty years, on sleepless nights they would have asked themselves, was it all worth it? Successful, financially secure, they could look forward to a comfortable retirement. Still, the sadness, the pain persisted. It is a feeling of a loss so immense that it makes the present seem absurd. Their struggles were essentially rendered irrelevant in face of the banality of having survived while an entire people were wasted. It served no useful purpose to continue.

On our way home from Poland Freda and I made an unplanned four-day stop in Austria. After impoverished Warsaw, Vienna struck me as an opulent, self-satisfied city. I learned that the Allies spared the historic inner city, full of palaces and museums, from bombings. Someone at headquarters was determined to preserve the cultural heritage of the Austro-Hungarian monarchy.

Adolf Hitler was an Austrian by birth. A greater proportion of Austrians than Germans joined the Nazi party. To this day the Austrians persist in the claim that they were Hitler's victims. Though prosperous, they have not been inclined to offer pensions to concentration camp survivors.

Saturday morning we went to a synagogue listed in the phone book as Beth Adath Israel. I walked into an old building, saw two guards, and climbed two flights of chipped, grey stone stairs. Faced with three sets of doors on the landing, I chose the one behind which there was a faintly familiar murmur. I entered, donned a yarmulke made of a heavy plush material, and looked around. A group of men, mostly elderly or middle-aged, were seated on or standing next to some long benches. They glared at me. Behind a high partition, through three small openings, I could see the heads of shawled women. The faces around me seemed foreign. I quietly closed the door behind me as I left. This, I learned later, was a synagogue attended by Jews from Iran.

At the next synagogue, a dozen blocks away, a young man standing beside a uniformed guard asked to see our ID. A somewhat heated discussion ensued. We wanted to know why we were being given the third degree, while the Israeli security guard demanded to know what had made us decide on this particular shul. Exasperated, I explained that we had just come from another shul. He retorted that this congregation was 'political' and that our best bet was to go to the big synagogue. I couldn't pin him down as to what he meant by 'political.' In we went. The synagogue was to the left of a paved courtyard where children aged five to about eleven were playing, all dressed in their Saturday best. Inside, all was white, blue, and gold, and new. Not a big room, but decorated in good taste, and with a high ceiling supported by pillars. There were chairs and tables rather than benches. Services were conducted in the Orthodox tradition. A lot of the men were bearded and had earlocks, *pais*. The women were in the gallery above. Small children kept running in and out. An old man from Safed, Israel, was haranguing the congregation in Yiddish. During the reading of the Torah, I shook hands with a number of the men. A young man named Ricki, a goldsmith by trade, said that the congregation was composed mainly of Hungarian and Czechoslovakian Jews. The synagogue had been rebuilt on the grounds of a Hebrew school. On the vacant lot next door there had once been a synagogue but it was burned down by the Nazis. Ricki explained that his father was in the wholesale jewellery business, but that he himself preferred to work with his hands. The congregation appeared to be prosperous.

We rushed over to the main synagogue in downtown Vienna but were too late for the services. The synagogue, with a domed ceiling and highly polished curved benches, was elegant in every respect. In the adjoining hall a Bar Mitzvah luncheon was in progress. I estimated that there were about three hundred people sitting at long tables covered with white linen tablecloths. Few people were leaving, so I imagined that the entire congregation had been invited to the celebration. At the centre table a plump boy was standing beside his father, shaking hands with well-wishers. Everything was as it should be.

We left shortly thereafter. Some time later we saw two Hasids hurrying from the shul. It was possible that the Bar Mitzvah feast lasted through the afternoon.

To visit three places of worship on the same Saturday morning was excessive. My research, however, showed that the Jews of Vienna in 1991 had very good reason to like it there.

On our return home in late October, we found things quite the same as we had left them. The air conditioner had to be repaired; a girl had been raped on the GO train; the mail dispute wasn't quite over; and no one cared who won the World Series, since the Blue Jays had lost the league championship to the Twins in five. We were invited to a luncheon in honour of upcoming nuptials. Our lawyer had sent a fax saying that he was giving up his practice but would help us find a replacement to take care of our problems. The recession persisted: a statement from the bank contained more bad news.

Even our four-day stay in Vienna had not diminished the agitation I felt. I came back wanting to share our experiences but, when showing photos to friends and trying to explain the scenes, I found that I had little to say beyond bland descriptions: 'Along this street I used to walk to school' or 'This is where we used to play.'

The mail brought pictures and cards from Zanycki, the Polish farmer near the Belarus border whose 'Babcia' had been Jewish: the photos were of the funeral and the impressive headstone; one showed Zanycki and his two very blond children at the site. A series of psalms in Polish, in a neat, even hand, were also included. He wrote that Kagan, the old Jewish cemetery keeper, was ill; an 'unlucky person,' he said. Zanycki himself couldn't make a living, as there was an imbalance in the cost of growing vegetables and the price the product brought at the market. He wondered if it was feasible for him to come to Canada to work for a year or so.

Shoshi, one of the Israeli kids, wrote that Auschwitz had made her realize for the first time what went on in that 'dreadful war.' She had to decide soon whether to postpone her upcoming army service in order to continue her studies in architecture or get it over with now. Shoshi, gentle, sweet, and pretty, added a post-script, 'Have you got a boy for me?'

The occupants of apartment 13, number 6 Gdańska in Łódź, Mrs Kowalczuk and her son, sent a pretty Christmas card with the greeting, 'Best wishes to you and your family.'